T0272196

mmm... Manitoba

mmm... Manitoba

The Stories Behind the Foods We Eat

Kimberley Moore and Janis Thiessen

UNIVERSITY OF MANITOBA PRESS

mmm . . . Manitoba: The Stories Behind the Foods We Eat
© Kimberley Moore and Janis Thiessen 2024

28 27 26 25 24   1 2 3 4 5

All rights reserved. No part of this publication may be reproduced
or transmitted in any form or by any means, or stored in a database
and retrieval system in Canada, without the prior written permission
of the publisher, or, in the case of photocopying or any other
reprographic copying, a licence from Access Copyright,
www.accesscopyright.ca, 1-800-893-5777.

University of Manitoba Press
Winnipeg, Manitoba, Canada
Treaty 1 Territory
uofmpress.ca

Cataloguing data available from Library and Archives Canada
ISBN 978-1-77284-041-4 (PAPER)
ISBN 978-1-77284-043-8 (PDF)
ISBN 978-1-77284-044-5 (EPUB)
ISBN 978-1-77284-044-5 (BOUND)

Front cover design by David Drummond
Interior design by Jess Koroscil

Printed in Canada

This book has been published with the help of funds provided by the Social Sciences and Humanities Research Council of
Canada, University of Winnipeg, and in-kind donations by University of Winnipeg's Oral History Centre and Diversity Food
Services.

The University of Manitoba Press acknowledges the financial support for its publication program provided by
the Government of Canada through the Canada Book Fund, the Canada Council for the Arts, the Manitoba Department
of Sport, Culture, and Heritage, the Manitoba Arts Council, and the Manitoba Book Publishing Tax Credit.

With love
to the Manitoba Food History
Canine Cluster and Poirot

The QR (quick response) codes included in each section of this book lead to *mmm. . . Manitoba*'s companion website, http://www.manitobafoodhistory.ca which features the results of the Manitoba Food History Project—including interactive digital maps, episodes of the *Preserves* podcast, ArcGIS Story Maps, and a soundscape—arranged as supplements to each chapter.

Contents

List of Recipes

mmm...
MANITOBA

INTRODUCTION

The Manitoba Food History Project

Though it has existed for most of her life, Janis Thiessen did not visit Ichi Ban Japanese Steak House in downtown Winnipeg until March 2018 when her niece's son asked to go there for his birthday.[1] She was both entranced and confused by the place. The kitschy decor, the menu items reflecting the high-end dining of an earlier generation, the flashy show put on by the chefs as they cooked at your table—how could this place still exist in the hipster era of avocado toast and third-wave coffee that had arrived in Winnipeg with Parlour Coffee and Thom Bargen?[2] She had to know more. She learned that the restaurant's designer had been the head of food services at Caesars Palace in Las Vegas; that their famous chicken liver appetizer probably owed its origins to the Jewish background of the restaurant founders; and that some of Winnipeg's most celebrated contemporary sushi chefs can trace a lineage back to one of Ichi Ban's former head chefs. It was not the story she had anticipated finding when she began her research on the restaurant.

Figure 1. Royden Loewen, Colin Rier, and Arshdeep Kaur eating at a table beside the Manitoba Food History Truck. Photograph by Kimberley Moore, 2019.

We hope readers of this book will experience many similar moments of surprise and wonder as they encounter unexpected stories that make them re-evaluate their understanding of the history of Manitoba (and, indeed, of Canada). As we've told reporters, "We have a rich food history in this province and food is the gateway to talk about every other aspect of history. The hope is that even people who don't care about history, or who at least don't think they care, will nonetheless be attracted to the [Manitoba Food History] project because they do like food."[3] This book is organized as a collection of photographs, biographies, maps, recipes, and historical chapters that you can dip in and out of, rather than as a linear or chronological history of the province. The companion website, http://www.manitobafoodhistory.ca, features interactive digital maps, our Manitoba food history podcast *Preserves*,[4] and some digital stories and soundscapes. We want readers to take their time exploring the wide range of ways that they can encounter the history of our province through food.

This food history project has its origins in some of our previous research. After writing *Snacks: A Canadian Food History*,[5] Janis wanted to continue using oral history methods to study food history, and, during her appointment as the University of Winnipeg Oral History Centre's (OHC) associate director, had the opportunity to begin working more closely with OHC staff Kent Davies and Kimberley Moore, who were experimenting with digital modes of disseminating oral history as public history. We secured a grant from the Social Sciences and Humanities Research Council of Canada (SSHRC) to study two important historical research questions: How has food been produced, sold, and consumed in Manitoba since the founding of the province in 1870? How have those processes changed over time?

Here, we do not narrowly define "food production" as agriculture or "food producers" as farmers. We use the term "food producer" to encompass *all* makers of food, whether large scale for profit (e.g., farmers) or small scale for domestic reproduction (e.g., home cooks), and in opposition to the term "food consumer." While these two terms are not mutually exclusive, we follow the usage of respected food studies scholars such as the editors of *Conversations in Food Studies,* the SSHRC-funded Social and Economic Dimensions of an Aging Population (SEDAP) researchers, sociologist Priscilla Parkhurst Ferguson, and historian Jessamyn Neuhaus (to name just a few).[6]

This book is meant to be a complement to our oral history archive and project website, not a comprehensive summary or analysis of all the food history research we have conducted to date. It draws on some, but not nearly all, of the oral histories we recorded for this project, as well as archived oral histories conducted by others. For the seven chapters that follow, we chose topics that highlight what we believe to be some of the most significant (or the most enjoyable!) aspects of Manitoba food history that we encountered during the course of our research these past several years. Chapter 1 tells the story of Winnipeg's Ichi Ban Japanese Steak House, examining the history of racism against Asian Canadian restaurateurs on the Canadian prairies as well as the question of "authenticity" in food traditions. Chapter 2 explores the origins of two Manitoba food institutions—the Fat Boy (a house-made burger topped with chili) and the local restaurant chain Salisbury House—in the context of the popularization of ready-made food in Winnipeg. Much of the food production in this province happens not on farms or in factories but in the home kitchen; Chapter 3 thus uses the Canadian prairie phenomenon, the "perogy lady," to study the history of food regulation. Chapter 4 explores the differing definitions and traditions of barbecue within Manitoba, including among the newcomer Filipinx community, thereby providing a glimpse into that community in Manitoba. Chapter 5 describes our time in Churchill and deconstructs some colonialist assumptions about the North. Our research team chose to visit Churchill, the northernmost readily accessible community in Manitoba, because we wanted to avoid the tendency when writing about the province to focus exclusively on the more populated southern regions. Chapter 6 examines the history of manomin as an example of a broader (and often ignored) history of Indigenous agricultural production. Chapter 7, the concluding chapter, explores the historical reimagination of contemporary Indigenous food through a tasting menu created by Peguis First Nation chef and culinary instructor Steven Watson. Accompanying these seven chapters are relevant maps, photographs, recipes, and mini-biographies of recipe contributors.

To conduct some of the oral histories that form part of the research for this book, we decided to use a food truck as a mobile oral history lab—an admittedly "unconventional vehicle for research and community engagement."[7] Combining the strengths of the Philadelphia Public History Truck, the StoryCorps MobileBooth, and the contemporary food truck phenomenon,

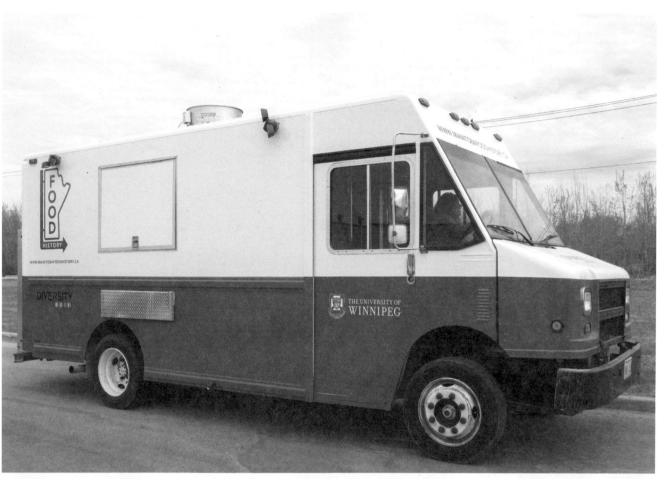

the Manitoba Food History Truck travelled the province, providing a venue for Manitobans to cook samples of foods memorable to them while we interviewed them about their lives and recorded their oral histories.[8] As Kimberley said in an article in the *National Post*, we were "not only interested in recipes that are your favourite or that are nostalgic and very rose coloured. It can also be something you hate with a passion."[9] After only two summers, however, our food truck's travels were ended by COVID-19.

Deciding that you want to use a food truck as a mobile history lab is one thing. But buying, equipping, and operating a food truck, we learned, comes with a ridiculous number of challenges, many of which we had not foreseen.[10] Fortunately, our university's vice-president of research has a background in the restaurant industry. On his recommendation, we found a used food truck on Kijiji, the online classified ads site. Our university's purchasing system is not well adapted to making major purchases from online classified ads, so that took some time to navigate! But buying the truck was only the beginning of our challenges. The truck was vandalized before we could use it. We have had years of work trying to secure various permits, and we're grateful that we partnered with our campus food provider, Diversity Food Services, who managed that process for us. Janis became certified as a food handler, but creating the documents with our university Workplace Safety and Health committee to record our safety training of students and project employees, while obviously helpful and essential, was almost overwhelming in scope. Getting the truck safetied, repaired, and winterized; deciding on a project logo and a truck design; vetting businesses to do all these necessary tasks—Janis's time in the project's first year or so was spent more on paperwork than on research. But the experience has been more than worth it. The Manitoba Food History Project could have developed only in

Figure 2. Side view of the Manitoba Food History Truck. Photograph by Kimberley Moore, 2018.

Figure 3. Side view of the Manitoba Food History Truck at the Manitoba Sunflower Festival in Altona. Photograph by Kimberley Moore, 2019.

Figure 4. Rear view of the Manitoba Food History Truck. Photograph by Janis Thiessen, 2021.

Figure 5. Rear view of the Manitoba Food History Truck, with Darwin Gaspar, Kent Davies, and Sarah Story. Photograph by Kimberley Moore, 2018.

a place like the University of Winnipeg (uw), where we have been supported by the combined expertise of the Oral History Centre, Diversity Foods, and the uw Research Office.

Food history is a familiar entry point for many of us into more complex historical subjects and questions of migration, identity, gender, ethnicity, politics, and health (among others). The Manitoba Food History Project thus contributes not only to our understanding of the history of food in Manitoba but the history of Manitoba (and Canada) as a whole.

Historian Gerald Friesen observes that Manitoba was "a Métis settlement when it entered Confederation in 1870."[11] Winnipeg, the provincial capital, had only 200 residents in 1871; by 2021, it had three-quarters of a million.[12] Friesen observes that "the physical appearance of Winnipeg was marked by a high degree of residential segregation by class" by the mid-1880s.[13] This residential segregation persists to the present day: neighbourhoods are organized more around class than ethnicity. Winnipeg's West End and North End have long been working-class neighbourhoods, though the particular ethnic composition of that working class has changed over time. The West End's primarily Greek, Italian, and Icelandic newcomers of the first half of the twentieth century moved to wealthier neighbourhoods as their children and grandchildren became more prosperous. They were superseded in the West End by Nigerian and Filipinx newcomers, as well as urban Indigenous residents. The North End's Jewish and Ukrainian populations were similarly succeeded by Indigenous and Southeast Asian residents. Some ethnic enclaves in Winnipeg persist (such as Russian Mennonites in the suburb of North Kildonan), while others are more recently established (such as the Asian community along Pembina Highway near the University of Manitoba). Each of these groups (as well as many others) contributed to the foodways of this province, bringing their traditions from elsewhere, adapting them to the conditions they found here, and learning from those who became their new neighbours.[14]

It is these foodways that we strive to document: the history of food manufacturing, production, retailing, and consumption from the creation of the province in 1870 (sometimes even earlier) to the present day. This is valuable research, as food and beverage processing is the largest manufacturing industry in Manitoba; almost a third of total manufacturing in Manitoba is produced by the food processing sector, and one in eleven jobs in the province is dependent on agriculture and related industries.[15] As historians and labour scholars Susan Levine and Steve Striffler observe, "food and work together raise significant questions about the industrial imaginary, gender and labor, the hidden nature of reproductive labor, the history of markets, and the relationship between agricultural and industrial labor. We clearly need more histories of the food industry—not only farm workers and migrant labor or meatpacking and poultry plants but the giant food processing, distribution, and retail industries that took form during the twentieth century."[16] But we need not only the history of the sites of capitalist production. Food making occurs not only on the farm and in the factory but in the kitchen; home cooks should also be seen as important food producers. A food history of Manitoba, then, allows investigation of domestic reproduction; of the many ways in which industrial capitalism transformed the agri-food system; of the various networks between various food producers and retailers in Manitoba; and of the role of gender, ethnicity, migration, politics, and health in Manitoba history. Food is an entry into all these stories, all these histories; the more fully we can understand the past, the better we can make choices for our future—not only regarding food security and regulation, but racism, sexism, and colonialism.

Food history in particular, and food studies in general, have become popular areas of scholarship of late. Published works in these fields have proliferated in the last few decades.[17] Many of these works are popular histories that engage minimally with either historiography or theory, or short business articles related to very narrow interests; Steve Penfold's history of the franchising of doughnut shops is a rare and welcome exception. Few of these books incorporate insights from such fields as labour history, oral history, or business history. Recent works by Michael Pollan and Eric Schlosser have captured the attention of the North American public, highlighting the health dangers of the typical North American diet.[18] These works, too, offer a limited historical approach to their subject matter.

The Manitoba Food History Project is part of the increasing interest of food historians in oral history, and emerged in part from Janis's earlier work in both fields.[19] There is a growing body of literature (including Rebecca Sharpless's *Cooking in Other Women's Kitchens* and Steven Penfold's *The Donut*) as well as research groups (the Southern Foodways Alliance at the University of Mississippi's Center for the Study of Southern Culture and the Culinaria

Research Centre at the University of Toronto Scarborough) combining food history and oral history.[20] The usefulness of oral history in documenting the business history of food production is demonstrated by an oral history project begun in 1998 by National Life Stories at the British Library. These interviews, as Polly Russell says, reveal "new information about how decisions are taken and business conducted through and by individuals who are, of course, part and parcel of those structural forces and logics that determine food production."[21] The project includes more than 300 interviews (150 digitized and available online, together with photos, letters, and other documents) with those people involved in the production, manufacture, and consumption of food in twentieth-century Britain.[22] The Manitoba Food History research project is generating a similarly valuable online archive. Its great strength, like that of the British Library collection, is its focus on "cultural practices and narratives" when business historians in particular have focused instead on "where labor, capital, cost, and waste manifest."[23]

For the Manitoba Food History Project, oral history does not serve merely (and simplistically) as a source of factual information. Rather, the methods and theories of oral history and the study of memory, as exemplified by the studies of Alessandro Portelli, Alon Confino, Michael Frisch, Jacques LeGoff, Paul Connerton, and others, are an integral part of our interpretive approach.[24] These scholars argue that interviews are about much more than collecting facts: the ways in which interview participants tell their stories (including 'misremembering' details) reveal much about people's values and how they make sense of the world. As Tracy K'Meyer and Joy Hart observe, oral histories "are heavily mediated and constructed documents that convey stories shaped by the circumstances under which they are created. . . . [B]y examining the recurring content, themes, and ways of organizing a narrative . . . we can begin to understand the collective story, especially how it reflects individual and community consciousness, identity, and values."[25]

To date, we have archived sixty-eight oral histories as part of this project. Those people we interviewed included commercial food processors (five), restaurant owners (twelve), beer brewers (two), coffee roasters (one), food truck operators (five), grocers (eight), farmers and greenhouse operators (seven), leaders/members of cultural organizations (nine), scholars (five), food transportation workers (two), rural agricultural specialists (five), chefs (thirteen), and Manitobans

ETHNIC ORIGIN	TOTAL
First Nations	140,250
Inuit	1,145
Métis	88,305
Other North American origins	138,630
British Isles	397,130
French	121,360
Western European (except French)	238,620
Northern European (except British Isles)	81,335
Eastern European	262,205
Southern European	49,690
Other European	2,120
Caribbean	11,715
Latin, Central and South American	27,705
Central and West African	16,505
North African	3,880
Southern and East African	15,315
West Central Asian and Middle Eastern	12,890
South Asian	61,300
East and Southeast Asian	137,450
Oceania	1,655
Total - Ethnic or Cultural Origin	1,307,190

Table 1. Selected ethnic or cultural origins of Manitobans 2021. Source: Statistics Canada, Table 98-10-0355-01 Ethnic or cultural origin by gender and age: Canada, provinces and territories, DOI: https://doi.org/10.25318/9810035501-eng.

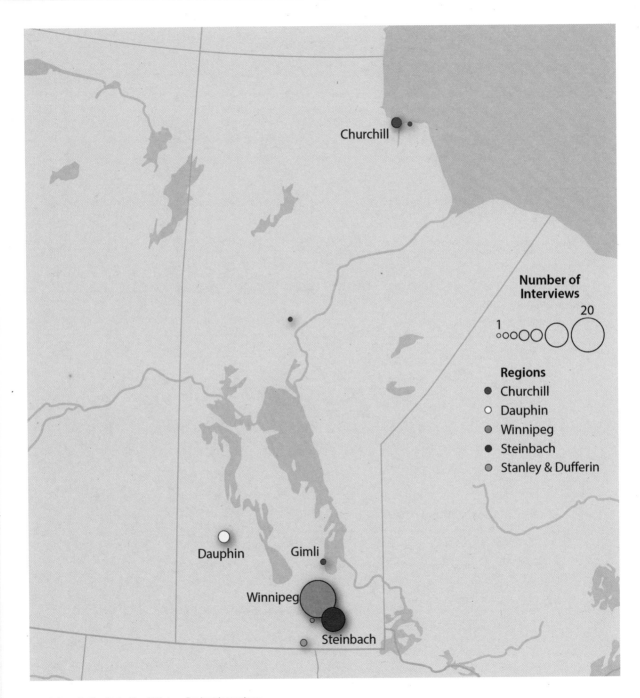

Churchill

Number of Interviews

1   20

Regions
- Churchill
- Dauphin
- Winnipeg
- Steinbach
- Stanley & Dufferin

Dauphin   Gimli

Winnipeg

Steinbach

Map 1. Manitoba Food History Project interviews.

who volunteered to cook aboard the Food History Truck (seventeen); many of these fit into more than one category. Interview participants came from a variety of backgrounds: Filipinx, Mennonite, Japanese, British, Anishinaabe, Ukrainian, Chinese, German, Salvadoran, Greek, Swedish, Icelandic, Spanish, Kanyen'keha:ka (Mohawk), and Italian, to name a few. Manitoba is a diverse province (as the 2021 Census reveals), and these oral histories reflect that fact.

With growing attention in the oral history community to the potential risks of interviewing comparative strangers alone in their homes, the Food History Truck provided a safer environment because it is a semi-public space.[26] It also posed an effective alternative to burdening volunteers with the task of finding their way to the UW campus and to our Oral History Centre interview room. Informed and written consent for these oral history interviews was obtained, in accordance with the Tri-Council Policy Statement on Ethical Conduct for Research Involving Humans (TCPS 2). Questions asked of interview participants included the following (as relevant):

- What are your earliest memories of eating the recipe you are preparing for us on the Food History Truck?

- What memories do you have of your parents eating or serving this recipe?

- How has your use of this recipe changed over time?

- In what ways is the recipe you are preparing for us on the Food History Truck distinctly Manitoban? To what extent does that matter to you?

- What have been the critical issues faced by the Manitoba agri-food industry, in your opinion?

- How did you become involved in the agri-food industry?

- How has your business changed over time?

- What have been the critical issues faced by people in your industry, in your opinion?

- What were the most significant changes in the history of your business? What made them significant?

- How has/have your product(s) changed over time?

- How have your relationships with suppliers changed over time?
- How has advertising in your industry changed over time?
- Describe your job: what is a typical work day for you?
- What gave you the most satisfaction in your work experience(s)? What did you learn from these experiences?
- Were you ever frustrated by, or did you experience any conflict with, your work experience(s)? How was it resolved?
- How did you feel about and what was your involvement in [various events, such as changes in company ownership or product lines]?

Best practices in oral history (as recommended by the Oral History Association) require that interviews be conducted face-to-face, that interviews be recorded in a format that will withstand the test of time and changes in technology (necessitating use of a particular digital recording format), and that interviews be deposited in public archives for consultation by other researchers. With participants' permission, oral history interviews have been archived at the University of Winnipeg's Oral History Centre; digital audio recordings are accompanied by a summary, index, transcript, consent form, archival release agreement, and (often) photos.

The Manitoba Food History Project has given numerous research and educational opportunities to undergraduate and graduate students at the University of Winnipeg. While we worked to get the Food History Truck ready for its first summer on the road, Janis taught a combined honours–graduate student seminar in Canadian social history that focused on Manitoban food history. Students described their work: "In addition to traditional course readings and discussions, we prepared dishes that connected to our learning, and took field trips to local food producers. In the course, we learned how food history connects to all disciplines and provides an important perspective that is often ignored. The goal of the course was to conduct an oral history interview and use it to produce a podcast or a digital map for The Manitoba Food History Project website."[27]

Janis also created an experiential field course in Food History at the University of Winnipeg: the Manitoba Food History Truck, HIST-3504. Undergrad students enrolled in this course researched the food history of Manitoba in the Manitoba Food History Truck, interviewing people while they cooked, and published their findings as ArcGIS Story Maps on our project website or as episodes of our *Preserves* podcast. We first offered this course in the summer of 2019 with the cooperation of Winnipeg Public Libraries, who kindly hosted our Food History Truck at the Sir William Stephenson Library in Winnipeg's Burrows-Keewatin neighbourhood. The distancing restrictions of COVID-19 required that we cancel the course in the summers of 2020 and 2021, unfortunately. We were able to offer the course for a final time in June 2022 on the University of Winnipeg campus. Both courses were heavily dependent on assistance from Kent and Kimberley (Kim) at the UW Oral History Centre, who were responsible for designing and delivering instruction on oral history, interviewing, audio recording, storytelling, story maps, and podcasting.

The Food History Truck began its explorations of Manitoba in 2018, with a three-week residence at Steinbach's Mennonite Heritage Village. We chose Steinbach as our first venture since Janis was familiar with the area, having lived there during her high school and undergraduate years. Importantly, it was within easy driving distance of Winnipeg, should we encounter any practical difficulties operating the truck that would require the assistance of our knowledgeable partners at Diversity Foods. Subsequent trips with the truck were at the invitation of organizations that had seen media reports of our project, including two stays at the St. Norbert Farmers' Market that same summer. We had contemplated taking the truck to Montreal for our roundtable at the Oral History Association conference, but it was simply too great a distance. So we presented there without it.

The following year—knowing that provincial histories tend to focus on southern regions—the team took the train to Churchill, the northernmost town in Manitoba. There we spent ten days learning about the region as well as eating snow goose, cloudberry jam, "Dene dogs," Arctic char, and fire-roasted caribou. That summer of 2019 also marked the debut of the two-week HIST-3504 Manitoba Food History Truck field course, as well as invitations to travel with the Manitoba Food History Truck to the Altona Sunflower Festival and Dauphin's National Ukrainian Festival to gather interviews.

Figure 6. Sharon Steward slicing vegetables inside the Manitoba Food History Truck. Photograph by Kimberley Moore, 2019.

The global COVID-19 pandemic grounded the truck in the spring of 2020. We had been invited to conduct interviews on board the truck at the Threshermen's Reunion in Austin. We also had planned that University of Winnipeg students in the Indigenous Summer Scholars Program (ISSP) working with our project would interview people from their communities. Pre-pandemic interviews by ISSP students at Winnipeg Indigenous restaurants Connie's Corner Café (now closed) and Feast, as well as the Chinese restaurant in Pikwitonei, had been cancelled for students' personal reasons; now the university's COVID-19 research protocols made interviews almost impossible. All in-person oral history interviewing ended. The HIST-3504 course, which we had planned to hold at Winnipeg's Osborne Library, was also cancelled. Student research assistants worked from home to make more than fifty archived interviews accessible by documenting and preparing metadata, summaries, session logs, and transcripts. It was difficult to have our truck grounded and much of our research effectively halted for two successive summers. But, as Kim explained, "We had a solid foundation as a team for a situation like this because, as much as we rely on each other and constantly communicate about the project and what needs to happen next, we are all kind of wildly independent. There is no typical day. . . . The food truck is a marvelous and volatile beast where you don't always get to dictate what happens, so a fair bit of this project is just dealing with situations as they arise. Similarly, with COVID, you can't change the fact of this situation, but you can find ways to cope."[28]

Our project has had many part-time and short-term team members. Sarah Story served as coordinator for the first year of the project. Scott Price was a graduate research fellow during the second year. Several undergraduate and graduate students have worked with us: Amber Ali, Jackson Anderson, Ashley Cross, Emma Dubeski, Madison Herget-Schmidt, Michaela Hiebert, Aidan Kingston, Madrin Macgillivray, Quinn MacNeil, Rochelle Richards, and Daniel Nychuk. Students in several of Janis's undergraduate courses assisted in archiving the project's oral histories, creating digital stories, and writing podcast episodes. Caitlin Mostoway-Parker and Alyssa Czemerynzki transcribed the recipes that appear in this book. Alyssa Czemerynzki also wrote most of the biographies. But the project's core team is the three of us: Kent Davies, Kimberley Moore, and Janis Thiessen.

Figure 7. Janis Thiessen seated on a rock at Cape Churchill. Photograph by Kimberley Moore, 2019.

Figure 8. Kent Davies recording sound while Kimberley Moore takes photos at Cape Churchill. Photograph by Janis Thiessen, 2019.

Figure 9. Kent Davies prepares the digital recorder for Anna Sigrithur. Photograph by Kimberley Moore, 2018.

Figure 10. Kimberley Moore in the driver's seat of the Manitoba Food History Truck, taking a photo of herself in the side mirror. Photograph by Kimberley Moore, 2018.

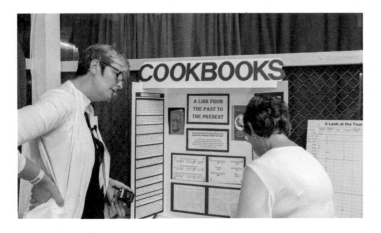

Figure 11. Janis Thiessen with Joyce Sirski-Howell and her Ukrainian Canadian cookbook display at Canada's National Ukrainian Festival in Dauphin. Photograph by Kimberley Moore, 2019.

Kimberley Moore (adjunct professor and programming and collections specialist at the University of Winnipeg's Oral History Centre [UW OHC]) and Kent Davies (adjunct professor and audio technician at the UW OHC) have specialized skills that contributed greatly to the success of this project. Since the founding of the University of Winnipeg's Oral History Centre in 2012, Kent has provided faculty, staff, students, and affiliate OHC members with the equipment, technical support, learning tools, and resources needed to complete their oral history research projects. In addition, he assists in the development and preservation of the OHC's projects and digital archive. He has an extensive background in radio broadcasting. Kent has worked on many digitization projects, and is the researcher behind the Harvest Moon Oral History project.[29] He is the producer and co-host of the project's podcast *Preserves* and the creator of the soundscape "What Is Northern Food?"[30]

Kimberley Moore has a Master of Arts in Oral History from Concordia University where, after obtaining a BA (Hons) from the University of Winnipeg, she continued her education in public history and in the preservation of oral history collections. Kim develops and coordinates the UW OHC's oral history workshops and co-manages the OHC's archival collections. She created the websites for the UW OHC and the Harvest Moon Oral History project, and teaches story mapping with ArcGIS, a web-based mapping software system. In addition to her technical skills, Kim has expertise in the methodological, ethical, and technological challenges of doing oral history, preserving interviews, and making them accessible; and teaches the OHC's Introduction to Oral History workshop series. She is the co-author of this book, the project's website

Figure 12. Janis Thiessen and a reporter standing outside the Manitoba Food History Truck, with Kent Davies inside the truck. Photograph by Kimberley Moore, 2018.

designer, the editor of the project's Stories of Food in Place, and the project's photographer (among many other things).

Janis Thiessen is a professor of history at University of Winnipeg and former associate director of the UW's Oral History Centre. Her first foray into food history began with her third book, *Snacks: A Canadian Food History*. She is the project's principal investigator and the other co-author of this book, and is as surprised as anybody that we conducted historical research with a food truck.

Our goal in writing this book is simple: we want you to have a good time enjoying food. Maybe you will learn some history along the way, or see an aspect of Manitoba food in a new light. We want to lead you with food through some of Manitoba's past, and, with stories, maps, photos, and recipes, illustrate that it is more nuanced, more interesting, and more complicated than perhaps we have been led to believe. We are interested in the history of food itself but also in what the history of food teaches us about the histories of domesticity, immigration, government policy, ethnic identity, and so many other aspects of life in Manitoba.

We are serious about our research. But we are also serious about exploring new methods of reaching new audiences. This book and its companion website and podcast are some of the ways the Manitoba Food History Project is striving to do so. We hope you enjoy this taste of Manitoba history.

CHAPTER ONE

Number One

The Japanese term for "Number One" is "Ichi Ban," which is also the name of a Winnipeg restaurant. In the heart of the downtown rests an unusual indoor Japanese garden. Walk through a door and down the stairs, and you enter its artificial environs, complete with ceramic-roofed tea house. Imitation cherry trees in full bloom are filled with automated birds. A low bridge carries you over a gentle stream, past bamboo, lanterns, flowers, Asian statuary, and a small water wheel, to a grass-green carpet. Here you are met by a kimono-clad server, who guides you to one of eight padded red chairs at a communal table that surrounds a flat metal plate. Behind this cooktop is your host and chef for the evening, dressed in a toque blanche, who greets you with a dazzling display of knifework. Steam rises from the surface of the grill, as your chef juggles salt and pepper shakers, dramatically flipping ingredients through the air and into serving bowls. As you watch this theatrical preparation of your dinner, you sip a cocktail, served in a ceramic geisha or buddha that you take home as a souvenir of this unique experience.

This is Ichi Ban Japanese Steak House. It opened in 1973 at 189 Carlton Street, across from Winnipeg's Convention Centre, as part of the newly built full-block Lakeview Square, which was then the largest commercial development in downtown Winnipeg.[1] Advertising their restaurant as "the best tasting show in town," the restaurant's owners and investors

explained that the restaurant's name means "Number One."[2] These were a small group of Jewish businessmen from Winnipeg and Las Vegas: Wally Guberman, owner of Winnipeg restaurants Caesars Palace and Pancake House as well as the retail chain The Place for Pants; Sam Linhart, executive vice-president of Lakeview Development; Jack Levit, president of Lakeview Development; Oscar Grubert, owner of multiple Winnipeg restaurants, including Champ's Chicken, Butcher Block, Mother Tucker's Food Experience, and the Palomino Club, and president of the Canadian Restaurant Association; and Nat Hart, celebrity chef and corporate vice-president of food and beverage for Caesars World.[3] Management of the restaurant was initially in the hands of Shoichi (Mike) Fujii, a Tokyo native who had experience in Japanese steak houses in Las Vegas, San Francisco, Chicago, and New York, including with Rocky Aoki's Benihana, the restaurant chain that introduced Japanese teppan yaki (iron plate cooking) to the United States.[4]

How did a Las Vegas celebrity chef become involved in a Japanese restaurant in Winnipeg? Steven Hart, Nat Hart's son, explained: "Jack and Yetta Levit were in Las Vegas, and they met my dad. They were staying at Caesars [Palace], I believe, at that time. And Jack was telling Dad, you know, he's looking for somebody who can do something with—he's got this Lakeview Development property on Hargrave Street and he's looking to develop it."[5] According to Steven, the pair were well matched: "Jack was an extremely smart numbers person. He was a cultivator, and a very good numbers person. But he had met his match when he met my dad, because my dad was . . . you could not talk to him about food and beverage unless you knew what you were talking about in food and beverage, because he was a concept man."[6]

Nat Hart had a remarkable gastronomic background. He had studied culinary arts at Le Pointe School of Cuisine in Paris and Lucerne Food Service School in Switzerland.[7] He was maître d'hôtel at Caesars Palace in the 1960s; in the 1970s, he became corporate vice-president of food and beverage for Caesars World, Inc. (owners of Caesars Palace, the first themed Las

Figure 13. Executive chef Mike Fuji; Jack Levit, President Lakeview Development; Nat Hart, President/owner Ichi Ban Japanese Steak House; Winnipeg Mayor Stephen Juba at opening night Ichi Ban Japanese Steak House chain Winnipeg, Manitoba, Canada. UNLV Archives, Nat Hart Professional Papers, 1930–2000, MS-00419, Box 10, Folder 12.

Vegas hotel).[8] Known as Vegas's first celebrity chef, he was responsible for the creation of the famed Bacchanal Room at Caesars Palace in 1966. This ostentatious eatery featured toga-clad servers presenting seven-course meals to diners while giving them shoulder massages. "Oh my gosh," a former customer recalled, "it was like an orgy."[9]

The ostentatiousness of Las Vegas's Bacchanal Room was reincarnated in a new context in Winnipeg's Ichi Ban. The restaurant was promoted as a show to watch as much as a place to eat.[10] "You know what's better than eating a great steak?" one advertisement asked rhetorically. "Eating a great steak and watching a great show. Not only does every ICHI BAN chef prepare the finest prime sirloin for you but he puts on a truly wizardly act as he's doing it. Catch a performance today. What other sorcerer can offer you such magnificent steak? What other steakhouse can offer you such magnificent sorcery?"[11] In any restaurant, as described by food scholars Norman Peng, Anne Chen, and Kuang-peng Hung, dining "can be an art form that gratifies multiple human senses."[12] That is particularly the case in teppan yaki restaurants, where chefs interact directly and continuously with their customers.[13] In a different article, Chen, Peng, and Hung write that these chefs "evoke diners' fantasies and feelings through their interpersonal skills, creativity, and technical skills."[14] Diners' needs at Ichi Ban would be attended to not only by chefs and servers but by the first point of contact—a reservation system used to track specific customers' preferences such that, as Nat Hart said, "at any time, we may go to any given day since Day 1 of opening, and discover where someone sat and who took care of them."[15]

Opening night at Ichi Ban saw local and international celebrities, including Winnipeg mayor Stephen Juba and the entertainer Liberace.[16] The exoticism of the new restaurant was promoted in Hart's plan for the opening-night invitations, which were to be written on rice paper in both Japanese and English "in a thick script so that the English has a Japanese appearance." These were to be hand-delivered to distinguished guests by a Japanese woman dressed as a geisha: "The effect would be tremendous—particularly when she walks up to the City Editor of a newspaper, bows, and hands over the invitation. Any editor's curiosity would be aroused."[17]

Hart's flair for the theatrical and his attention to detail were complemented by his knowledge of Japanese cuisine, which he had learned in the course of his work feeding casino guests. When a high roller from Japan came to gamble at Caesars Palace, Hart would contact

Figure 14. Promotional photo of executive chef Mike Fuji, Ichi Ban Winnipeg. Special Collections & Archives, University Libraries, University of Nevada, Las Vegas (hereafter UNLV Archives), Nat Hart Professional Papers, 1930–2000, MS-00419, Box 9, Folder 15.

KUGEL

9 oz.[18] wide egg noodles

¼ pound butter

1/3 cup sugar

1 tsp. vanilla

½ pound cream cheese

4 eggs

1½ cups milk

2½ cups canned crushed pineapple, drained

Cook noodles in large pot of boiling salted water. Do not overcook. Drain. Mix all the other ingredients together. Add the noodles and toss carefully. Place mixture in a buttered 9 x 12-inch pan and bake in a preheated 325 degrees oven for 45 minutes or until top is well browned.

Hannah Robinson, "Collection Highlight: Nat Hart Professional Papers," blog post, UNLV Special Collections and Archives, 18 August 2014, https://www.library.unlv.edu/whats_new_in_special_collections/20 (accessed 14 December 2018).

Figure 15.
Matchbook cover
promoting Winnipeg's Ichi
Ban Japanese Steak House.
Purchased from eBay.

that person's favourite restaurant in Japan and then hire its chef to come and cook for the high roller while they gambled in Las Vegas. Working together with these expert Japanese chefs in the Caesars Palace kitchens, Hart could learn about Japanese cuisine at a time before the present-day plethora of cookbooks and cooking shows. Hart's son Steven described the process:

> If you bring a fellow in from Japan and he eats certain types of food that we do not have in America, before he comes, you would talk to the casino credit exec junket rep—whoever handles that property with you in your hotel—and find out from him where that Japanese fellow in Japan likes to eat. What is his favourite restaurant? And then what you would do is—this is now in the old days—what you would do is, you would contact that restaurant and that chef and say to him, "We would like to invite you to our hotel in Las Vegas, okay, to cook for this person who comes to your restaurant." And he would tell us what ingredients he needs and what types of foods he wants to cook with. And by doing that, you develop a recipe from another country. . . . Today, you can pick up a book, a good Japanese book, and you can learn real Japanese food. Or on the Internet. You know, the times have changed. But that's the way they did it in the old days.[19]

In 1964, Hart was invited by the Government of Japan to design the restaurant and menu for the Japanese pavilion at the World's Fair in New York.[20] While there, he met Hiroaki "Rocky" Aoki, creator of the Benihana Japanese Steakhouses, and learned about teppan yaki. That experience led to Hart's creation of the Ah'so Japanese Steak House at Caesars Palace in Las Vegas, the Hyakumi Japanese Steak House in Atlantic City, and Ichi Ban Japanese Steak House in Winnipeg.[21]

Teppan yaki, the focus of Ichi Ban, is a particular style of Japanese cooking. Steven Hart explained: "There's two types of

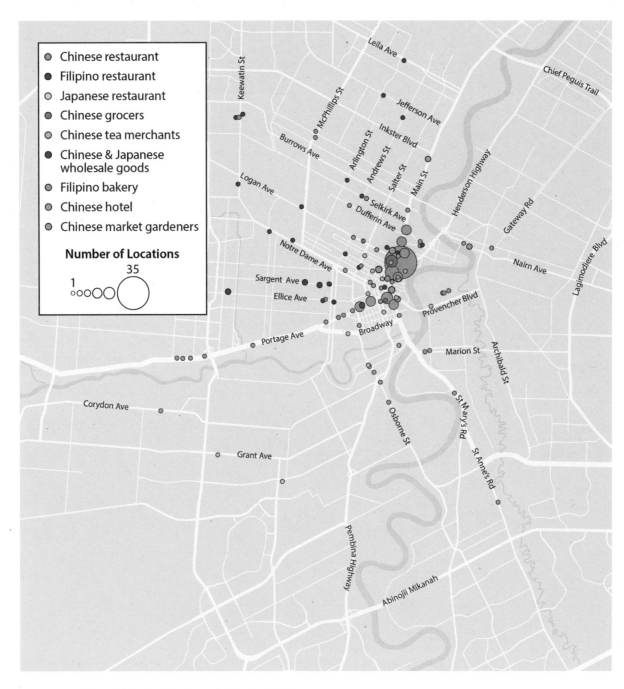

Map 2. Selected Asian food businesses in Winnipeg, 1880–present.

Legend:
- Chinese restaurant
- Filipino restaurant
- Japanese restaurant
- Chinese grocers
- Chinese tea merchants
- Chinese & Japanese wholesale goods
- Filipino bakery
- Chinese hotel
- Chinese market gardeners

Number of Locations
1 ●○○○○ 35

Map labels: Leila Ave, Keewatin St, McPhillips St, Jefferson Ave, Chief Peguis Trail, Burrows Ave, Arlington St, Inkster Blvd, Andrews St, Salter St, Main St, Henderson Highway, Gateway Rd, Logan Ave, Selkirk Ave, Dufferin Ave, Nairn Ave, Lagimodiere Blvd, Notre Dame Ave, Sargent Ave, Ellice Ave, Provencher Blvd, Portage Ave, Broadway, Marion St, Archibald St, Corydon Ave, Osborne St, St Mary's Rd, St Anne's Rd, Grant Ave, Pembina Highway, Abinojii Mikanah

Figure 16. Liberace with Ichi Ban serving staff in kimonos, Winnipeg. UNLV Archives, Nat Hart Professional Papers, 1930–2000, MS-00419, Box 9, Folder 15.

Japanese food: there's American-style Japanese food—like everything else— and there's Japanese food. Okay, sushi and sashimi are Japanese foods, but of course, they may be made a little bit different in America than they are in Japan. . . . So what we were serving in the Ichi Ban was not Japanese food, it was American-style Japanese food."[22] Teppan yaki was invented in Japan in the 1940s by Fujioka Shigetsugu of Kobe's Misono restaurant to appeal to American soldiers.[23] Winnipeg restaurant reviewer Cynthia Wine described the teppan as a large rectangular metal plate that "is heated from below by a gas jet aimed at its centre. This method allows the centre to become very hot for fast cooking and leaves the outer edges of the grill for a kind of holding-warming area. Huge, hooded fans over the grill whisk away cooking smells and extra heat."[24] Teppan yaki restaurants proliferated across North America in the 1960s, made popular by the restaurant Benihana.[25]

Benihana, the first teppan yaki restaurant outside of Japan, was opened by twenty-five-year-old Rocky Aoki in New York City in 1964.[26] It became a nationwide American chain by the end of the 1970s. Ichi Ban's menu and restaurant decor were very similar to Benihana's. Japanese Studies scholar Katarzyna Cwiertka observed, "customers were seated around a large steel griddle plate where the food was cooked in front of their eyes. The four food items—steak, filet mignon, chicken, and shrimp—could either be had as entrée items or in combinations, accompanied by bean sprouts, zucchini, mushrooms, onions, and rice. The interior [of the restaurant] was an authentically detailed Japanese country inn, constructed out of building materials gathered from old Japanese houses, shipped in pieces to the United States, and reassembled."[27]

ICHI BAN COCKTAILS

"Geisha Girl" Cocktail (Original)

¾ oz. lime juice

½ oz. sugar

½ oz. orange juice

½ oz. pineapple juice

½ oz. blue curacao

1 oz. vodka

"Geisha Girl" Cocktail (Revised)

¾ oz. dry gin

1 oz. sake

¾ oz. cherry brandy

½ lime

¾ oz. grenadine

"Buddha" Cocktail

¾ oz. lime juice

2 oz. orange juice

¾ oz. orgeat

¾ oz. gin or vodka

¾ oz. rum

¾ oz. brandy

Box 9, Folder 8, Nat Hart Collection, MS-00419, Special Collections & Archives, University Libraries, University of Nevada, Las Vegas; Tent drink card, unaccessioned material, Nat Hart Collection, MS-00419, Special Collections & Archives, University Libraries, University of Nevada, Las Vegas.

In Ichi Ban's planning stages, Nat Hart intended to serve complete dinners including appetizer, soup, tempura, salad, main course (chicken, beef, fish, or a combination of beef, lobster, and chicken), vegetables, rice, fresh fruit, and dessert (either ginger or mandarin ice cream).[28] Thus Ichi Ban would serve a more extensive complete dinner than either of their North American Japanese restaurant competitors (Benihana in the United States and Kobe Japanese Steak House in Vancouver), or their high-end dining competition in Winnipeg (Oliver's Restaurant, La Vieille Gare, the Rib Room, and Rae & Jerry's). This elaborate multi-course meal was called the "Imperial Dinner." Its final iteration included soup, salad, rice, vegetables, entrée, and Japanese green tea. Ichi Ban's chicken livers became its best-known appetizer, sautéed in a special sauce with mushrooms and onions:

> STEVEN HART: And by the way, I understand they took the chicken livers out. Which is a big no-no! The chicken livers are one of the greatest things to eat, served the way we had it with our secret sauce.
>
> JANIS THIESSEN: They're still there. It's just now it's a choice [for the customer], it's not automatic.
>
> STEVEN HART: Uh-huh. Right.[29]

This liver dish may seem more Jewish than Japanese, but Asian restaurants in western Canada have a long history of adaptability to their environs. As English literature scholar Lily Cho observes of the Chinese Canadian restaurant, "it is strangely visible and yet invisible—a sign of the passing of time and the death of prairie life, and yet still one of the last places where one can find a proper beef dip sandwich."[30]

One of the most innovative contributions of Ichi Ban to Winnipeg's restaurant scene was its use of fresh vegetables. Consider this critique from Cynthia Wine in 1972: "Which brings me to my favorite fruitless appeal. Oliver's is another of our luxury restaurants which treats vegetables as a garnish instead of a food, presenting, instead of fresh vegetables in season, their icky canned or frozen substitutes. Fresh vegetables are offered à la carte at $1 a serving."[31] Ichi Ban not only used fresh vegetables in every Imperial Dinner but prepared them before the diners' eyes. Journalist Gene Telpner noted, "They use fresh ingredients, they make an occasion of every meal, and their prices are not outrageous. Ichi Ban is still one of the better examples

Figure 17. Ichi Ban's chicken liver appetizer. Photograph by Janis Thiessen, 2023.

of its kind, its gardens and waterfalls still novel and refreshing, if bizarre, after all these years."[32]

The restaurant's design might be viewed as nostalgic Orientalism. *Ciao!* magazine's review said, "The décor at Ichiban reflects the way North America viewed Japanese culture circa 1973," and remains largely unchanged: "red chairs on wheels, faux leather tabletops, and plastic dishes. Only a sushi bar has been added to reflect more recent awareness of Japanese cuisine."[33] Local food critic Marion Warhaft, writing in 1991, declared, "Some might call Ichi Ban's ambiance corny. I find it pleasant."[34]

Some beautiful original elements of the restaurant's decor have fallen away over the years. Nat Hart and son Steven Hart personally designed and built much of the restaurant, working with local Winnipeg businessmen Ivan Berkowitz (Monarch Wear, H.I. Marketing) and Melvin Manishen (Empire Sheet Metal Manufacturing). Nat had built the furniture for his own home, all in a Japanese style.[35] Steven Hart had learned how to build and design, becoming a millwright.

JANIS THIESSEN: [looking at a photograph of the restaurant interior at its opening] It's a beautiful, beautiful restaurant.

STEVEN HART: Is it still? Yeah?

JANIS THIESSEN: It is, yeah. It seems to be very unchanged.

STEVEN HART: Is there still a lot of foliage in there?

JANIS THIESSEN: Not as much. [looking at the photo] I'm surprised by the cherry trees that seemed to be there.

STEVEN HART: So here's something that—little things are what make a restaurant great, okay? Number one: consistency, okay. When you build, and when you operate, and your food should be consistent, right? Concepts are very important. You're talking about a cherry tree. So what we did was . . . you get a little hobby motor

Figure 18. Interior of Ichi Ban, Winnipeg. UNLV Archives, Nat Hart Professional Papers, 1930–2000, MS-00419, Box 9, Folder 15.

with a shaft and you solder on a piece of—well, we used little regular metal hangers. Cut a piece of hanger, and put a little hobby store birdie on it. With music going every so often, incorporated into the music. . . . You could hear a *vhing!* and you could see that bird up in that cherry tree going around. I don't know if they still have that.

JANIS THIESSEN: I have not noticed that, no. That's amazing.

STEVEN HART: Little things that we used to do in order to make the restaurant more authentic. And that was the concept there, you're out in a garden area. That's why there is still green grass down there. There's a wooded area up above, that would be the [restaurant] front of the house. The Japanese house is the kitchen side that you're looking at when you come in. That back part would be the house. You're coming out of the house which is from the kitchen, really. And you're going into the backyard, which is the garden, and then the terrace part up above. That was the concept. . . . So when you walked into the property, you came down [the stairs], and then you either went into the bar, or you crossed over the bridge . . . and you went into the dining room.[36]

Such creativity helped disguise some of the more obtrusive structural elements of the building. Steven Hart recalled:

We actually built the trees ourselves. Those were columns [supporting the building]. . . . These columns are actually the trees. So what we do is, we take a column and we put chicken wire all around it, bend it where we want to bend it to make a form. And then we just take plaster of Paris—that's what's on there—and we just put the plaster of Paris on there, let it dry, and then we paint it to the texture and to the colour that we want to make it look like. And [we] did the same thing with branches and stuff with wires.[37]

San Francisco's Otagiri Mercantile and Vancouver's Capilano Trading imported quality Japanese ceramics for the restaurant.[38] "Beautiful Otagiri plates. All the [table]ware. The teapots: Otagiris. We used to have—they loved teapots, and it's cold in Winnipeg, and a lot of people tried to put them underneath their jackets and take them out. And of course, we had to nicely tell them that they weren't for sale."[39]

Just around the corner from the interior artificial Japanese garden of Ichi Ban, in the centre of Lakeview Square, is an exterior real Japanese garden. Created in 1974 with the assistance of the Government of Japan and the Setagaya Ward of the City of Tokyo, the garden is in honour of the latter's association as a sister city of Winnipeg.[40] It, too, is not what it once was. Described as a Hayashi (wooded) garden, the plan was for it to contain more than ninety metres of streams,[41] "reflecting pools, stone lanterns, formal flower beds, and an authentic Japanese Tea House."[42] There is no teahouse. A small waterfall creates one small stream that flows under a stone slab bridge to a tiny pond—or it would, if the water was turned on. Trees and plants abound, though some beds have been filled with chips of wood or stone instead of vegetation.

Near this garden, and next door to Ichi Ban, was a second themed restaurant developed by the Harts for Jack Levit's Lakeview Square. The Grande Canal of Venice was an Italian restaurant. Steven Hart described the perimeter of the restaurant as having "a façade all the way around there: this was the port of Venice."[43] The façade was of a number of cafés, each accommodating a table of diners and with a different theme. In the centre of the restaurant floated two huge boats, six to seven metres long—"In actual water, just like Dad did with the Cleopatra's barges at Caesars Palace," Hart said.[44] Students from the Manitoba Opera school and elsewhere were employed as servers to sing while waiting tables.[45] An Italian prep chef was hired to cook and plate individual meals well in advance, each of which would then be placed in a blast freezer. A day's worth would then be transferred to a cooler to thaw for that day's service; orders were heated in a microwave before serving. The Grande Canal was not a success. The singing stopped, the restaurant was renamed Café Mediterranea, and the menu was changed twice.[46] Steven Hart had one explanation for its failure: "This [restaurant concept] did not go very well with Canadian people, because Canadian people like steak and beer."[47] Local food critics had other explanations: "That Winnipeg is really only a steak town is a cliché but, for some restaurateurs, it has become a cop-out. The blame for the failure of Café Mediterranea's continental menu does not belong in our laps. It belongs in the kitchens of Café Med/La Grande Canal of Venice. It's not that Winnipeggers won't accept continental or 'different foods,' it's that Winnipeggers are learning to reject poor food, whether or not it has a fancy name."[48]

While Chinese restaurants have a long history in western Canada, Japanese restaurants were a rarity in Winnipeg until the late 1980s, as they were in much of the world outside of Japan.[49] The first Japanese restaurants in Europe were established in the 1970s, but until the 1990s, as Cwiertka commented, "Japanese cuisine was too unfamiliar and too expensive to attract local clientele" on that continent.[50] Ichi Ban, not surprisingly, made a deliberate effort to educate their customers. They provided "do-it-yourself chopsticks" that hinged the two sticks together for ease of use by beginners.[51] The restaurant listed and defined their menu items in their advertisements: "Properly prepared *sashimi*—sliced raw fish—is one of the glories of Japanese cuisine. *Sushi* is simply sashimi or other fresh ingredients rolled in vinegared rice. For neophytes, veggie or shrimp variations are sure to get you hooked."[52] Restaurant reviewers informed their readers of what to expect when dining at Ichi Ban: "The soup spoon is alabaster china and the rest of the dinner is eaten with chop sticks. The rice can be managed easily if you pick up the bowl."[53] Other educational efforts included participation in the Folklorama Festival, Winnipeg's festival of ethno-cultural diversity. Ichi Ban chefs provided cooking demonstrations at Folklorama's Japanese pavilion in 1976.[54]

Historically, Ichi Ban is the second Japanese restaurant to be created in Winnipeg, though the history of Asian restaurants in the city is much longer. In 1936, sixty-nine of the 288 restaurants, lunch counters, and other dining establishments in Winnipeg—almost a quarter—were operated by those the *Winnipeg Tribune* referred to as "Orientals."[55] The earliest mention of a specifically Japanese restaurant in Winnipeg is a report of a court case in 1903: James Lawson, the proprietor of a restaurant on Portage Avenue East, was sued by his contractor for failure to pay for repairs.[56] The restaurant is identified by the *Free Press* as Japanese, while the *Tribune* describes the proprietor as Chinese. The restaurant's cuisine was neither, apparently. Lawson was in court again later that year, but this time as the plaintiff. Three American customers ordered waffles, described by the reporter as "a catchy dish when served with genuine maple syrup"

Figure 19. Entrance to Ichi Ban, Winnipeg. Photograph by Janis Thiessen, 2020.

Figure 20. Japanese garden at Lakeview Square, Winnipeg. Photograph by Janis Thiessen, 2020.

Figure 21. Chef Sadao Ono with a plate of sashimi. Photograph by Janis Thiessen, 2021.

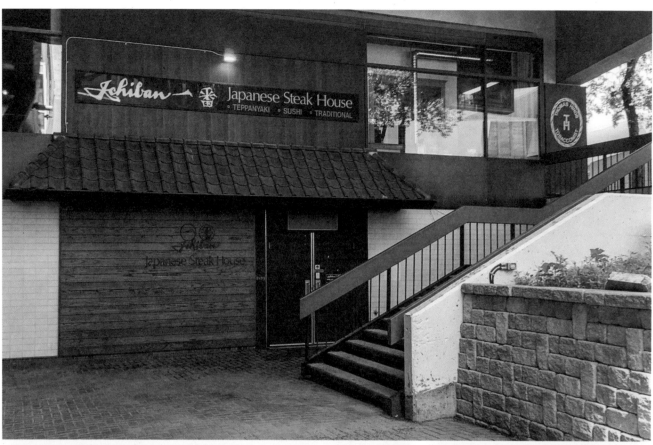

that was "not generally in vogue on this side of the line." Angered by the price, the Americans proceeded to "smash things in general."[57]

The first Japanese newcomers to Canada arrived not in Manitoba but in British Columbia in 1877.[58] The population of Japanese Canadians in Manitoba was miniscule before the Second World War: in 1931, there were only fifty-one in the province. During the Second World War, Japanese Canadian civilians (and, in lesser numbers, Ukrainian Canadians, Italian Canadians, and others) were incarcerated in violation of their civil rights and liberties.[59] More than 20,000 Japanese Canadians were relocated from Canada's west coast and their property confiscated; of these, 782 were incarcerated, and 1,053 were forcibly relocated to Manitoba. Many of the Japanese Manitobans were ordered to work on sugar beet farms.[60] Art Miki, former president of the National Association of Japanese Canadians and one of the Japanese Canadians so relocated from British Columbia to Manitoba, was instrumental in securing an apology and compensation from the Government of Canada for these actions in 1988.[61] Historians Rhonda Hinther and Jim Mochoruk note, however, "It is no exaggeration to say that ever since the earliest community members' arrival, the lives of Japanese Canadians had been unequally regulated and circumscribed by formal and informal racist manoeuvring on the part of white government officials, union members, citizens' groups, and others."[62] The Japanese Manitoban population remained low for decades after the war: only 1,161 in 1951, and 1,335 in 1971.[63]

It is therefore not surprising that traditional Japanese food was not readily available in Winnipeg for decades.[64] Japanese food could be purchased from Central Family Co-op on King Street, founded by Genji Otsu, Harold Hirose, and Ichiro Hirayama in 1947; it folded in 1956.[65] Japanese cuisine also was offered at occasional dinners held by various Winnipeg organizations in the 1950s and 1960s. The YMCA Crucible Club, for example, offered a Japanese Canadian "Ethnic Night" in 1952, with food prepared by local Japanese Canadians, who also performed dances and songs and gave demonstrations of flower arranging. The *Winnipeg Free Press* reported, "Japanese food was served. Probably most of the visitors were familiar with 'chow mein' but the rest of the food was excitingly new to them. The appearance of the various foods was deceptive. 'Osushi' look like pink tea-sandwiches, but they are seasoned rice coated with sea weed or egg or soya paste. 'Omanju' looks like a thick, shiny little pancake, but it has a sweetened bean paste inside that makes it taste more like a confection. One food looked like potato chips, but it tasted like caramel-coated popcorn. 'Yokan,' however, looks like gumdrops and tastes like gumdrops."[66] A meeting of the Manitoba Home for Girls Auxiliary in 1961 served both Chinese and Japanese food, prepared by women from Winnipeg's Chinese United Church and the Nisei Canadian Women's Club.[67] The Dakota Motor Hotel offered a "sukiyaki night" in 1967, featuring "Japanese girls in native costume" cooking the food tableside on fifty electric frying pans.[68]

It was not until 1963 that the first restaurant in Winnipeg advertised itself as offering Japanese cuisine. This was Purple Lantern Restaurant, owned by Howie Young. Operating until at least 1965 at 114 Higgins Avenue, across from the CPR station, it offered Chinese, Japanese, and American food, describing itself as "Simple But Exotic—Small But Exquisite."[69]

Opening a decade later, Ichi Ban was thus the second restaurant in Winnipeg to feature Japanese cuisine. Unlike the short-lived Purple Lantern, however, Ichi Ban created an opening for a broader range of Japanese food offerings in the city, partly by cultivating a clientele and partly by helping establish a network of Asian Canadian chefs who would go on to open their own Japanese restaurants.[70] In 1979, Tokyo Joe's Bulkoki House (132 Pioneer Avenue) was the next Japanese restaurant to open in the city. Its owner, Joe Lee, combined his Korean background with his experience cooking Japanese food at Ichi Ban to design his restaurant's menu.[71] Lee was the first to serve sushi and sashimi in Winnipeg,[72] offerings that local food critic Marion Warhaft did not then appreciate: "Unquestionably for special tastes (not mine)." Describing sushi as "a bland rice and cooked fish combination wrapped in seaweed," she advised, "If you're curious, try half-orders. The presentation is so attractive they're almost worth ordering as a feast for the eyes alone."[73] Hers was not an unusual view among many North Americans at the time, though tastes were changing: "If it's slimy and raw, don't eat it, right? Wrong,"[74] noted the *Free Press* a year earlier. Ichi Ban and Tokyo Joe's were joined in 1980 by Yamato Restaurant, headed by Sam Aoyama. Yamato offered sushi only on Tuesdays, but by then food columnist Marjorie Gillies was providing instructions for the enterprising home sushi chef in the pages of the *Tribune*.[75] Chef-owner Sadao Ono, a former head chef at Ichi Ban, opened Winnipeg's first sushi bar, Edohei, in 1987.[76] Ono became the mentor of many of Winnipeg's best-known sushi chefs, including Laotian Canadian chef Cho Venevongsa of Wasabi and Japanese Canadian chef Masa Sugita of Masa and Izakaya Edokko.[77] Sugita partnered with Chinese Canadian chef Edward Lam to open Miyabi and Yujiro, and Lam went on to open Gaijin Izakaya and Saburo Kitchen. By 1994, Ichi Ban was advertising itself as not just a Japanese steak house but also a sushi bar, and in 1996 was offering all-you-can-eat sushi.[78] Slowly, Marion Warhaft and other Winnipeggers began to embrace Japanese cuisine: "Twenty years ago [the 1980s], while the rest of the world was being swept by sushi, we weren't. At that time the only sushi we could find was at Yamato, and then only as a sometime thing. . . . Today [the year 2000] we have several Japanese restaurants, and all of them serve sushi daily, in quantity," Warhaft wrote, declaring Yamato's sushi "sublime."[79]

The diversity of Asian Canadians in Winnipeg's Japanese restaurant scene is noteworthy. Steven Hart recalled of Ichi Ban's first years: "We could not find Japanese people [as employees]—we found a few. So, what we did was, we put ads in the paper. We were able to get a mixture of Chinese, mostly, and Filipino employees to work there."[80] The restaurant's ads recruiting employees in the 1970s asked for individuals familiar with Japanese language and culture. The ads' language was a result of warnings from Ichi Ban's publicists: "Wording is quite important since you cannot specifically ask for Japanese staff. This would amount to discrimination. However, with suitable wording, you can make it fairly obvious that you are interested primarily in recruiting Japanese staff."[81]

The Orientalist assumption that all Asians were interchangeable, reflected in the *Free Press*'s misidentification of Lawson's restaurant as Japanese and the early hiring practices of Ichi Ban, was part of a long and troubling history of racism in Canada. In 1912, Saskatchewan passed An Act to Prevent the Employment of Female Labor in Certain Capacities, preventing "any white woman or girl to reside or lodge in, or to work in, or, save as a bona fide customer in a public apartment thereof only, to frequent any restaurant, laundry or other place of business or amusement owned, kept or managed by any Japanese, Chinaman or other Oriental person."[82] Punishment upon conviction was to be a fine of up to one hundred dollars or imprisonment of up to two months. Identical legislation was passed in Manitoba in 1913 but not proclaimed into law.[83] British Columbia had similar legislation; only Chinese managers and proprietors were

INSIDE OUT
MAKI-ZUSHI

SUSHI RICE:

2½ cups Japanese short grain rice

3 cups water

5 tbsp rice vinegar

1 tbsp mirin (rice wine)

3 tbsp sugar

2 tsp salt

Wash rice under tap water until clear. Bring water to a boil in a pot, reduce heat, and boil rice for 5 minutes. Then lower heat and steam rice for 12–15 minutes. Remove rice from heat.

Combine all other ingredients in a separate pot and heat gently until sugar has dissolved, stirring gently. Set aside this sushi seasoning.

Transfer cooked rice to hangiri (wooden tub for sushi rice preparation) or a large, wide bowl. Run a shamoji (broad wooden spatula) through the rice to separate grains while slowly adding sushi seasoning.

Fan the rice to cool at room temperature, then cover with damp tea towel and use as soon as possible.

INSIDE OUT MAKI-ZUSHI:

cooked and seasoned sushi rice

½ sheet of nori (roasted seaweed)

wasabi paste

masago (smelt fish roe)

tobiko (flying fish roe)

sliced avocado

crab stick

Prepare small bowl of vinegared water (1 part vinegar to 2 parts water). Place nori horizontally on sudare (bamboo rolling mat) covered with plastic wrap. Coat hands thoroughly in vinegared water, then pick up sushi rice and spread evenly over nori, leaving a ½-inch strip bare at the far end of the nori. Carefully flip the nori so the rice is on the sudare and the nori is facing upward.

With your finger, smear some wasabi in a horizontal line across the end of the nori closest to you. Place strips of avocado and crab stick on the wasabi, and sprinkle with masago.

Pick up the corners of the sudare closest to you and roll away from you. The strip of nori that you left bare will form a seal for the roll. Remove the sudare and slice the roll into even pieces, wiping the knife blade with a damp cloth before each cut. Sprinkle with tobiko.

Sadao Ono

Interviewed by Janis Thiessen and Kent Davies, cooking class at the Food Studio, Winnipeg, MB, 15 November 2021.

JANIS THIESSEN: Chef, can I ask you about when you opened Edohei? I had been reading in the newspaper that, when it opened, the restaurant reviewers didn't understand what sushi was in Winnipeg. So was it hard for you for the first year?

SADAO ONO: Very, very hard. Because nobody had—now everybody knows sushi and eats fish, but when I opened that was very hard.

KENT DAVIES: It's really hard to imagine [laughs].

SADAO ONO: Yeah. When I opened Edohei, two TV stations come and film that . . .

JANIS THIESSEN: How long did it take before that turned around and people realized what you were doing?

SADAO ONO: Ohhhh. Probably . . . very popular starting in five or six years, easy.

MARIA ABIUSI [owner of the Food Studio]: Wow! That's a long time.

SADAO ONO: Yeah.

The son of a rice farmer, Sadao Ono trained as a sushi chef in Tokyo, moving to Vancouver in 1972 and Winnipeg in 1975.[84] A former head chef at Ichi Ban restaurant, he opened Winnipeg's first sushi bar, Edohei, in 1988.[85] He became the mentor of many of Winnipeg's best-known sushi chefs, including the owners of Wasabi, Masa, and Izakaya Edokko. He closed Edohei in 2012 but did not fully retire.[86] Instead, he has served for years as sushi chef at Folklorama's Japanese Pavilion, teaches classes at the Food Studio, and offers special-order ramen and bento box meals that sell out quickly at the Japanese Cultural Association of Manitoba.[87]

CHICKEN KARAAGE

1/3 cup Japanese soy sauce

2 tbsp sake

25 grams grated fresh ginger

900 grams skin-on boneless chicken thighs,
cut into bite-sized pieces

170 grams potato starch

vegetable oil for frying

½ lemon, sliced into wedges for serving

Whisk the soy sauce, sake, and ginger together in a bowl to create the
marinade. Add chicken and mix well to coat. Cover and refrigerate for
1–4 hours.

Heat 1 inch of oil in a heavy-bottomed pot to 170°C. Dredge marinated
chicken in potato starch to coat evenly. Fry coated chicken in batches,
being careful not to overcrowd the pot. When chicken has an internal
temperature of 71°C, transfer it to a paper towel-lined rack or plate to rest
for a few minutes before serving.

singled out, however.[88] Saskatchewan's Act was amended in 1913 to apply only to Chinese Canadians, and again in 1919 to apply only to restaurants and laundries, whoever the owners.[89] Such racist laws were a response to moral panics about white slavery,[90] but also a response to the Canadian labour movement's exclusionist policies. The passage of the Saskatchewan Act had been requested by trade unionists "and others interested in social and moral reform" and was upheld in the courts in *R. v. Quong-Wing* in 1914, a case involving two Chinese Canadian restaurant owners in Moose Jaw.[91] Even the One Big Union entertained a resolution that they be "opposed to the patronage of restaurants owned and operated by Asiatic [*sic*] . . . and support the hotel and restaurant employees in establishing white help exclusively in all hotels and restaurants or other licensed premises where food and refreshments are served."[92] Ontario had similar legislation, preventing Chinese Canadian owners of factories, restaurants, and laundries from employing white women from 1914 to 1947, though it was apparently in effect only from 1927 to 1929.[93]

In the early 1920s, both Winnipeg and St. Boniface city councils were interested in similarly restricting the ability of Chinese Canadian employers to hire white women within their city limits.[94] Winnipeg City Council had been petitioned in 1921 for the passage of such legislation, and it was recommended by the Committee on Health.[95] The province, as City Solicitor Jules Preudhomme declared, had passed but never proclaimed such legislation,[96] but amending the city's Charter would allow Winnipeg to authorize such restrictions within their borders.[97] And so in 1923, An Act to Amend the Winnipeg Charter was passed, allowing the city to pass a bylaw prohibiting employment of women in businesses owned or managed by Chinese Canadians.[98] According to the *Winnipeg Evening Tribune*, St. Boniface City Council decided in 1923 to investigate "the problem of white help employed in Oriental restaurants on the advice of Mayor Swain, who thought it was about time that something was done to avoid such a condition. Winnipeg's bylaws will be gone over to see what it has done towards this problem."[99] Though there was much debate, no such bylaw was ever created in Winnipeg.

Support for these racist proposed restrictions came from Winnipeg Chief of Police Donald Macpherson, the city's License Inspector, the Winnipeg branch of the Great War Veterans' Association, as well as F.H. Barber, vice-president of the Asiatic Exclusion League.[100] The latter argued that employment restrictions should apply not just to the Chinese but to "all

Orientals."[101] This argument was consistent with the racist aims of the Asiatic Exclusion League, whose primary aim was "To work for a White Canada" and "To Eradicate the Oriental Menace by every means in our power."[102] The Consul General of China protested Winnipeg's proposed bylaw, describing it as "unnecessary" and "unjust legislation," and a "disgrace to China."[103] As had happened with the Saskatchewan legislation, Winnipeg's city solicitor suspected that any proposed legislation would have to *regulate* employment of women by Chinese employers rather than completely restrict it.[104] Lawyers representing the Chinese Nationalist League requested as much, though they couched their argument in racist terms in their letters to Winnipeg's city solicitor:

> When the Chinese as a whole are compared with other foreigners it seems to me that they would, as good and law abiding citizens, be far in advance of anything that we get from Central or Southern Europe. . . . Whether or not the Chinese are desirable citizens is scarcely open for discussion. The fact is they are here, and it would seem to me that our duty would be to treat them in the same manner as other citizens are treated and in this way endeavour to assimilate them with the rest of the population at as early a period as possible.[105]

Another letter from the same lawyers, written a couple of years later, asked: "Greeks, Italians and other foreigners are engaged in the restaurant and fruit business and if they are allowed to employ female labor, why should not the Chinese. . . . It cannot be said that they are not law-abiding citizens, or that they do not compare favorably with other immigrants. Take for example the Galicians who are probably more so than [any] other class before the criminal courts."[106]

City Council members, however, according to the *Manitoba Free Press*, decided that their singling out of Chinese Canadians was justified "in view of the fact the Orientals are given different treatment to others by imposition of a head tax by the Dominion government."[107]

Legislation notwithstanding, many restaurants across Manitoba engaged in racist hiring and advertising practices for a quarter-century, declaring "only/all white help employed" as both a qualification in "help wanted" ads and as an assumed attraction for customers.[108] Some were particularly flagrant: "White Help—White Treatment. . . . You'll be thought more of if you think more of the place where you dine."[109] Such racist actions did not pass without critique at the time. As early as 1915, A.L. Driver wrote the *Manitoba Free Press*, decrying efforts to "draw the color line" and declaring "it is bad for a city the size of Winnipeg and a country noted for freedom and fair play to all members of the human race to let such things pass unobserved." The editors of the paper ran his letter under the dismissive heading: "From a Colored Man."[110]

Decades later, it was people of non-Japanese background who were the first to establish restaurants in Winnipeg offering Japanese cuisine: Howie Young's Purple Lantern Restaurant, Jack Levit's and Nat Hart's Ichi Ban Steak House, Joe Lee's Tokyo Joe's Bulkoki House. Much as Starbucks paved the way for third-wave coffee, these restaurants taught Winnipeggers to appreciate what was, for many, an unfamiliar cuisine.[111] Increased global travel, whether experienced personally or vicariously (the *Winnipeg Free Press* published numerous exoticized stories of tourist trips to Japan in the 1960s and 1970s), fostered desires for "authentic" experiences of Japanese food in Winnipeg restaurants. So-called ethnic restaurants like Ichi Ban, according to writer Dan Aviv, "provide an opportunity for individuals to indulge in the proprietor's ethnicity, to safely sample of the Other without need of a passport."[112] But Ichi Ban did not always fare well in these debates over traditionalism and authenticity, as some believed the kitschy decor overwhelmed its efforts in the kitchen. One of Cynthia Wine's reviews in the *Winnipeg Free Press* stated, "Perhaps not unwittingly, the menu seems almost incidental to the theatre in which it's consumed. At the Ichi Ban, one is struck immediately by the flamboyance of its decoration."[113] And yet these same critics also could be circumspect about the mootness of the question. Wine continued:

> "But is it authentic?" insisted a man who telephoned last week. Well, the question calls into play a practical argument: How authentic can one expect it to be? One can't find real French bread in Winnipeg because we simply don't have French flour. . . . So, I suppose the Ichi Ban isn't completely authentic but, most of the time, the food we've had there has compared well with other Teppan Yaki meals we've had in Japan and the United States. Teppan Yaki offers the best compromise for a person who is looking for "something different" but who doesn't really want to find it. None of the food you eat at the Ichi Ban will be unfamiliar to you. All that is different is the choreography of its preparation.[114]

Ichi Ban's founders and developers themselves did not see their restaurant as authentically Japanese. But teppan yaki, it may be argued, *is* authentic Japanese cooking. It was developed by Japanese chefs in Japanese restaurants looking to appeal to a broader clientele. It is not a case of, as Aviv says, "the dominant culture exoticizing, fetishizing and commodifying non-dominant cultures."[115] To insist that teppan yaki is not authentic or traditional necessitates the question: At what point in time do you want to freeze a tradition? And to what purpose?

Edward Lam, current owner of Yujiro Restaurant, makes this point about tradition very clearly. Reflecting on his Chinese Canadian food background, he observes, "We don't have sweet and sour chicken balls; we don't have them. We don't have dry ribs; we don't have deep fried wings; we don't have those. . . . But, are they good? They're good."[116] Cuisines develop over time in response to the creativity of chefs and the kitchen staff, to the changing composition of clientele, and to those customers' changing tastes. Lam says:

> Yes, yes, tradition is always good but you don't—see, that's why it's really a confusing word nowadays. I remember, six years ago, I did an interview with the [*Winnipeg*] *Free Press* and all I'm saying is "Yujiro or Miyabi is traditional Japanese restaurant." Traditional. I kept saying "traditional, traditional." Last year I did another one: I tell them "it's traditional with a contemporary mindset." There's no more just traditional, because people don't really want only traditional. And also, should we say, how many people in Winnipeg know what is traditional Japanese food? I can say it's traditional. Even Japanese people could come in and say "I don't even know what is really traditional nowadays." You know? You think Kaiseki [Japanese multi-course haute cuisine] is traditional but today Kaiseki is different. All the Japanese restaurants are all different now; there's no "only traditional."[117]

What matters, then, is not whether a food is traditional or authentic (again, which tradition? preserved at what point in time?). The question of authenticity is also a racist one. American Studies scholar Martin F. Manalansan IV comments: "Immigrants encounter notions and questions of authenticity because they are almost always seen as strangers being slowly integrated into the preexisting 'native' culture."[118] But all that matters is whether the food tastes good. As Edward Lam says:

I think anybody that can take something small or even big and magnify it to make a statement of it should be known. Because it's not just something that you can say, "I pick up a street food, and because I'm Momofuku [David Chang's famous culinary brand], because I'm [Iron Chef Masaharu] Morimoto, I can make it happen"—no. There is a lot of work in between to modify it, to make everything taste good. Let's say Mokoto Ono [son of Edohei's chef Sadao Ono], not every plate he punches out is successful, maybe just a few. But that few was so outstanding. The commitment, the research, the hard work behind that, that make all the chefs say, "This is a good chef." Somebody that can commit that much and do that hard of work, that is a good chef. He can do it this time, and can do it next time. That has become what they say a good chef; but not necessarily every dish, every plate is good.[119]

Lam's words remind us that it is *this* tradition of Japanese food in Winnipeg that Ichi Ban can take some credit for. Cynthia Wine observes Ichi Ban itself "seems very much an expense-account, special-occasion restaurant, which makes no pretence about its commercialism, even down to the crockery which is for sale by the exit. But all of that is fine: The food is good, the surroundings are fun and it is all very good theatre."[120] As the English translation of the restaurant's name declares, "Ichi Ban—number one."

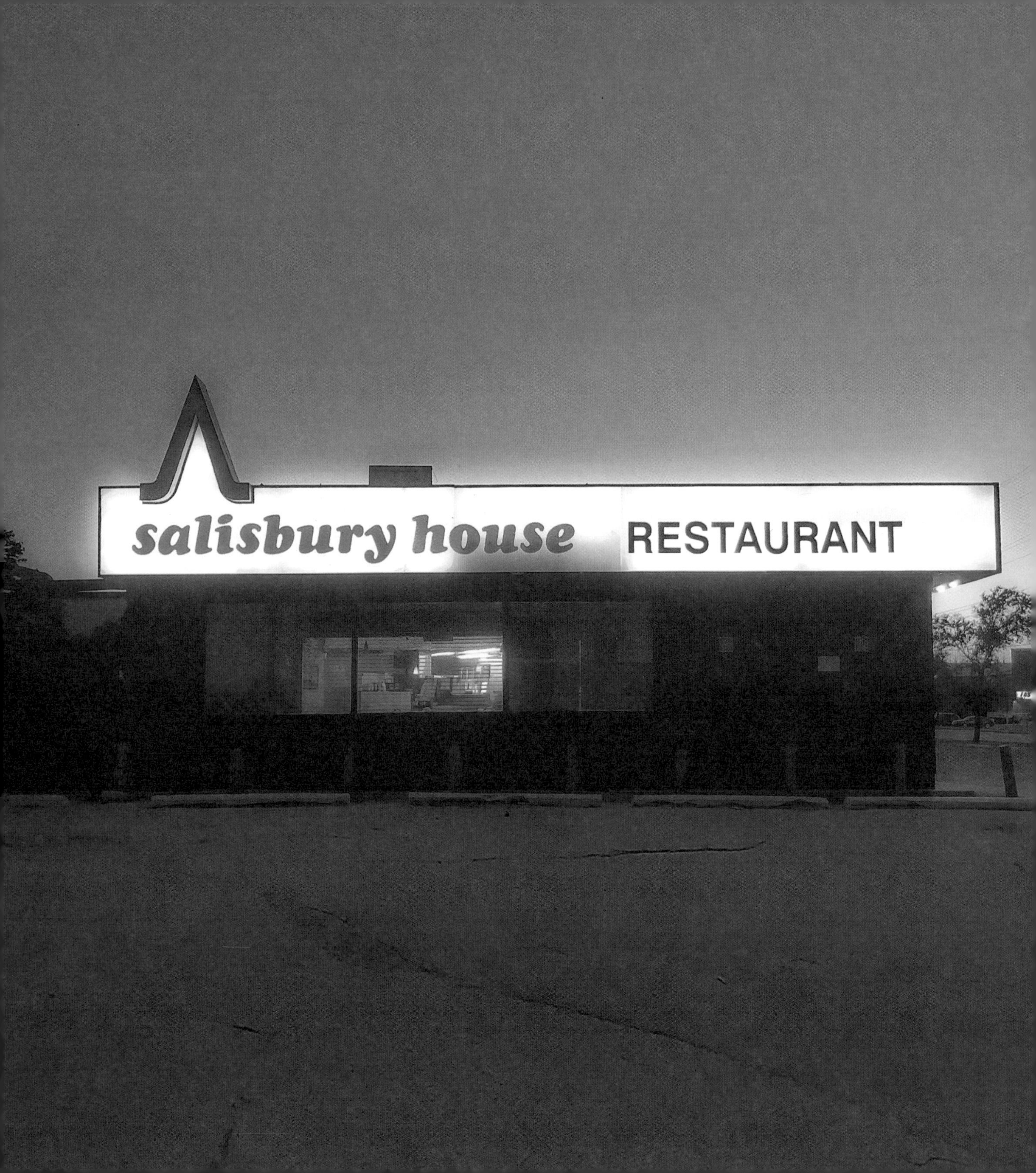
salisbury house
RESTAURANT

CHAPTER TWO

Fat Boys and Nips

Throughout the Manitoba Food History Project, we have explored the idea of "local food" and the malleable parameters one can apply in defining what that means. This chapter tells the story of two Manitoban food phenomena: the Fat Boy and the Nip. While those people unfamiliar with Manitoba's menu offerings may side-eye a suggestion to indulge in one or the other, locals will recognize both as two varieties of hamburger: the Nip being the signature burger of local franchise Salisbury House—or Sals, as it is commonly called— and the Fat Boy, which defies proprietary claims, served exclusively by Greek-owned drive-ins.[1]

The Fat Boy is a fully dressed burger topped with what locals call "chili" but which lacks beans and has hints of cinnamon. This meat sauce is the defining characteristic of the Fat Boy. Although this Greek chili is served on burgers at several different spots, there is a remarkable consistency to the taste, regardless of which drive-in you order from. Do not, however, mistake the chili-topped burger at Salisbury House to be a Fat Boy. Although it is described on the

Figure 22. Salisbury House at 1860 Ellice Avenue, taken in 2020 shortly before the location was permanently closed. Photograph by Kimberley Moore, 2020.

menu as "smothered in chili meat sauce," it is not "Greek chili" and, thus, it is rather a "Chili Nip."[2] Apart from its name, we are hard-pressed to find any truly unique characteristic of the Nip. Charitably, it is the fried onions, which have been a constituent part of the burger since at least 1945.[3] The Nip comes in several classic variations—Nip (grilled onions), Mr. Big Nip (raw onions), Cheese Nip (grilled onions and cheese), Chili Nip (grilled onions and meat sauce)—as well as a few modern additions, such as the Bacon Mushroom Swiss Nip, a "Gourmet" Nip with onion and garlic aioli, a Veggie Nip, and the Big Earl, a three-patty burger (named for Sals proprietor, and two-time rescuer, Earl Barish), which, in the menu's description, is accompanied by a dare.[4]

That a few notable Greek-owned drive-ins and Salisbury House (and their respective Fat Boys and Nips) have survived into the twenty-first century is somewhat bewildering, considering the rapid pace at which dining trends evolve and individual eateries appear and vanish. The longevity of these establishments might be their most remarkable characteristic. These two institutions have endured for the better part of a century by employing very different strategies: Salisbury House has survived through ceaseless evolution and adaptation over a period of ninety-one years, while Greek-owned drive-ins have endured for over sixty years largely by staying small and never changing a thing.

The focus of this chapter is primarily Winnipeg, partly due to the scarcity of sources and stories from outside the Perimeter Highway, and partly due to space constraints. (The history of Greek-owned restaurants in Manitoba could easily be a multi-year research project in its own right.) However, these stories reach into other parts of Manitoba. Although Greek-owned drive-ins are mostly confined to Winnipeg, you can find Fat Boys in a few surrounding areas such as Portage La Prairie (Jimmy's), Headingley (Nick's Inn), Gimli (Country Boy), and Winnipeg Beach (Johnee's). Although Sals primarily operates in Winnipeg now, there have been past locations in Selkirk, Steinbach, Thompson, Flin Flon, Norway House, Kenora, Moose Jaw, Calgary, and Fargo, North Dakota.[5] Despite our having conducted exhaustive research, the story told in this chapter largely relies on evidentiary fragments and individual memory, both of which are subject to omissions, errors, and in some cases embellishment. While we cannot claim that herein lie the indisputable facts of the past in their entirety, there is enough to begin this story—which is as true as it can be under the circumstances. To fill in the gaps and illuminate the errors, more research is necessary; there are more data to quantify; there are more family keepsakes that await rediscovery; there are more stories to hear.

Charting the evolution of the various types of ready-made food service through the nineteenth and twentieth centuries, from street food to fast food, is challenging. It is not a linear evolution. Trends in food sales, including menu offerings and the spaces in which they were sold, were adapted and combined any which way that proprietors imagined to be profitable. Any effort at tracing this evolution according to restaurant type is quickly frustrated by lunch wagons called cafés and diners, diners called restaurants, lunch bars called grills, diners called drive-ins, and various other combinations of these labels. In Manitoba, general trends through the decades become apparent in piecing together bylaws, the records of the Manitoba Companies Office, and news fragments. However, these evidentiary fragments rarely speak to the details of these places. They do not tell us (beyond names) about their owners, answer questions such as what was on the menu, or inform us of who dined there. But together with the work of local community historians, journalists, reporters, and filmmakers, personal keepsakes, and eBay memorabilia, and the memories of those who were there, it is possible to gain a clearer picture of the conditions under which Salisbury House and Greek drive-ins emerged in Manitoba. Situating the available fragments within a much larger story of food for "mass eaters"[6] within North America illustrates how Salisbury House and the drive-in restaurant were each a product of their time, how broader trends influenced the development of Winnipeg's own food service landscape, and ultimately how these two institutions emerged under uniquely Manitoban conditions. Coincidentally, considering these conspicuously named burgers in a larger context also reveals that both had a common point of inspiration: the "Coney Island Red Hot," which is not a hamburger at all but a kind of hot dog.

The many incarnations of Salisbury House within the City of Winnipeg illustrate the relentless evolution of ready-made food vendors in a single restaurant franchise. Depending on the neighbourhood and the decade, Sals has been a lunch counter, cigar stand, diner, commissary, drive-in, full-service restaurant, and market store. Each of these iterations, and their locations, speaks to a phase in the dining industry's evolution, as food moved out of the home kitchen and into the streets to meet the demands of an evolving urban landscape and the workers who occupied it. As the population grew, workforces changed, and technology and infrastructure evolved, types of ready-made food (and the accommodations built to serve it) multiplied. An incomplete list of Salisbury House locations over time includes several locations in downtown Winnipeg, several more in the suburbs, two in bus depots, in the McLaren Hotel on Main Street downtown, on the ground level of the cylindrical Garry Street parkade, inside Minto Armouries, in Investors Group Stadium (where the Winnipeg Blue Bombers play football) and Shaw Park (where the Winnipeg Goldeyes play baseball), at the Winnipeg International Airport, and on l'Esplanade Riel, the pedestrian bridge between downtown Winnipeg and the francophone community of St. Boniface.

For those who have spent most of their lives in Winnipeg, the Salisbury House restaurant is part of the fabric of the city. It has served us butter-flavoured hash browns at weekend family brunches, provided us with tin ashtrays when we needed a place to drink endless coffee and chain-smoke cigarettes, and importantly, fed us at several twenty-four-hour locations whatever our drunken hearts desired after the bars closed at 2:00 a.m.[7] But like anything that is ever-present, a certain apathy has often surrounded Salisbury House.[8] Perhaps this is owing in part to the fact that from the time that founder Ralph Erwin sold it in 1979 until 2001, the Manitoban restaurant chain had not been locally owned.[9]

So, in 2001, when a group of prominent Winnipeggers banded together to purchase the franchise, and Salisbury House was on front pages across Canada, a local enthusiasm for the restaurant ignited.[10] The group included the Winnipeg Goldeyes Baseball Club owner (and soon to be Winnipeg mayor) Sam Katz,[11] Earl and Cheryl Barish, The Guess Who's band manager, Lorne Saifer, and its lead singer, Burton Cummings.[12] The headline in the *Globe and Mail* declared: "Rock Royalty Buys Winnipeg 'Crown Jewel,'"[13] Sals launched an official website,[14] and Cummings promptly embarked on a sixteen-restaurant tour, at which he performed and signed autographs in an attempt to rekindle Winnipeggers' affection for the franchise.[15]

Despite the *Globe and Mail* headline's hyperbole, Cummings's association with Salisbury House resulted in something of a cult following. Both Cummings and Sals are concurrently adored in earnest and embraced in irony by locals—they are part of Winnipeg's iconography.[16]

This is visible in local works of art such as the short film *Fahrenheit 7-11* by Walter Forsberg and Matthew Rankin; the album release announcement for band Ultramega's *Panis Angelicus*; the cover of musician Smoky Tiger's *Corporal Compliance*; and a wooden ornament crafted by Winnipeg North of Fargo artist Roy Liang on which the Louis Vuitton monogram has been modified by swapping the initials LV with images of Louis Riel, a stylized Winnipeg Jets logo, the Confusion Corner junction,[17] and the Salisbury House's peaked roof.

By 2005, with Salisbury sur l'Esplanade Riel as the first occupant of the newly constructed Esplanade Riel's restaurant space (situated midway across the pedestrian corridor) the restaurant seemed to once again occupy a central place in Winnipeggers' hearts.[18] However, this novel location, with its French signage, Burton's baby grand, a Harley Davidson motorcycle,[19] and Winnipeg's "million-dollar toilet,"[20] was not immune to the troubles that came with operating a restaurant in the middle of a bridge, particularly in Winnipeg's winter.[21] Despite the fanfare that came along with this location's opening, the franchise was also not immune to the market forces that exert pressure on most food service establishments.

Although it reported "revenues of over $15 million"[22] at the time of the ownership change in 2001, by 2006 Salisbury House was on the brink of receivership. Investors called an "emergency shareholders meeting" at which Dickie Dee Ice Cream founder Earl Barish was appointed president and CEO.[23] With Barish at the helm, the restaurant doubled down on its Manitoban identity and on the nostalgia factor that investors had attempted to inject in the early 2000s. The walls of Salisbury House became an exhibit of past locations, staff, former City of Winnipeg mayors, and various local celebrities. Today, there are even two locations at which you will find dedicated corners of Manitoba memorabilia entirely unrelated to the restaurant, or even to food.

The most recent additions to Salisbury House consist of the entirely reconstructed Pembina Highway location (which includes the mid-century lunch counter and stools from the original restaurant at this location), a Manitoba Music Memorabilia Exhibit in its front entrance, and a liquor licence, which permits it to boast a selection of local craft beer, including Salisbury House's own "Red Roof Lager."[24] The Portage Avenue location has a similar exhibit of local sports memorabilia. In 2020, in response to the strain and limitations the COVID-19 pandemic placed on restaurants, Salisbury House launched the Sals Market, an extension of the commissary on King Edward Street. From Sals Market you can order "Heat and Eat Meals" for delivery, stop in to pick up some Winni Buns,[25] or drive up and order a piece of wafer pie to eat in your car, courtesy of the COVID-safe car hops introduced at this location in 2021.[26] These twenty-first-century additions are part of a ninety-year history of constant adaptation. Salisbury House has been turned every which way but loose in the effort to keep it alive and thriving.[27] Although the number of Salisbury Houses has been reduced to seven restaurants, all in Winnipeg, the nostalgic draw has a clear and effective impact. If you visit a Salisbury House, you will inevitably overhear other patrons regaling the defenceless waitstaff with personal memories of the locations they've ritually patronized, and for how many decades they've been doing so.

Salisbury House founder Ralph Erwin was born in Burwell, Nebraska, in 1903, the only son of a railroad engineer and a dressmaker. An actor by trade, Erwin began travelling with Chautauqua companies (a form of touring entertainment) at the age of seventeen. Although Erwin wanted to leave the circuit, he lost the coin toss that would determine if he'd be released from his acting contract and subsequently made his way to Canada with the Ellison-White Chautauqua company.[28] As Erwin biographer Patrick Donohue details in *The Erwin Story*, Erwin would go on to become the manager of his own acting company, and established a studio in Winnipeg.[29] For the next decade, the Martin Erwin Players would travel the prairies until, "the Depression and the talkies administered the death blows" to the Chautauqua circuit.[30] His career as a producer over, Erwin joined his wife, Helen, in New York, to consider how he might next make a living. He thought of the times when he and Helen would stop at White Castle restaurants in New York for burgers after a show, or at a Greek restaurant for a "Coney Island Red Hot, a little hot dog, two and a half inches long, with sauce on it, in a bun,"[31] and recalled that in his acting days in Canada, he'd found a lack of "cheap, tasty, food, especially late at night."[32] Hamburgers in particular were hard to find. So, he returned to Winnipeg to establish his own Canadian restaurant to remedy this.[33]

The name of the Salisbury House, and of the Nip, came to him in a roundabout way. Between news articles and the Salisbury House's website, the story varies, but *The Erwin Story* includes the tale. Believing that the word "'hamburger' had a crass sound that wouldn't appeal to Canadians," Erwin thought they'd prefer something a little more British. He recalled that chopped beef was called "Salisbury steak" but did not think "steak" had enough appeal. As Donohue writes, "One night, while walking the streets of New York, Ralph and Helen heard the 'zip, zip' sounds of a shooting gallery they passed. Something like that would do the trick, he thought. They decided that the hamburgers would be known as Salisbury Nips."[34] The name of his restaurant followed.

Erwin set out for Canada with Helen, but after stopping in with her family to visit, they decided it would be better for her to stay in the U.S. and work while he established the business. When he arrived in Winnipeg, he'd returned to a familiar area of town, near the train station at Main Street and Broadway Avenue. Despite there already being several restaurants in the area,[35] the first Salisbury House opened in 1931 on Fort Street as a hole-in-the-wall lunch counter. As described by Donohue, "It was only 11 feet wide and 65 feet long, and although it had once been a restaurant, it was now abandoned and grubby."[36] Receiving financing from the gas company for equipment, Erwin placed a griddle, a hot dog machine, and a Silex coffee maker in the front window.[37] According to his biography, "The entire menu of Salisbury House consisted of a Salisbury Nip, coffee, and pies. Chili followed in short order."[38] In time the menu expanded in response to customer demands. In the first year of business, Erwin did not earn much. He hired an employee, thinking it would be more profitable to remain open all night. Preoccupation with his fledgling business had prevented Erwin from writing to his wife for some time. Concern brought his mother-in-law—without notice and without Helen—to Winnipeg in 1932; she began cooking in the restaurant the night she stepped off the bus.[39]

The following year, Erwin opened a second location at 254 Kennedy Street, and began to advertise in local papers, emphasizing Sals' late hours: "After the Dance have a Nip and a Silex Coffee."[40] In 1933, a third location opened at Broadway Avenue and Osborne Street. By then, at least one restaurant was flattering Sals by imitation. Freddies, located at 764 McDermot Avenue, advertised both "Haddad's Nips, and Silex coffee."[41] In 1934, the original hole-in-the-wall on Fort Street was shuttered and was replaced by a lunch counter in the downtown bus depot on Hargrave Street.[42] A year later, the first location opened outside of Winnipeg in Flin Flon in

FLAPPER/WAFER PIE

Crust:

375 mL (11/2 cups) graham wafer crumbs

80 mL (1/3 cup) brown sugar

60 mL (¼ cup) melted butter

Filling:

6 egg yolks

125 mL (½ cup) white sugar

60 mL (4 tbsp) cornstarch

1 L (4 cups) whole milk, scalded

10 mL (2 tsp) vanilla

Meringue:

6 egg whites

45 mL (3 tbsp) white sugar

2 mL (½ tsp) cornstarch

15 mL (1 tbsp) graham wafer crumbs

Preheat oven to 175 ° C (350° F). Reserve 1/3 cup of graham wafer crumbs for topping. In a small bowl, mix remaining graham wafer crumbs, melted butter, and sugar, then press mixture onto sides and bottom of 8-inch cake pan. Bake 8 minutes.

In a saucepan, prepare filling by mixing sugar, cornstarch, and flour. Gradually stir in milk. Boil 2 minutes over medium heat while whisking until mixture thickens. Remove from heat and slowly stir in beaten egg yolks. Return to heat and boil 1 minute. Remove from heat and add butter and vanilla. Pour into baked pie crust.

To prepare meringue, in a small bowl beat egg whites until soft peaks form. Beat in sugar a little at a time until meringue is glossy. Spread over pie filling to meet edges of crust. Top with reserved graham wafer crumbs. Bake at 425° F for 5 minutes or until meringue is brown. Cool at room temperature 3 hours before serving.

Alison Gillmor, "Wafer? Flapper? Open Wide and Say 'Sals,'" *Winnipeg Free Press*, 7 November 2012, https://www.winnipegfreepress.com/arts-and-life/food/wafer-flapper-open-wide-and-say-sals-177603771.html (accessed 13 May 2023).

northern Manitoba, and in the 1940s Sals followed Manitoba cottagers to Kenora, Ontario, where it established two more locations.[43]

Ralph Erwin opened the first Salisbury House in 1931, early in the rise of restaurants in Winnipeg. But even then, there was already ample competition. While the main street cafés, hotel coffee shops, and saloons had been a part of the streetscape since the previous century,[44] the demand for ready-made food had been steadily increasing from the late nineteenth century on. By the postwar years there was more demand for affordable, quick meal options, and more variety, than ever before. Lunch wagon, snack cart, grill, lunch bar, café, commissary, coffee shop, cafeteria, diner, drive-in—all aimed to serve the "mass eaters" of Winnipeg who had limited budgets, limited time, and other places to be. For the most part, these establishments were physically indistinct from one another: a small space, a grill, a counter lined with stools, and a few tables along the wall. In *Roadside Restaurants* John Jakle and Keith Sculle note that, "by the 1920s the format hardly varied at all in this type of restaurant."[45] While the names on the signs varied, most people would associate this classic floorplan with that of a diner.

Despite taking their name from the dining cars on passenger trains, the mid-century diners we know were not plucked off trains and dropped into the streetscape. In the late nineteenth century, while opulent dining cars (diners) on trains were serving the travelling leisure class, Walter Scott was carrying a basket of provisions through the street in Providence, Rhode Island, selling a small assortment of pre-made fare to passersby. As demand for his ready-made food grew, he invested in a pushcart to meet it. In 1872, the cart no longer sufficed, and Scott modified a freight wagon. Just large enough to accommodate Scott and his provisions, the freight wagon featured a pass-through window cut into each side. Scott parked on the street and served sandwiches, boiled eggs, and pie, from both sides of the cart, from sunset until four o'clock in the morning. The evolution of the diner occurred over several decades—off the rails and in the streets of the eastern United States—beginning with this night lunch wagon.[46]

At this time in North America, increasing real estate values in the city meant that the working class was living further away from its core, and often had to travel further from these newly created suburbs to work. As historian Megan Elias explains in *Lunch*, the "emergence of the industrial economy in North America and Europe produced both the working-class lunch—brief, frugal and not eaten at a table—and the business-man's lunch—prolonged, copious, and taken in great comfort."[47] There were cafés, and saloons also offered free lunch to drinking customers (often subsidized by brewers),[48] but, as Katherine Turner describes, increasing numbers of European immigrants "brought European urban traditions of local food businesses and street foods."[49] Pushcarts and lunch wagons emerged in the streets as a more convenient option, particularly for night-shift workers, which included everyone from industrial employees to hospital staff.[50] Turner contextualizes street sellers like Scott as purveyors of "inexpensive meals away from home, [who] enabled workers to avoid packing a lunch or returning home to eat."[51]

The night lunch wagon business in the eastern United States became increasingly popular, spreading across Rhode Island and Massachusetts. Lunch car owners became manufacturers, and their designs increasingly well appointed. The modest lunch wagon grew to feature ornately painted white wagons with tile flooring and stained-glass windows.[52] Cooking stoves were added, allowing menus to expand, and amenities like exhaust fans and toilets provided a more comfortable environment for patrons.[53] The basic layout, a counter lined with stools and a few tables along the wall, remained. From 1872 into the 1930s, menu offerings grew along with the carts, and alongside night lunch wagons emerged (daytime) lunch cars, cafés, (hot) dog wagons, and grills. The prefabricated structures transitioned from wood to steel framing, and their wheels no longer served for roving the streets but rather to transport the structures to a preferred lot where they could be parked and operate all hours of the day. While nobody knows which manufacturer adopted the name first, the switch from "lunch wagon" to "diner" is thought to have been spurred by a 1924 article written about a lunch car in Chicago, in which the author suggested that the lunch wagon's dining environment was on par with the comfort and class of a train's dining car, and therefore ought to adopt the name.[54]

The original night lunch wagons gave way to the diner. By the 1940s, wagons that continued to operate in the street—although once considered a higher class of provision than peddlers or pushcart sales[55]—came to be associated with undesirable late-night patrons and gastrointestinal upset. But forces larger than bad eggs hastened their decline. As more acceptable forms of retail emerged on permanent foundations, roving vendors of any kind

Figure 23. Salisbury House matchbook cover advertising locations in Winnipeg, Selkirk, Kenora, and Fargo. Purchased from eBay.

were increasingly limited by civic bylaws. In addition to public health standards, other regulatory efforts were implemented through bylaws that, according to historian Daniel Bluestone, "clearly favored a modern, rationalized, efficient system of commerce that would serve higher realty values, higher urban densities, and the unrestricted circulation of people and store-bought commodities."[56]

In Winnipeg, this effort to regulate the city is evident by the late nineteenth century. Market Square, established in downtown Winnipeg in 1898, provided a centralized marketplace for produce sellers to vend their goods. Larger, centrally located department stores, such as Robinson and Co. and Eaton's, were overtaking street vendors and stalls as preferred retail locations. Bluestone posits that department stores and other more specialized retail forms "contributed to the ebbing of street life while setting up both the conditions and the demand for the redefinition of the street itself as a traffic artery."[57] Streetcars were introduced in Winnipeg in 1882 to facilitate the movement of customers to and from retail concentrated in the centre of the city.

Early City of Winnipeg bylaws requiring peddlers to take out licences were aimed at combating fly-by-night salespeople who were not residents of the city of Winnipeg.[58] Gradually, bylaws evolved to incorporate all roving vendors. Health regulations grew increasingly strict, and annual licences to carry on business became more expensive.[59] In Winnipeg, fees for operating a peddler's wagon, whether on foot, drawn by beast of burden, or motorized, were costly. The city of Winnipeg seems to have struggled with determining what reasonable fees were in 1904, repealing a proposed fee of fifty dollars for those on foot and seventy-five dollars for those with beasts or motors, and decided on a more affordable twenty-five dollars and fifty dollars, respectively.[60] By 1928, bylaws were much more specific and required peddlers to be moving at all times "except while actually engaged in making a sale to a customer."[61] By the 1930s, no business was to be conducted before 6:00 a.m. or after 10:00 p.m.[62] However, despite increased regulation and fluctuating licence fees, carts and wagons remained an affordable option for those entering the ready-made food sales business.

There is no available evidence to confirm the existence of *night* lunch wagons on Winnipeg's city streets. Deducing whether or not there were lunch wagons at all from sources such as the *Henderson's Directories* and City of Winnipeg bylaws of the era is nearly impossible, as all street-sellers were simply labelled "pedlars" without distinction as to what was being peddled. A 1908 bylaw passed in the City of Winnipeg stated that henceforth anyone selling items intended "for food for man," including "hawkers waggons" be subject to current health standards and inspection, which hints at a mobile food trade but is unfortunately not specific enough to determine if this meant ready-to-eat items.

In the 1900s, Manitobans would have been aware of the booming lunch cart trade, as it had become part of popular culture. Those who had not travelled to see one in person would have consistently encountered them in the media in short stories, news tidbits from American cities, comic strips, the movies, and even song, from the late 1800s into the 1940s.[63] And, although the records of the time are largely ambiguous, there is evidence of one entrepreneurial-minded individual who did try to bring night lunch wagons to the streets of Winnipeg and the difficulty he encountered in attempting to establish this type of business in Winnipeg.

In March 1903, C.S. Parker applied to the City of Winnipeg Licencing Committee, seeking permission to operate two lunch wagons "between the hours of 7 p.m. and 6 a.m.": one near Portage Avenue and Main Street, and the other near Main Street and Higgins Avenue.[64] Almost a month later, the *Winnipeg Daily Tribune* reported that the City of Winnipeg's Licencing Committee, after receiving the city solicitor's opinion on the matter, declared that the City had "no power to grant such licences," and that "to permit traffic to be so impeded would be against public policy."[65] The night lunch wagon business appears to have died before it lived in Winnipeg. But, in accordance with the 1908 bylaw, the good citizens of Winnipeg paid the required fees and operated other conveyances such as food carts and wagons in the streets during the day.[66] Cart and wagon operators occupied a space in Winnipeg's food economy similar to that of "household food entrepreneurs" described in Chapter 3 of this book. There are a few notable differences: first, cart operators appear to have been primarily men, and, unlike Manitoba's perogy pinchers, they did not operate underground but rather in broad daylight, serving the lunch crowds in Winnipeg's streets. As with the perogy-making cottage industry, few written records of lunch carts and wagons exist. There are no advertisements in newspapers for these owner-operated businesses, which had no need for staff, no fixed address, and no need to advertise. Despite the lack of written or visual records, we do know that wagons operated on Winnipeg's streets, as their stories have been preserved through family keepsakes and local legends.

The origin story of Winnipeg's beloved C. Kelekis Restaurant is a well-documented part of Winnipeg's collective civic memory. C. Kelekis Restaurant was a classic diner: a neon sign out front and an orange-topped u-shaped counter lined with stools inside. It operated in Winnipeg's North End from 1945 to 2012. Like today's Salisbury House, its long roots in Winnipeg's past nourished a deep nostalgia, which emanated from the wood-panelled walls lined with photographs of familiar and famous faces. The Kelekis Restaurant interior included a rich oral tradition of diners sharing stories of their long-time patronage, and its exterior featured a mural that shared the diner's origin story.

Chris Kelekis, the restaurant's founder, immigrated to Canada from a Greek community in Turkey in 1913, settling in Winnipeg in 1918. The Greek community in Manitoba is small (only 0.7 percent of the population in 2021) but has had an outsized presence in the Winnipeg food scene; many people loaned each other funds to establish diners when they found themselves excluded from bank loans and professions due to prejudice.[67] Like many other Greek immigrants, Kelekis started in the food business selling popcorn and peanuts from a pushcart.[68] His business grew into a confectionery and fruit store, Radio Confectionery at 680 Victor Street in Winnipeg's West End.[69] It was there that Chris Kelekis had the idea to branch out into french fry sales. He converted a Model T Ford into a "chip wagon" and launched Kelekis Chips into the streets of Winnipeg.

In short order, he added hot dogs and corn on the cob to his menu.[70] Kelekis's chip wagon was a success, and in 1943 and 1945 he and his wife, Magdalene, opened two restaurants in

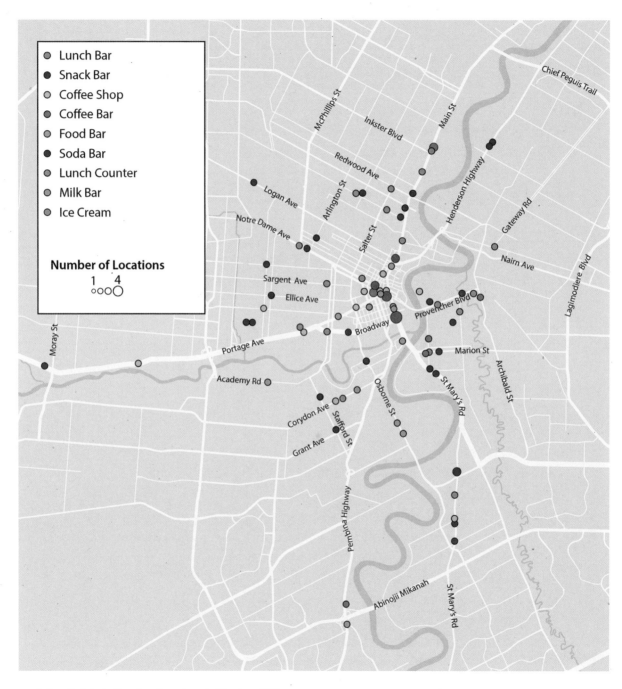

Map 3. Selected lunch and snack spots, Winnipeg, 1951.

Legend

- Lunch Bar
- Snack Bar
- Coffee Shop
- Coffee Bar
- Food Bar
- Soda Bar
- Lunch Counter
- Milk Bar
- Ice Cream

Number of Locations
1   4

Winnipeg's North End.[71] The second, at 1100 Main Street, initially a fish and chips shop, would eventually grow to become Winnipeg's beloved Kelekis diner. The only remaining (publicly available) visual evidence of the chip wagon is in photographs of the restaurant's mural, which featured an artist's depiction of the Model T chip wagon. However, there is photographic evidence of another wagon that was feeding Winnipeg's snackers during this period, which was owned and operated by an equally Winnipeg-famous family.

In the spring of 2019, the Manitoba Food History Project interviewed Anthony Faraci, owner of Faraci Foods, which includes the Bannock Factory, Faraci's Pretzel & Fry Factory, Faraci Food's Italian Streatery, and food trailers that serve everything from bannock to Paul's Original Pizza Snack.[72] The Faraci name might be familiar because Anthony's great-uncle, Paul Faraci, invented the Pizza Pop in a Sargent Avenue restaurant in the 1960s. After interviewing Anthony, Emily Gartner and Trent Brownlee contributed their research to the *Preserves* podcast episode "Paul's Original Pizza Story," which tells Paul's story and the story of the Pizza Pop.

Anthony graciously cooked for us in one of the Faraci food trailers while telling the story of his business and his family's history of food service in Winnipeg. As an aside during this 2019 interview, Anthony remarked that his great-great-grandfather had also been in the food truck business, so to speak:

> EMILY GARTNER: This isn''t the first food truck/trailer in your family. I saw a picture online of a great-great-grandfather.
>
> ANTHONY FARACI: Yeah, it was a relative way back when. . . . Peanuts and ice cream, or something like that. It was a horse and buggy trailer, so that was, I guess, the original food trailer, pulled by one horsepower.[73]

Although in the context of this interview, this was all but a passing remark, through further email correspondence with Anthony Faraci, and digging through available sources, we were able to determine the following: Faraci and his family are not certain of all the photograph's details, but believe it is of Anthony's great-great-grandfather, Sam Guarino. The Faraci family's food history in Winnipeg extends at least as far back as the 1930s. In 1939, Sam Guarino lived at 390 Colony Street.[74] Although at this time his occupation is not listed, a Chas [Charles] Guarino, Sam's son, is listed as his employee.[75] In 1940, Sam is listed as among the fruit vendors in the city directory at 390 Colony Street, his home address. Guarino's wooden, horse-drawn cart resembles the early models used by Scott and Buckley. Cleanly stenciled lettering advertises: "Fresh Roasted Peanuts," "Nut Bars and Chewing Gum," "Ice Cold Drinks," and in larger lettering front and centre below the window, "Ice Cream & Fruit, 5¢," items that were commonly sold from carts at that time.[76] By 1943, Sam Guarino had opened a market at Portage Avenue and Furby Street.[77] In 1946, Sam had moved to Winnipeg's West End and was the proprietor of Malkowich Fruit and Vegetable at 515 Ellice Avenue.[78] The *Henderson's Directories* do not reveal the rest of Sam's story, but Anthony's family recalls that he later manufactured sugar cones for ice cream in Winnipeg. Sam's daughter (Anthony's great-grandmother) Michelina Guarino married Anthony's great-grandfather Phil Faraci.[79]

Although from a public health and permits standpoint, street sellers were a nuisance, the conditions at the turn of the century ensured mobile food vendors were patronized by the public—in particular the lunch crowd—and were profitable for their owners.[80] In 1936, when the City of Winnipeg decided to regulate lunch wagons after all—and subject them to inspection under the purview of the city health inspector—it appears that it was as much to limit their existence as it was to "permit" them. But high urban density in central Winnipeg, the need for people to earn a living, and the simple convenience of ready-made food ensured there was a market for this type of business.[81] The lunches offered by hotel saloons wouldn't have been a suitable option for many, including white-collar workers and an increasing number of women.

As the stories of Kelekis and Faraci illustrate, many who entered the food business followed a path from pushcart to wagon to restaurant, sometimes over more than one generation.[82] The same 1936 *Tribune* article that announced forthcoming regulations for lunch wagons suggested they "be applied to booths in buildings as well." Providing a tally of "victualling" establishments in the city, it hinted at the rise of another kind of food service: "It was reported that there were 515 premises in the city listed to do 'victualling.' These included 200 restaurants, 88 lunch counters, the balance being drug stores, groceries, and confectionaries with lunch counters, fish and chips shops, department stores, bakeries with eating accommodation, dance halls and clubs. Of the premises 69 were operated by Orientals."[83]

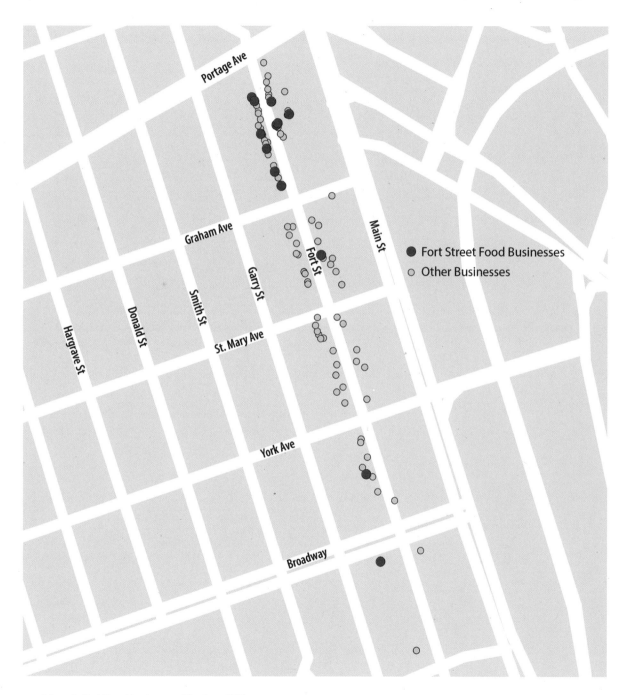

Map 4. Fort Street businesses, Winnipeg, 1932.

Figure 24. Sam Guarino's snack wagon, date unknown, Winnipeg. Photograph courtesy of Anthony Faraci, Winnipeg.

As work in the city changed, so did lunch. By the mid-1930s, the restaurant business in Winnipeg was booming, whether the city Licencing Committee was ready or not. Pushcarts, lunch wagons, and lunch counters were emerging with the influx of settlers to Winnipeg, who were using what skills they had to earn a living, and types of food service evolved according to regulation, culture, and demand. The main street cafés modernized, and soda fountains began to incorporate more fare into their menus. Manitoba's brief flirtation with alcohol prohibition (1916 to 1923) would have disrupted food service in saloons, forcing these establishments to adopt new foodways or close. A significant number of these "victualling" establishments catered specifically to lunch crowds, noon and night.

As industrial workplaces moved farther away from the city's core, families moved to the suburbs, and restaurants followed them. Although many industry workplaces adopted an in-house canteen model of providing lunch, family-run restaurants, specifically diners, emerged adjacent to these workplaces. For example, in the late 1950s and early '60s, there were two in a predominantly industrial area of St. Boniface that served lunch to workers in the area around Central Grain Company Elevator, the Union Stockyards, and Canada Packers.

Kim's grandparents' restaurant, Adolphe and Sally's Diner, was located in a small enclave of Belgian Canadians on the corner of Archibald Street and Plinguet Street. The restaurant was situated on the southwest corner of the intersection, on the tail end of Plinguet Street amongst no more than half a dozen houses, a church, and cemetery. The restaurant was on the ground floor, and the family lived upstairs. Her mother recalls workers from Central Grain Company Elevator being frequent lunch customers, as well as some from Winnipeg's Loveday Mushrooms, including owner Mr. Loveday. There was also the El Toro at 874 Marion Street, owned by Joe and Roma DeGagné. It is memorialized in the film *El Toro*, in which director Danielle Sturk resurrects her grandparents' restaurant, using animation and oral history, and permits viewers to travel through the decades of family memories about the diner. While the film doesn't depict what inspired Sturk's grandparents to open the El Toro, one narrator recalls, "most of the business was the meat-packing people and the truckers."[84] Diners like these served blue-collar workers and those travelling (for business or pleasure) on the road and highway systems that expanded in the 1950s.

Restaurateurs who remained in Winnipeg's inner city started lunch counters and lunch bars and other "quick lunch" stops to meet the demands of an ever-growing lunch crowd of downtown workers.[85] Within names registered with the Manitoba Companies Office between 1930 and 1962, there were upwards of 300 separate locations offering variations on lunch in cafés, lunch counters, food and snack bars, and grills.[86]

Although the automobile was popularized by the 1920s and some enterprising individuals such as Chris Kelekis were using them to advantage in their food businesses, mass adoption of the automobile did not occur until the postwar years. Families who could afford to own their means of transportation had the freedom of travelling according to their timetables.[87] Destination travel by car increased, and the city began to change shape to appeal to motorists.[88] Highway food stands and early drive-in restaurants had emerged in tandem with increasing automobile sales in the United States beginning in the 1920s. New restaurants were set back from the sidewalk to feature ample parking, and drive-in restaurants of all shapes and sizes emerged in both cities and towns. Jessie G. Kirby, co-founder of the barbecue restaurant chain Dallas Pig Stands Company, observed: "people with cars are so lazy, they don't want to get out of them to eat."[89]

"Architecturally," John Heimann writes, "the drive-in [invented] itself as it went along."[90] Those that emerged in 1920s America were humble and had barely more than a driveway that led up to a modest stand. Chain restaurants like the Pig Stand in Texas hired "runners" and A&W introduced "tray boys" to carry orders out to customers.[91] By the 1930s, future-oriented optimism was visible in modern architecture, which was increasingly designed around auto-mobility.[92] In the 1930s, there was experimentation in form. In Los Angeles, architects hired to design drive-ins experimented with a variety of novelty architecture (including apples, pigs, teepees, and castles), as well as clean, modern designs that included circular buildings (360-degree parking!), curved corners, and towering neon signs. Although the Depression did not considerably slow the growth of the drive-in, the Second World War did: procuring restaurant equipment became more difficult, employees were harder to come by, and recreational travel slowed.[93] But with the end of the war, drive-ins picked up where they left off, serving an even larger population of automobile owners who were eager to consume. In the U.S., the drive-in began to lose steam in the late 1950s, and by the mid-1960s was "breathing its last gasp" as food varieties and market competition increased.[94] Heimann explains, "The term drive-in now came to mean any restaurant that accommodated a car, but not necessarily service in your car."[95] Many abandoned car-hop service, which was expensive, and scaled back to become walk-up windows instead.[96]

It was at this moment in history that Winnipeg was ready for the drive-in: a logical fit, considering Manitoba's kilometres of highway and ample urban surface parking. When the drive-in arrived in the latter half of the 1950s, it would become immensely popular throughout Manitoba, in both rural and urban areas. Drive-ins appeared in most Winnipeg neighbour-hoods, from the city centre to the city's edge, and became a common addition to many small towns along rural highways. Anywhere that Manitobans were driving, a drive-in was erected to accommodate them—and they ranged from the humble stands with hardly any parking at all, to large restaurants with even larger parking lots. The most ostentatious drive-ins were a distinct product of the modern era: small buildings with long stretches of canopy-covered parking that, at night, glowed in the light of towering neon signs and back-lit menu boards. Of the numerous drive-ins established in Winnipeg through the 1950s and 1960s, many of the smaller independent locations failed within the first two years. Some disappeared altogether, and some changed ownership and rebranded once or twice before closing. Seventy years later, many of these buildings remain part of the Winnipeg streetscape. Many are no longer drive-ins, and with a discerning eye you can spot convenience stores with suspiciously large parking lots, or a stretch of canopy that shelters nothing in particular. But there are several, both urban and rural, that have endured. They have changed imperceptibly, if at all, since they opened.

Ralph Erwin claimed to have operated the first drive-in in Winnipeg, at the Salisbury House located at the corner of Broadway Avenue and Osborne Street, in 1933.

> The ingenious idea occurred to [Erwin] to open up a drive-in on the vacant lot behind the property. "It was along one side of the filling station," Ralph says. "I paid no rent on it or anything like that. I just walked in and used it."
>
> Ralph acquired a type of tray that slipped across the back seat of the car. In no time, the place was doing a roaring business. One day, Ralph was walking up Broadway from the University [of Winnipeg]. As he approached Osborne, he noticed there was a traffic jam, and the police had been called out to direct traffic. One of the policemen turned to Ralph and pointed to the vacant lot by the filling station. "There seems to be a lot of traffic over there. Look at the cars driving in and out. What's going on up there, do you know?"
>
> "I haven't got any idea," Ralph answered.
>
> He thought, "Oh boy, here we go again." The traffic problem was eventually straightened out. "That was Winnipeg's first drive-in," Ralph says. It was probably one of the first in Canada.[97]

Whether the details of Erwin's story are strictly true or not, a Salisbury House was nonetheless one of the earliest drive-ins in Winnipeg; the modern, purpose-built Ellice Avenue location opened in 1954.[98] Sketches for the Ellice Avenue location (which you can view on the wall of many Winnipeg Salisbury Houses) feature a modern building with a circular glass entranceway.

Early ads soliciting car hops for the location stated only married women need apply, as manager Bill Neville had observed, "married girls are more stable, they can cope with difficult customers and part time work suits them."[99] In 1956, an ad appeared for "8 additional staff required for new Salisbury Drive In, Stafford at Pembina."[100] In addition to the Salisbury House, there were other franchisees that went all in on the drive-in. A&W established its first location in Canada in 1956, and where there is now a Junior's on Portage Avenue and Langside Street, there was Emmett Kelley's Carnival Drive Inn.

Dan Ritchie was an early and enthusiastic investor in the drive-in business in Winnipeg. Many people in Manitoba will remember him as Commodore Ritchie, or Captain Dan Ritchie, the captain of the *River Rouge* "inland cruise ship." Ritchie was born in Battleford, Saskatchewan, and after serving in the Second World War, he began working in food service in Toronto before moving to Winnipeg. In 1954, Ritchie and his brother Lorne pooled their savings to start a catering company. Continental Caterers went on to have cafeterias in Winnipeg workplaces, including the Canada Post building, Winnipeg Transit, City Hydro, and the Sherwin Williams paint plant.[101] Ritchie and his brother would open the first of three Millionaire Drive Inns in 1959, after buying in to the Sno-Cap Root Beer franchise. The McPhillips Street location was a spectacular, modern drive-in, complete with canopy and a towering neon sign featuring "an illuminated chef in tails, 35ft high, holding in each hand the drive-in's specialties, a large hamburger and a Sno-Cap Rootbeer," reported writer George Legris.[102] The Millionaire's canopy, under which hung internally lit menu boards, could accommodate twenty-six cars, in addition to another "three quarters of an acre" of parking lot.[103] While we couldn't find much information on the locations in St. Vital (St. Mary's Road and Dakota Avenue) and Pembina Highway, or about the other branch of the franchise, the Sno-Cap Drive-In at 312 Nairn Avenue, they were likely quite similar to the Millionaire in light of its being a franchise operation.[104] In 1967, the Sno-Cap rebranded as the River Rouge Drive-In.[105] The Millionaire on McPhillips was purchased in the 1980s by McDonald's, which remains there today.

Between 1901 and 1941, over 15,000 Greek immigrants made their way to Canada. In the 1950s, this number jumped significantly: 8,594 Greek immigrants arrived in Canada in 1951 alone.[106] Of those who made their way to Winnipeg, many would establish restaurants. Some

Figure 25. Photograph of the Millionaire Drive Inn on McPhillips Street, Winnipeg, showing the ten-metre-tall neon sign and canopy-covered parking. Archives of Manitoba, Government Photographs, CH 0267, GR3552, 61-7 Millionaire Drive In [sic], 1961, ZZ 10-2-4-1, 61-7 / ZZ 10-2-1-1.

were first-generation immigrants, but by the 1940s there was a generation of Canadian-born Greeks entering the restaurant business. While most had humble roots, beginning in small places like restaurant kitchens and lunch bars, many went on to operate some of Winnipeg's most well-known and memorable restaurants including Kelekis Restaurant, Willie's Place, the Paris Restaurant, the Manhattan, the Town and Country, Johnny G's, the Pony Corral, Junior's, and Rae and Jerry's, among *many* others. In the late 1950s, Greek restaurateurs played a significant role in ushering the drive-in trend into Winnipeg dining.

John Ginakes arrived in Canada in 1954, four years after his brother Demos (Jimmy). Johnny G is one of Winnipeg's most well-known restaurateurs. Best known for the eponymously named restaurant Johnny G's, he has also been involved (with partners) in several of Winnipeg's well-known eateries including Manhattan and the Town and Country Night Club. The Ginakes brothers' first restaurant was a lunch counter, Danny's Quick Lunch at 864 Main Street. They would later open the Thunderbird Drive-In on McPhillips Street.

In 2018, Zachary Hamilton interviewed John Ginakes and Demitris Scouras, son of Red Top Drive Inn founder John Scouras. From this interview he produced the *Preserves* podcast episode "Burger Town," which provides a twenty-two-minute glimpse into the business network of Winnipeg's Greek community through the perspectives of two generations. However, the beginning of that story originates one generation earlier.

Hamilton's 2018 interview with Ginakes and Scouras and an interview conducted with John Calogeris by Janis Thiessen in 2019 describe the generosity of spirit in the Greek community and among its restaurateurs. For Demitris Scouras and John Calogeris, this generosity is exemplified by their fathers, who are the same generation as Ginakes. Both recount stories that their fathers told about taking responsibility for educating and assisting those Greek Canadians who came after them. Calogeris recalls that his father would help other Greek Canadians wanting to establish restaurants: "If someone was struggling, or didn't know. . . He would tell them, 'Look. I will come to where you are, and I will set you up.' And he would."[107] Scouras remembers his father similarly, and how he spoke about those who had helped him: "So, some of the stories that I remember my dad telling me—and you [speaking to Ginakes] can probably attest to this—when a new Greek immigrant, a new young boy, would come to the city, a lot of the current people who lived here that started a restaurant or were in a restaurant would take them under their wing and bring him in, give him a job, whether it was a dishwasher . . ."[108]

John Ginakes anchors his personal story in the Greek community—one which, at the time of Ginakes's arrival in Winnipeg, was based in Winnipeg's downtown and the culturally diverse West End, which was home to many recent immigrants. Ginakes remembers the "old timers" who welcomed him and his brother Jimmy, who would extend their hospitality to those who had just arrived, knowing they had no family or connections.[109] Ginakes describes this generosity as the Greek principle of *philoxenia*: one lives by extending hospitality and helping those in need. City directories, news clippings, and obituaries reveal what philoxenia meant in practice: a close Greek community existed in Winnipeg in both friendships and business partnerships that spanned generations. The many, many Greek-owned restaurants in Winnipeg show a community that helped each other in a variety of ways: through job opportunities and training, partnering, investing, or simply sharing knowledge.

There are two restaurants in particular that are important to Winnipeggers and have been most often connected to the origins of the Fat Boy burger: the Red Top Drive Inn at 219 St. Mary's Road, and vj's Drive Inn at 170 Main Street. Both the *Winnipeg Free Press* and cbc Manitoba have paid tribute to these restaurants over the decades, interviewing their owners and including both in articles detailing Winnipeg's oldest, or most beloved, restaurants. Although there have been efforts to explore the origin of the Fat Boy to date, the question of where it came from has never been conclusively resolved.

As to why it became known as a Fat Boy, cbc reporter Cory Funk got to the bottom of this in 2019 by interviewing Gus Scouras. Scouras explained that he and his brothers had never called it that. The burgers at Junior's and Red Top were called the Lotta Burger and Big Boy, respectively. But over time, their customers just started calling them the Fat Boy. Gus Scouras credited another St. Boniface drive-in owner for adding the Fat Boy to a menu: Mike Lambos, who bought the Dairi Wip Drive-In (383 Marion Street) in 1959 after leaving the Red Top. The name clearly stuck, and by the 1970s the Fat Boy begins to appear in newspaper ads for various local establishments.[110]

But the mystery of who decided to put chili on these burgers is much more confusing and difficult to solve. It is only after considering several versions of the story, and fact-checking the details in each, that it becomes clear where the points of confusion are, and how the origins of the Fat Boy drifted away from history into mystery. In the following pages, we visit the restaurants and the three generations of players involved.

According to John Scouras's obituary, Gus and George Scouras came to Winnipeg in 1949, having made their way west from Fort William, Ontario; their younger brother, John Scouras, joined them in Winnipeg in 1954.[111] As Funk reported, the brothers were working for their uncle in Fort William at the Coney Island Restaurant in 1950, where Gus "learned to make the meat sauce his uncle slathered on hot dogs and spaghetti."[112] By 1955, about only five years after arriving in Canada, George and Gus Scouras were managing Herb's Lunch Counter and Confectionery at 374 Colony Street and Herb's Restaurant at 376 Edmonton Street.[113] Gus Scouras (with partners) would go on to establish Junior's Drive Inn at 170 Main Street in 1957. Gus and George Scouras then established the Big Boy in 1958, and in 1960 they founded the Red Top Drive Inn (with partners Leo DaDalt and George Depres). More than a drive-in at first, the Red Top Plaza was also home to a car wash and by 1966 had added a sporting goods store. The small red and white building (with limited seating) and its towering neon sign are Winnipeg institutions. Its red and white interior is largely the same as it was when it opened, except for the gradual expansion of the photographic "wall of fame." Vicky Scouras had been wary of making changes to the restaurant, for fear that customers would not like it.[114] When John Scouras (who had been the face of the Red Top since 1968) died suddenly in 2007, his obituary was featured prominently on the first page of the "City and Business" section of the *Winnipeg Free Press*.[115] When Vicky Scouras sold the restaurant in 2018, after the untimely passing of her son Peter (who had taken over after John died), the sale of the restaurant was also a feature in Winnipeg's news media.[116] It was purchased by Stavros Athanasiadis, owner of Corydon Avenue's Santa Lucia Pizza. The headlines of the *Winnipeg Free Press* and *CBC Manitoba* reporting the sale of the Red Top read: "New Owner Promises Red Top Will Stay the Same" and "Winnipeg's Iconic Red Top Drive-In Will Stay the Same, New Owner Says."[117]

Figure 26. Photograph of the Red Top's neon sign at the entrance of the Red Top Restaurant and Plaza, 219 St. Mary's Road, Winnipeg. Photograph by Kimberley Moore, 2022.

Nick Calogeris immigrated to Winnipeg in 1939, having made his way north from Los Angeles. He doesn't appear in Winnipeg directories much, but before entering the restaurant business in Winnipeg, he had worked for the Canadian National Railway "on the trains, as the head chef," John Calogeris (Nick's son) said in an interview.[118] His obituary simply states that he operated several restaurants in his lifetime.[119] After opening a restaurant in Winnipeg Beach called the Carousel, Nick Calogeris went on to be part of several Winnipeg restaurants including the Manhattan, the Original Food Bar, BBW Restaurant, and Kit-Kat Grill. He was also the founder of VJ's Drive-Inn.[120]

According to the business registration docket filed in 1958, Nick Calogeris partnered with Gus Scouras in the Main Street Junior's location and is listed as co-proprietor with Gus Scouras.[121] In 1964, Gus Scouras left the Main Street Junior's location. Nick Calogeris (with new partners) would remain at the Main Street drive-in. In 1981, Nick Calogeris rebranded, changing the name to VJ's.[122] John Calogeris began working in the restaurant in the 1980s. He inherited his father's share of the business in 1989 and has continued to run it since then. Though Nick Calogeris and Gus Scouras decided to pursue business independently of one another, each took something from their partnership—a burger topped with Greek chili.

Depending on where you look, you'll find that both Scouras and Calogeris are credited with inventing the concept of the Fat Boy.[123] John Calogeris credits his father: "My father started that. He was the pioneer of that. No one else knew of that. . . . The recipe was his own; he had many recipes. I have the original one locked away that he [wrote] for me before he passed away. . . . He had half a dozen recipes, my mother said, and he gave them out. He never gave them the original one."[124]

Figure 27. Red Top Restaurant. Photograph by Kimberley Moore, 2022.

In his interview with John Ginakes and Demitris Scouras (John Scouras's son), Zachary Hamilton cut straight to the chase in inquiring about where the idea for Greek chili on burgers came from. But the discussion stopped short after a response from Ginakes, whose memory could not quite reach back the entire seventy-some years. Ginakes recalled:

> Who brought the chili here, was a gentleman from Port Arthur, Fort William. Peter . . . What was his name? . . . He was the originator, who opened up the Original Food Bar. I forget his last name, what it is. He brought the chili in town. Somebody from Thunder Bay, Port Arthur. . . . Then afterwards they passed it around, they passed around the recipe to. . . . Some people they were willing to give the recipe, some people they developed their own—because if you have something good to use you don't want to give it to somebody else. So, this is the same thing with anybody else, you have a recipe, and you try to keep it to yourself. But the majority, one Greek would give it to another Greek.[125]

Although Hamilton "got a little less intrigue and mystique" than he'd expected, Ginakes's having connected the Fat Boy's chili origins to the Original Food Bar created a new avenue of inquiry. Scouring the Companies Office records, obituaries, decades of news features about drive-ins, and the Winnipeg *Henderson's Directories* extending back to the 1930s did not reveal any evidence of a man named Peter affiliated with the Original Food Bar, or enough evidence to decisively name an inventor of the Fat Boy. What this exercise ultimately did was extend the generations-deep web of familiar Greek names and decades of Greek-owned restaurants in Manitoba even further. It also revealed a series of coincidences and shed some light on the context in which the Fat Boy emerged.

In the mid-1930s, there were two "Coney Island" restaurants in Winnipeg: Original Coney Island, and Coney Island Lunch (which, confusingly, is sometimes also called the Original Coney Island Lunch).[126] According to writer Erick Trickey, these restaurants drew their names not from Coney Island amusement park in New York but rather from the early twentieth-century diners in Michigan, popularly known as "coney islands," which were known for their Coney Dogs: a hotdog, garnished with onions and mustard, topped with a "savoury meat sauce."[127] In *Coney Detroit*, Katherine Yung and Joe Grimm recount the legend that the Coney Dogs—also called Coney Island Hot Dogs, Coney Island Hots, or Coney Island Red Hots—

WINNIPEG GREEK CHILI

2 tbsp. olive oil

2 lbs. lean ground beef

1 tbsp. ground cumin

2 tsp. unsweetened cocoa powder

1 tsp. turmeric

½ tsp. red pepper flakes

2 cups beef broth

4 garlic cloves, minced

2 tbsp. chili powder

1 tbsp. dried oregano leaves

1 tsp. celery seeds

1 tsp. cinnamon

2 cups tomato juice

¼ cup cornmeal

Heat oil in Dutch oven over medium heat. Add onion and garlic, sauté until translucent, about 10 minutes. Add ground beef and cook until brown. Add chili powder, cumin, oregano, cocoa, celery seed, turmeric, cinnamon, and pepper flakes, and stir 3 minutes. Add tomato juice and broth and bring to a boil. Reduce heat and simmer until liquid reduced by a third, about 1½ hours. Add cornmeal and stir 2 minutes.

"Like Junior's Chili," recipe contributed by Debbie Saske, *Winnipeg Free Press,* 30 May 2007, D5.

Peter Scouras

RED TOP BURGER PATTY

2 lbs. lean ground beef

1 Spanish onion, diced

1½ cup breadcrumbs

2 eggs

2 tbsp. pepper

salt

Mix all ingredients in a large bowl. Salt to taste. Portion into 3.5–4 ounce balls and flatten into patties.

Peter Scouras was the son of John and Vicky Scouras. He took over management of the restaurant with his mother when his father died suddenly while on vacation in Greece in 2007. Red Top had been founded in 1960 by his uncle Gus Scouras and a few business partners as a takeout restaurant; ownership soon settled in the hands of Gus and John.[128] The restaurant was featured on the Food Network's program *You Gotta Eat Here* on May 18, 2012.[129] Scouras died on vacation in Costa Rica in 2017, aged 33.[130] A year later, the restaurant was sold to Stavros Athanasiadis, owner of Corydon Avenue's Santa Lucia Pizza.[131]

Original Coney Island Lunch, 564½ Main st. We specialize in Spaghetti, Chili Con Carne, Red Hots and Hamburger. Quick Service.

Figure 28. Advertisement for Coney Island Lunch (later the Original Food Bar) specialities, including "Spaghetti, Chili Con Carne, Red Hots and Hamburger." *Winnipeg Tribune*, 1 March 1935, 18.

Figure 29. Still of the Original Food Bar's neon sign, as it appears in the film *49th Parallel*, directed by Michael Powell, Columbia Pictures, 1941. Used with permission.

were spread across the eastern U.S. by Greek and Macedonian immigrants in the 1900s and 1910s,[132] who took their inspiration from Coney Island after having passed through, or hearing stories about it after arriving in the U.S. The meat sauce used to top Coney Dogs is modelled after saltsa kima, a tomato-based meat sauce commonly used on spaghetti in Greece.[133] As Jane and Michael Stern elucidate in *500 Things to Eat Before It's Too Late and the Very Best Places to Eat Them*—just like the Fat Boy at Greek-owned drive-ins in Winnipeg—it is the "beanless chili," with its "sweet hot twang [and] marked Greek accent,"[134] that makes the Coney Dog special. And just like the Fat Boy's Greek chili, the recipes for this meat sauce are handed down through the generations and kept as closely guarded secrets.[135] This is also the case in Thunder Bay, where "coney sauce" is a staple served at many of the local diners. As Adam Waito explained, of those from Thunder Bay: "We love Coney Sauce: a sort of meaty chili sauce poured over hot dogs and burgers,"[136] which has been served by restaurants such as McKellar Confectionary (established 1926) and the Westfort Coney Island (established approximately 1950).

Winnipeg's Coney Island Lunch at 564½ Main Street first appears in Winnipeg's *Henderson's Directory* in 1934. Tom Pagonis is listed as the manager in 1934, and the 1935 directory names Georges Saites as proprietor.[137] In 1937, Andrew Petrakos transitioned from employee to proprietor.[138] It is likely Andrew Petrakos whom Ginakes tried to recall in his interview.

Andrew Petrakos was born in Fort William, Ontario, and made his way to Winnipeg in 1935. Upon arriving, he found work at the Original Coney Island Lunch. An ad in the

Figure 30. Former parking canopy of the Sno-Cap Drive-In, facing the Red River at 312 Nairn Avenue. Photograph by Kimberley Moore, 2023.

Winnipeg Tribune from that year touts specialties of "Spaghetti, Chili Con Carne, Red Hots and Hamburger."[139] In 1940, the Original Coney Island Lunch replaced "Lunch" with "Food Bar," and in subsequent years dropped the "Coney Island," becoming simply the Original Food Bar.[140] Andrew's brother John joined him in running the restaurant in 1950, and they operated the Original Food Bar until they died, John in 1963 and Andrew in 1969.

Although it is most often the Scouras brothers and Nick Calogeris credited with establishing the Fat Boy in Winnipeg, Petrakos deserves his share of the credit—not for pioneering the practice of chili on burgers but for being part of its westward migration after having made its way north across the Great Lakes. Although none of these three men invented Greek chili, and neither were they the first to put it on hot dogs and hamburgers, their lives and business ventures intersected in such a way as to establish the foundation of its enduring legacy in Winnipeg. In the original docket filed with the Companies Office in 1957, Andrew Petrakos is named as the original partner of Gus Scouras at the Main Street Junior's. John Calogeris recalls how Andrew's son John Petrakos even came up with the restaurant's name: "Little John Petrakos was running back and forth. He [Petrakos] goes: "Why don't we name it after Junior, here?"[141] Petrakos sold the Junior's at 170 Main Street, along with its name and its recipes, to John Philopulos in 1970. In 1972, the business had grown to a second location.[142] Philopulos opened the Junior's at 558 Portage Avenue, where it remains in operation today, in addition to locations on St. Mary's Road and McPhillips Avenue.

Just as the increasing diversity of food and proliferation of restaurants stifled the drive-in in the U.S., the drive-in business in Winnipeg waned through the 1970s. A&W (one of the longest holdouts) abandoned curb service in favour of the drive-through in the 1980s. A McDonald's stands where the Millionaire Drive-Inn once was, and the canopy of the Sno-Cap Drive-In now shelters the inventory of a used car lot. These same factors inevitably contributed to the decline of Salisbury House.

In its current incarnation, there is nothing particularly distinctive about the food offerings at Salisbury House. Much like other family-oriented chain restaurants such as Smitty's, Denny's, and Perkins, its thick, colourful menu offers an assortment of all-day breakfasts, sandwiches, entrees, and burgers. As the Sals website states, "There is something for everyone at your favourite Sals."[143] There are seven remaining Salisbury House restaurant locations, plus the Sals Market. None of them are drive-ins, and none are open twenty-four hours, and all are located in Winnipeg.[144] Three locations closed permanently during the writing of this book: the Ellice Avenue and Steinbach, MB locations in 2021, and the Sals Express on Main Street and Matheson Avenue in 2022. This is the fewest number of Salisbury Houses since the 1950s. With the appearance of the Main Street location in the local real estate listings in February 2023, the last of Salisbury House's red-peaked roofs has been consigned to history.[145] With the gradual loss of many of Salisbury House locations within an increasingly diverse food-service landscape, it is difficult to imagine that even Earl Barish's inexhaustible enthusiasm for Sals and for Winnipeg can save it indefinitely. It is, after all, a business at heart. It will remain, in the style of the time, as long as it remains profitable. So too with the drive-ins that remain here, so long after the decline of this North American trend. These modest enterprises, the ones that, as Cory Funk described, "basically put up four walls, put up a few tables and [used] every inch of the restaurant,"[146] have endured, one suspects, due to low infrastructure costs and to the entrepreneurial wisdom imparted by John Calogeris: "When you work as hard as we do, you're best off owning [the property]. . . . We own our own land and business."[147] But there's no real reason to expect that they'll be around forever. Those who built them were successful in their businesses; they earned a living and were able to provide their children with more occupational choices; not all of them will be handed down to the next generation. Vicki Scouras sold the Red Top in 2018, and though this was happily to another locally known Greek restaurateur, the obsolete format of the drive-in amid new trends in food service poses a further threat. Peter Ginakes, current owner of the Thunderbird drive-in, recently voiced concerns for its future, faced with the possible development of a Starbucks drive-through on the adjacent lot.[148] Headlines announcing the (potential) closure of these institutions are most often met with a flurry of social media activity. Just as though seated in a booth at Salisbury House or C. Kelekis Restaurant, long-time patrons recount and reminisce about the restaurants in comment threads and social media apps. Even those who have never been, lament the loss of these institutions.

What makes the Fat Boy and the Nip unique—beyond their names—is that they belong to Winnipeggers. Though employing different business strategies, which over decades comingled

Figure 31. Salisbury House on Main Street and Matheson Avenue, the only remaining "red-roof" Salisbury House. Photograph by Kimberley Moore, 2019.

with community and nostalgia, each culminated in a pride of ownership particular to Winnipeg. In 1941 columnist George Freeman, in a reflection titled "The Trouble with Winnipeg," observed that many unique and quirky aspects of Winnipeg were irrelevant because "they aren't things [Winnipeggers] can boast to other Canadians about and feel smug about."[149] As Winnipeggers grapple with our perceived lack of national status in the geographic centre of Canada, and negative headlines that declare us frigid, racist, or impoverished (whether financially or culturally), as a city we fluctuate between self-loathing and boosterism.[150] We can boast about Fat Boys and Nips. On such occasions as when Canadian chef Matty Matheson was a guest on Los Angeles-based *First We Feast*'s "Burger Scholar Sessions," taken aback by the Nip's name and expressing love for "Winnipeg [and] Fat Boys,"[151] or when Toronto's The Wren pub had a "Winnipeg Fat Boy" special,[152] Winnipeggers can smirk. These are ours. You can find similar fare elsewhere, but if you want Fat Boys or Nips, you'll have to come to Winnipeg.

CHAPTER THREE

Unlawful Perogies

Ukrainian immigrants first arrived in Manitoba in 1891, settling throughout the province in the towns of Stuartburn, Whitemouth, Shoal Lake, and Dauphin as well as Winnipeg.[1] Perogies were one of the food traditions they brought with them. These dumplings were labour-intensive but also cheap to produce, and often eaten by Ukrainian Catholics on Fridays when their faith required them to abstain from meat.[2] As a food that was both affordable and filling, perogies were popular throughout the southern half of the province where Ukrainian Canadians lived in great numbers. As a "peasant food" not readily available in Manitoba restaurants until the 1970s, Manitobans, for much of the twentieth century, had either to make their own perogies or buy them from a local "perogy pincher."

Perogy pinchers are typically women who adapt their cooking skills to provide for their families not only by preparing meals for them but by (usually illegally) selling food made in their homes to others. The underground food economy[3] muddies the distinctions between familial, community, and commercial food, between domestic and marketable production. Household food entrepreneurs have a long history in Canada,[4] and many Manitobans have a

"perogy lady" from whom they buy homemade perogies. There is little information available about these women. As food studies scholar Irena Knezevic notes, "The fuzzy edges of informal economic activities make them difficult to study."[5] The occasional newspaper tribute, classified advertisement, or obituary is seemingly the only print evidence of their existence.

Many perogy ladies continued to produce perogies in their homes for sale well into their golden years. Stella Barta was described in the local newspaper as "Hadashville's perogy lady." At age seventy-five, she was "still going strong pinching and cooking those yummy perogies known well to the west in Winnipeg and to the east in Kenora."[6] Her home production was described by the journalist as "her perogy factory." Mary Stelmack was similarly labelled as Marchand's "perogy lady."[7] Jean Wensel taught perogy making at a Winnipeg high school's home economics class, and, as her obituary stated, "after retirement from Eaton's, went on to begin a small, home-based perogy and pie business. There was never a shortage of customers."[8]

Classified ads reveal the historical popularity of perogies as a cottage industry. An ad in the *Selkirk Journal* featured a twenty-quart dough mixer, described as "perfect for bakeries, restaurants, or perogy sellers."[9] Two unnamed but "experienced ladies" advertised in the *Winnipeg Free Press* that they were willing to "fill orders for delicious homemade perogies and holubchi" (holubchi are cabbage or, less commonly, beet leaf, rolls).[10] Others advertised that they had for sale "fresh cabbage rolls and perogies"[11] or "perogies & home-made bread."[12] One simply declared that they were willing to "make perogies on weekends."[13] These are only a few of the many perogy pinchers who, for decades, have sold perogies out of their homes in Winnipeg's North End, the Interlake, southern Manitoba, and the Parkland—indeed, almost every corner of the province, including Churchill. Ukrainian Manitobans from Birch River moved to Churchill and brought their food traditions with them.[14] Helen McEwan, peer coordinator at the local school, explained that Churchill has "a really strong perogy community. So, everyone has kind of their own traditional ways of doing things and there's [work] bees that get together [to make perogies] and stuff."[15]

Figure 32. Beet leaf holubchi, ready to serve. Photograph by Kimberley Moore, 2019.

Figure 33. Beet leaf holubchi, after rolling. Photograph by Kimberley Moore, 2019.

It is illegal to be a perogy lady in Manitoba; the province prohibits the preparation and direct sale of food from home-based businesses, whether through word of mouth or websites or social media.[16] Under the province's Farmers' Market Guidelines, only home-produced food that is not considered potentially hazardous food may be sold, and then only at a permitted market. Potentially hazardous food is defined as "any food that consists in whole or in part of milk or milk products, eggs, meat, poultry, fish, shellfish, edible crustacea, or other ingredients, including synthetic ingredients, in a form capable of supporting rapid and progressive growth of infectious or toxigenic micro-organisms, but does not include foods which have a pH level of 4.6 or below or a water activity value of 0.85 or less."[17] Permitted markets are "a short-term operation for the sale of produce and prepared food products under the direction of a designated Market Coordinator," such as farmers' markets, "flea markets, craft sales, bake sales and other such establishments." The market itself requires a permit; vendors at the market selling potentially hazardous food must have produced it in a permitted commercial facility such as a community kitchen. Potentially hazardous food includes "homemade perogies, cabbage rolls, sandwiches, and cream-filled pastries" but not "jams, jellies and pickles with a pH of 4.6 or lower." The sale of "unpasteurized milk, ungraded eggs, wild mushrooms, uninspected meat or poultry" is never permitted at such markets.[18]

To produce perogies and other potentially hazardous foods for sale in Manitoba, a commercial kitchen, a health permit, and regular public health inspections of facilities are required to ensure the safety of the products made.[19] The Public Health Act's Food and Food Handling Establishments Regulation requires those who "operate a food handling establishment" have a permit unless they produce only non-potentially hazardous foods.[20] This provincial regulation also restricts the ability of Indigenous hunters in the province to sell wild game, and prevents Indigenous restaurants from offering country food on their menus: only inspected meat may be sold in Manitoba. While individuals can process game animals and birds for their personal consumption without inspection, such game can be served to the public only with provincial permission "for special occasions or under special circumstances."[21] This regulation also places limits on the kinds of cheeses that may be produced in the province, as no unpasteurized milk products are permitted—a particular frustration for those attempting to carry on the tradition of Manitoba Trappist cheese making.[22]

Winnipeg's first bylaws addressing food were made shortly after the creation of the province in 1870. Grocers, taverns, and hawkers were licensed as early as 1874.[23] The city's first health inspector, D.B. Murray, was appointed in 1875; he also served as chief of police at the time.[24] A bylaw to establish and regulate public markets was enacted the same year; it was amended in 1877 to regulate who would be allowed to sell meat and fish, though a fish market was established the following year.[25] The first food, drug, and agricultural fertilizer inspectors in Winnipeg were appointed in 1894: Mac S. Inglis, Benjamin F. Fairclough, and Alexander Polson.[26] There must have been some issue with subsequent appointments, as a bylaw was passed in 1913 requiring that "all persons in future appointed as Sanitary Inspectors shall be properly qualified."[27]

Regulations governing perogy production and other types of "cottage food" or home-based food production vary from place to place.[28] Since 2016, Saskatchewan permits direct sale to the public of non-hazardous home-based foods; they are the only Canadian province to do so. Saskatchewan residents can now sell jam and cookies (for example) via social media directly to consumers, retailers, and wholesalers and not solely through farmers' markets. Home-based perogy sales are not permitted, however, as they are considered a potentially hazardous food.[29] In the United States, New Jersey prohibits all cottage foods, whereas Wyoming and North Dakota have virtually no restrictions on their production.[30] Policy analyst Jennifer McDonald surveyed 775 cottage food producers in twenty-two of the twenty-six American states that permitted cottage food production. She found that these producers were "primarily women who live in rural areas, have below-average incomes, and operate their businesses as a supplemental

BEET LEAF HOLUBCHI

1 cup heavy cream or half and half
½ tbsp salt
fresh dill
20–30 fresh beet leaves
bread dough

Pick beet leaves the night before cooking; rinse and let wilt overnight. Roll dough between hands to make a palm-sized elongated shape; wrap beet leaf around it. Dough should just be visible on the ends. Place on baking sheet and let rise slightly (about 1 hour). Bake at 365° F until slightly golden.

Cut baked beet holubchi into bite-sized pieces. Boil in cream with dill and a pinch of salt.

Betty Shumka

Interviewed by Janis Thiessen, Manitoba Food History Truck,
Dauphin, MB, 3 August 2019

BETTY SHUMKA: See, what I do is I pre-cook the cream a bit because I want it to thicken. So, I always pre-boil it a little. All I add there, just a little bit of salt and then I will throw in dill. Got some fresh from the garden this morning so dill is what makes this really good. So, while it's cooking down, I will demonstrate what I do.

JANIS THIESSEN: Smells great, but I mean, you can't beat cream and dill!

BETTY SHUMKA: No, you can't! No, you can't. My mother always used farm cream, real thick. So, I usually pick the beets the night before so it's kind of— The leaves get a little softer, you know, so it's easier to wrap them. So, what I do is I'll pick the beets the night before. I'll wash them, I'll put them on a towel to let them wilt. And then in the morning, I'll make the dough. And it's very easy. Ordinary bread dough. In Dauphin Co-op, they sell bread dough for the little old babas around here that don't want to make their own. And they buy the dough, and they make the beet buns because everybody has a garden around here. And basically, what I do is I just wrap it—like this.

JANIS THIESSEN: So, you've made a kind of a tube or, sorry, a long noodle, thick noodle?

BETTY SHUMKA: Yeah!

JANIS THIESSEN: Just roll it between your hands and then—

BETTY SHUMKA: Roll it between my hands.

JANIS THIESSEN: Put it a third of the way down the leaf and wrap it up.

BETTY SHUMKA: And wrap it up and this end always down. When I place them on a cookie sheet, I just do one layer at a time. When I put them on a cookie sheet, I'll put them a little bit apart like that so that they'll rise a little. I get my granddaughters to do this. They love it.

Betty Shumka was born and raised in Sifton, Manitoba, and comes from a Ukrainian background.[31] Her great-grandparents immigrated to the Sifton area in the early 1900s. Betty has a large family of nine brothers and sisters who lived on a mixed farm with all kinds of farm animals. She always helped in the kitchen from a young age.[32] Her favourite hobbies include cooking and baking.[33] Betty hosts dances in her community and always looks forward to hosting lunches during these events.[34] During any event, she loves to make foods ranging from perogies to cabbage rolls, among other traditional Ukrainian foods.[35] Betty enjoys gardening and has done so all her life. She enjoys making her dishes from scratch with simple ingredients.[36]

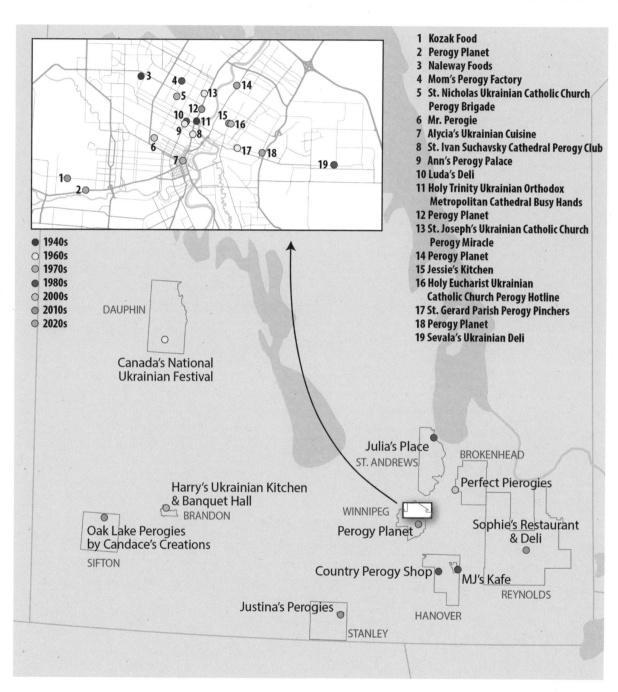

1 Kozak Food
2 Perogy Planet
3 Naleway Foods
4 Mom's Perogy Factory
5 St. Nicholas Ukrainian Catholic Church
   Perogy Brigade
6 Mr. Perogie
7 Alycia's Ukrainian Cuisine
8 St. Ivan Suchavsky Cathedral Perogy Club
9 Ann's Perogy Palace
10 Luda's Deli
11 Holy Trinity Ukrainian Orthodox
   Metropolitan Cathedral Busy Hands
12 Perogy Planet
13 St. Joseph's Ukrainian Catholic Church
   Perogy Miracle
14 Perogy Planet
15 Jessie's Kitchen
16 Holy Eucharist Ukrainian
   Catholic Church Perogy Hotline
17 St. Gerard Parish Perogy Pinchers
18 Perogy Planet
19 Sevala's Ukrainian Deli

● 1940s
○ 1960s
◉ 1970s
● 1980s
○ 2000s
◉ 2010s
◉ 2020s

DAUPHIN

Canada's National
Ukrainian Festival

Julia's Place
ST. ANDREWS

BROKENHEAD

Perfect Pierogies

Harry's Ukrainian Kitchen
& Banquet Hall
BRANDON

WINNIPEG

Perogy Planet

Sophie's Restaurant
& Deli

Oak Lake Perogies
by Candace's Creations

SIFTON

Country Perogy Shop

MJ's Kafe

REYNOLDS

Justina's Perogies

HANOVER

STANLEY

Map 5. Perogy makers in Manitoba.

occupation or hobby."[37] As a result, she argues, those "concerned about expanding female business ownership and improving rural well-being should consider expanding cottage food laws to encourage the industry to flourish."[38]

There are many reasons why someone might become a perogy lady, despite its illegality. Involvement in the informal food sector does not require specialization or large amounts of capital. It can be a way of generating income (with or without paying taxes). And it is a way to meet consumer demands not met by the formal food sector.[39] It can also be a way to support connections between rural and urban communities as well as within ethnic communities.[40] Cottage food production can be significant in some locations.[41] Tensions between cottage producers and the state have a long history: environmental scholars Rosemary Ommer and Nancy Turner note that there are points of similarity between twenty-first-century efforts to regulate the informal economy and Edward Palmer Thompson's discussion of the Black Acts in England; the "blurred boundaries between legal and illegal acts" are perhaps as evident to Manitoba's twenty-first-century perogy ladies as they were to England's eighteenth-century peasantry.[42] The modern informal economy, sociologist Bill Reimer argues, thus should not be viewed as "the vestiges of a previous level of development."[43] Rather, people like Manitoba's perogy ladies may be seen as integral parts of the formal economy, perhaps, as Knezevic says, even "contributing to cultural resilience."[44] Polish Canadian scholar Wiktor Kulinski would agree with this view: "Pierogi-making is an everyday performance that is both an act of preservation (or archive) and an active force that shapes the very heritage from which it draws (or repertoire)."[45]

Home-based or cottage food has been produced for sale in Manitoba for decades, but its postwar decline in popularity and its illegality meant that it rarely drew the attention of the media.[46] Seventy-five percent of sales at Jemy's Grocery (656 Aberdeen Avenue) were from home-produced food in the 1980s; owner Leticia Wenceslao sold fifty pounds (twenty-three kilograms) of barbecued chicken and 400 eggrolls weekly.[47] Similarly, Marianne Buza, owner of Barchet's Quality Meats & Groceries (866 Westminster Avenue), sold steak tartare to customers in the know in the 1980s: "No advertising, just word of mouth."[48] Thirty years later, the activities of Althea Guiboche, nicknamed the Bannock Lady, drew the attention of health authorities and local media. Guiboche gave away homemade soup and bannock to unhoused people in Winnipeg every week in 2012. A year later, the provincial health department informed her she could not do so without the proper permits, despite the fact that she wasn't charging for the food. She obtained the permits.[49] Her actions led to her receiving a Manitoba human rights award in 2014 from the Manitoba Association for Rights and Liberties, the Canadian Human Rights Commission, and the Manitoba Human Rights Commission.[50] Two years later, she ran unsuccessfully for the provincial Liberal party, losing to the NDP's Kevin Chief.[51]

Shortly after Guiboche's feting, another prominent Winnipeg home-based food seller made headlines. After almost twenty years of selling homemade spring rolls as a fundraiser for Canadians Helping Kids in Vietnam, Winnipeg tailor Tam Nguyen was forced to stop by Manitoba Health in 2014. While Nguyen believed "someone in the commercial spring-roll market complained about the charity's low-cost product undercutting them," Manitoba Health explained that the requirements for food handler certification and an inspected commercial kitchen were in place to prevent potential illness.[52]

Shortly thereafter, the province made two moves in an attempt to counteract these illegal sales of home-based food. First, five community centres in Manitoba received funding to develop commercial kitchens: Hadashville Recreation Centre, Austin Community Hall, Teulon Rockwood Centennial Centre, Gilbert Plains Community Hall, and Winnipeg's Riverview Community Centre.[53] Time and space in these kitchens could be rented by those wanting to produce home-based foods to be compliant with health regulations, reported the *Beausejour Clipper*, as the kitchens "are inspected and have a valid food-service establishment permit."[54] Second, the province posted a "notice to home-based food businesses" on their website, warning of a coming crackdown on those violating the Public Health Act.

> Please be advised that preparing and serving food from a home-based business for public consumption is prohibited. The sole exception to this is non-potentially hazardous foods sold at a farmer's [sic] market, flea market, craft sale or bake sale, in accordance with the Farmers' Market Guidelines. Any facility or location where food is prepared or served to the general public is considered a food handling establishment. This includes restaurants, grocery stores, bakeries, butcher shops, delicatessens, catering facilities, take-outs, mobile vending carts, farmers markets and temporary food events at fairs or festivals. The regulations that govern food

handling establishments require a commercial kitchen (not a residential home-based kitchen). They also require regular inspections by a public health inspector, an application for a health permit and continued compliance with the Food and Food Handling Establishments Regulation. Simply having a valid Food Handler Training Certificate is not sufficient. This Manitoba Health Protection Unit website illustrates the importance of food safety and explains reasons why these measures are required. . . . We will be actively seeking these types of home-based businesses; it is your responsibility to ensure that you are following the above mentioned laws and requirements to avoid enforcement actions.[55]

Advertising on social media of home-produced food for sale had drawn the attention of Manitoba's food inspectors, prompting crackdowns.[56] In response, the Deerboine Hutterite Colony decided to end their annual sale of home-produced food. They had been selling raw cookie dough and home-canned chicken (among other items) but chose to continue offering only fresh produce and caramel rolls (non-potentially hazardous foods) on a weekly basis.[57]

Complaints about illegal food producers rose again during the COVID-19 pandemic, as restaurants shuttered by the province's public health orders found their delivery model competing with people offering catering from their uninspected home kitchens.[58] Winnipegger Megan McGhie was one such caterer, selling pasta and meatballs made in her home while her hair salon was closed due to the pandemic: "I would never condone somebody in my business doing stuff like this—it feels very contradictory—but it's also become sort of a matter of survival. . . . Everyone else is doing it; I'm jumping on the bandwagon."[59] She stopped doing so when a local restaurateur threatened to report her to Manitoba Health. Over 250 complaints about home-based food businesses were filed with the province in the first five months of the pandemic; just over 100 had been filed in the entirety of 2019.[60] In response, the provincial government "created a new team of health inspectors" in December 2020 specifically to investigate home-based food businesses. Warnings and fines were issued; some home-based businesses moved their food preparation to inspected commercial kitchens.[61]

Many perogy pinchers use their talents legally in their local churches' inspected commercial kitchens to produce perogies for fundraisers. Food journalist Corey Mintz explains, "Your typical [church perogy making] group operates as part artisanal-food business, part charitable fundraiser and part social club, with volunteers coming as much to chat and catch up as to roll out, fill, crimp and package their dumplings."[62] Some Manitoba churches, like St. Joseph's Ukrainian Catholic Church, produce perogies only once a month.[63] Others, like Holy Eucharist Ukrainian Catholic Parish, produce vast quantities every week.[64] St. Gerard Parish makes 1,800 perogies a week, while St. Ivan Suchavsky Ukrainian Orthodox Cathedral produces 1,200 dozen perogies weekly. It can be a lucrative business: St. Ivan Suchavesky has 50,000 dollars in sales every year.[65] Joyce Sirski-Howell, a researcher in Edmonton who studies Ukrainian Canadian cookbooks, explained in detail how these church members produce these perogies:

> JANIS THIESSEN: So, in the Ukrainian Mennonite tradition I grew up with, the traditional way to do the perogies is boil them, then fry them a little bit, then cover them with a sauce made of . . . you fry farmer sausage, take that out, pour cream into the pan, stir it up with the drippings [to make schmauntfat] and put all that and some fried onions on top of the perogies. What is the proper Ukrainian way to serve perogies?

> JOYCE SIRSKI-HOWELL: Well, most of us—I mean, everywhere I've been—we would basically, we'd boil them, and we'd have perogy suppers at our church and we'd have 500 people come [laughs]. And it's a lot of pinching. We'd boil them. Now there's two theories: some people like to run cold water over them to kind of wash off some of the starch. My mother didn't do this, so I don't do it. And I think it's just a waste of one step and also, they cool them down in my mind but some people do that. But then we just put melted butter and fried onions, basically. And if it was during the week, they would have maybe used what we call shkvarka which is like bacon bits. But that would be the pork rind that would have been fried and thrown on.

> JANIS THIESSEN: I'm getting hungry now [both laugh]. You talked about, you know, 500 perogies. Can you talk a bit about what you know about that process of mass production of perogies within these sorts of community organizations or churches?

> JOYCE SIRSKI-HOWELL: Well, I'm very familiar with Edmonton, for example. We use a big mixer to mix the dough. I'm not just sure how many cups of flour they do at a time. And they actually invested in a machine that rolls out the dough for them. And then it's the men's job to roll that out. You can get table-mounted, I've seen table-mounted, little machines that are on a table and it's like a pasta machine basically. Like a pasta machine could do it, for rolling out. And then they cut them. And my mom made square ones so she didn't waste any dough. But most of the groups when they're selling them will cut them with a circular cutter. Which often [is] a tomato soup can! Works very well without too much effort of finding one and

makes the right size. And so, then they just reroll that dough into the next batch, the pieces [left over]. But they're very, very careful when they're cutting the dough that they don't waste a lot of dough to be rerolled again. They're very thrifty in that way, so it's not rerolled five times or anything. And they just do mass production. Like we have thirty women coming to make pyrohy.[66] And a lot of these churches sell them as a fundraiser for their organizations. And, they're no longer two dollars a dozen, you know, they've gone up a little bit. It's about fifty cents apiece or so. But when you take in your time, if your hours are worth something and you only want a few dozen, like it's worth making. And they're not little, they're a good size.

JANIS THIESSEN: Is there a proper pinching method or is it—?

JOYCE SIRSKI-HOWELL: You want to stick them, keep them together. And that's all part of the dough. Because you can't have a very firm dough because it doesn't stick. And so, it has to be fairly—not really sticky, but not firm because it doesn't hold. And rolling becomes a big thing, because if you roll too thin, then it can break and yeah.

JANIS THIESSEN: So, there's a lot of skill involved?

JOYCE SIRSKI-HOWELL: Oh right, and the amount of filling to put in, too! Because you don't want them looking hungry, so you have to have— And different people, some organizations will take a melon scooper and one person's job is to just make little melon balls [of filling] and they'll have a cookie sheet full of melon balls. And then that's the size that will fit their round and so they're very consistent in their size, proportion. So, if you were to weigh a dozen of them, they should all be fairly close in weight.[67]

Though commercially produced perogies became readily (and cheaply) available in the 1970s, there remained a demand for such hand-produced perogies.[68] A help-wanted ad in the *Winnipeg Free Press* from 1970 suggests that it was not just individuals but also restaurants that preferred the handmade perogy: "Perogies wanted. Any person willing to make 20 to 30 dozen perogies weekly in their home."[69] Manitoba has had a few Ukrainian restaurants that specialize in hand-pinched perogies. Alycia's was one such, pinching 12,000 perogies daily in Winnipeg's North End, and famous for its patronage by celebrities like John Candy.[70] Originally known as Alice's Restaurant, it was renamed Alycia's in the 1970s when it was purchased by Marion Staff, who thought the new name sounded better and turned it into a Ukrainian restaurant featuring perogies, kubasa, holubchi, and borscht.[71]

Russ Gourluck interviewed Sharon Staff and Roger Leclerc in 2009, who, at that time, were the owners of Alycia's.

RUSS GOURLUCK: Let's go back to the original restaurant. You were telling me earlier that just that little front part was the whole restaurant?

SHARON STAFF: Yes. It had six tables.

RUSS GOURLUCK: Six tables. So, it would seat, what? Twenty-four people?

SHARON STAFF: Yes.

RUSS GOURLUCK: And you said that she had an ordinary kitchen stove.

SHARON STAFF: Ordinary kitchen stove and fridge, yes. As if she were working out of her home.

RUSS GOURLUCK: And that was all just in that one little contained area. And she lived where?

SHARON STAFF: She lived in what we call now section A and B, which is the older part of the restaurant now. That was her living quarters.[72]
While Alycia's restaurant found ways to expedite the process of perogy making, they were still all made by hand.

RUSS GOURLUCK: How do you manufacture a thousand dozen perogies a day?

SHARON STAFF: We have as many as twelve people on the perogy line, rolling, pinching, boiling.

RUSS GOURLUCK: Do you use a machine of any kind?

SHARON STAFF: No.

RUSS GOURLUCK: You don't use a Hunky Bill [perogy maker] [laughs]?

SHARON STAFF: No. In fact, Mom used to use a glass to cut the perogies. And then—she thought this was just the greatest idea—somebody designed a sort of a rolling pin-looking thing that will roll out so many circles. So, you'll roll it out this way and you'll have them all cut. And you'll roll it out again and have them all cut.

RUSS GOURLUCK: But they're all formed and pinched by hand?

SHARON STAFF: Yes.

RUSS GOURLUCK: Which I think is, that's a good thing.[73]

COTTAGE CHEESE PEROGIES

Filling:
3 cups dry curd cottage cheese
3 egg yolks
salt and pepper to taste

Dough:
2 cups flour
1 cup milk
1 egg
salt to taste

Mix filling ingredients well and set aside.

Mix dough ingredients together, and roll into thin sheet. Cut circles using a cookie cutter or empty soup can. Place spoonful of filling in centre of dough circle; fold in half and pinch edges to seal.

Cook perogies in boiling water. They are done when they float to the surface. Serve with fried onions and schmauntfat [see Royden Loewen's schmauntfat recipe in this book].

Recipe from Margret Thiessen, mother of Janis Thiessen.

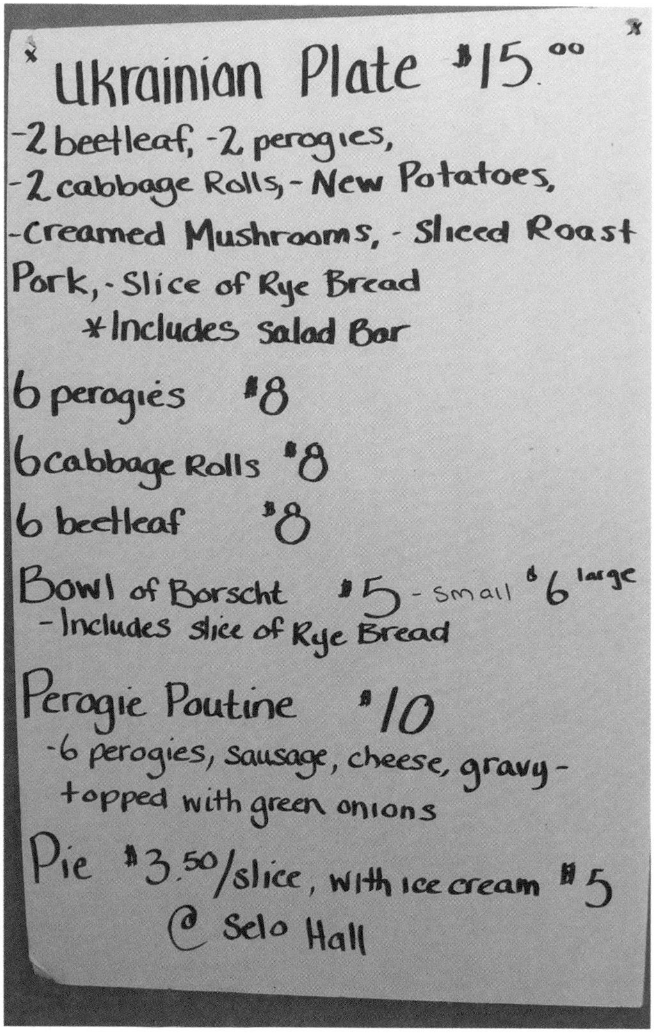

Ukrainian Plate $15.⁰⁰

-2 beetleaf, -2 perogies,
-2 cabbage Rolls, - New Potatoes,
-creamed Mushrooms, - Sliced Roast
Pork, - Slice of Rye Bread
*Includes salad Bar

6 perogies $8
6 cabbage Rolls $8
6 beetleaf $8
Bowl of Borscht $5 - small $6 large
- Includes slice of Rye Bread

Perogie Poutine $10
-6 perogies, sausage, cheese, gravy -
topped with green onions

Pie $3.⁵⁰/slice, with ice cream $5
@ Selo Hall

Figure 34. Close-up of the hands of Madison Herget-Schmidt as she places cottage cheese filling onto perogy dough. Photograph by Kimberley Moore, 2019.

Figure 35. Close-up of Madison Herget-Schmidt's hands as she pinches perogies. Photograph by Kimberley Moore, 2019.

Figure 36. A bowl of borscht prepared by the Cossack Camp of Canada's National Riding and Dancing Cossacks and Company, at Canada's National Ukrainian Festival, Dauphin. Photograph by Janis Thiessen, 2019.

Figure 37. Menu at Selo Hall, Canada's National Ukrainian Festival, Dauphin. Photograph by Janis Thiessen, 2019.

After Marion's death in 2004, the restaurant continued under the leadership of daughter Sharon Staff, son-in-law Roger Leclerc, and grandson Aaron Blanchard until 2011.[74] Blanchard reopened the restaurant in Gimli in 2016; an injury resulted in his mother-in-law, Colleen Swifte, taking over in 2017 and moving the restaurant further north to Arnes. The following year, Alycia's moved to the Royal Albert Arms in Winnipeg's Exchange District, where it eventually closed permanently.[75]

Sevala's Ukrainian Deli is another restaurant that features handmade perogies. It was founded in 1985; owner Sylvia Beck began by making perogies in her home when health issues forced her to leave her job. After a visit from a provincial health inspector, she converted her garage to a commercial kitchen. Sevala's expanded to two restaurant locations before consolidating and relocating to Winnipeg's Transcona neighbourhood in 1994. It is now a third-generation business producing 500 to 600 dozen perogies a day.[76]

For the perogy cognoscenti, handmade is the only way to go. Mass-produced machine-made perogies are eschewed for their thicker, tougher dough. This difference in dough is necessitated by the use of machines; as Bill Redekop describes in a *Winnipeg Free Press* article, "flour is sprinkled on the dough during production to prevent it from sticking to the metal."[77] As Perogy Pantry owner Linda Kostesky explained in the *Brandon Sun*, "There is no comparison between the hand-made product and bulk-produced supermarket perogies which she compares to 'chewing on a rubber eraser.'"[78]

Manitoba has two companies that produce machine-made perogies: Naleway Foods and Perfect Pierogies.[79] Naleway's origins are with Anne Naleway, who opened Anne's Grill in the Sutherland Hotel in Winnipeg's North End in 1942. Eventually the business transformed into a catering company on Selkirk Avenue (the North End's equivalent of Main Street), before shifting in the 1990s to catering and frozen food production. In 1998, the manufacturing side of the business was sold, and Naleway Catering (with its spinoff Perogy Planet) remained in the hands of grandson Rob Naleway.[80] Perfect Pierogies, located in Garson, Manitoba, modified their machinery to produce a perogy they believe rivals that of the seasoned church volunteer perogy pinchers. They produce a million every month.[81] By contrast, Canada's largest perogy producer, Cheemo, produces three million perogies a day.[82] Cheemo was founded in Edmonton in 1972 by Walter Makowecki, who bought his perogy making equipment in Moscow after seeing it showcased at Expo 67.[83]

The popularity of perogies has expanded well beyond the Ukrainian community in Manitoba, and resulted in a diversity of recipes as well as some innovative takes on this simple food. Joyce Sirski-Howell explains, "I did do some research when I was doing a workshop on perogies and I took about thirteen cookbooks and I made a chart of the ingredients. And there were only two recipes that were the same."[84] It seems everyone has their own preferred method for making perogies, which is a labour-intensive process, whatever the recipe. "It's getting more rare that people are actually making them themselves," Sirski-Howell comments. "I only want two dozen. Why am I going to take five hours of my time to make them, when I can buy them and they're pretty good."[85] She observes that some people reduce the tremendous work of perogy making by making a casserole instead. "So, you layer lasagna noodles, your cottage cheese, potatoes and layer it, and they bake it in the oven, and you've got a casserole, but it's like perogies without all the work. They call them lazy perogies."[86]

The history of Manitoba perogies demonstrates that food cannot be easily classified into binary categories such as domestic or commercial, private or public, legal or illegal. And as such, vast swaths of the province's food history remain unrecorded and unresearched. The illegality of selling perogies made in one's home kitchen—a time-honoured practice in this province—renders the history of the perogy lady all but opaque to the scholar. Oral history interviews simply do not exist of some of these contributors to food traditions of lesser prestige and sometimes questionable origin.[87] While provincial authorities have long sought to protect citizens from potential food poisoning (and businesses from unfair competition), Manitobans continue to trust their local perogy ladies.

CHAPTER FOUR

Ubiquitous Barbecue

Barbecue is a food that defies simple categorization. Is it an event, a communal occasion? Is it something you buy at a restaurant or "pit joint," a commercial product? Is it something you do in your backyard, a domestic meal? Is it specific to a particular culture or ethnicity? Never mind the many debates as to the differences between barbecuing, grilling, and smoking, or the use of charcoal versus gas. In Manitoba, barbecue has been all these things and more, especially for farmers, Black people, and Filipinx in diaspora. Filipina French writer Gema Charmaine Gonzales observes, "In our kitchenless migrant lives, a plate is never just a plate. It is a taste of home, a banquet of sensory memories, and a reminder of where we come from."[1] For many people, a plate of barbecue is particularly special.

The butchering of chickens and hogs was often a family or community activity on Manitoba farms. Southern Manitoba farmer Joanelle Wichers raised chickens for her family's

Figure 38. Piercy and Zena Haynes inside the kitchen of Haynes Chicken Shack in Winnipeg, 29 December 1975. University of Manitoba Archives and Special Collections (hereafter UMA), *Winnipeg Tribune* fonds, PC 18 (A.81-12), http://hdl.handle.net/10719/1885961 (accessed 24 May 2023).

consumption and butchered them every summer. Her children, including newspaper writer Geralyn Wichers, were involved in both raising and killing chickens. Geralyn fed and watered them as a young teenager and, on butchering day, was tasked with removing pin feathers and eviscerating the chickens. "To me that was a fun day," she recalled. "And then me and the two brothers would be out there, poking around. 'Dad, what's this?' 'That's the stomach.' 'Dad, what's this?' 'That is the spleen.'"[2] Grandparents from both sides of her family would work together with other family members; at the end of the day, thirty or forty chickens would be in the freezer to feed a family of six over the course of the year.[3]

Butchering hogs was more labour-intensive than chickens. Fall was a popular time of year for killing and processing pigs in Manitoba, right before the winter season that made storage of meat easier in the days before mechanized refrigeration. Relatives, friends, and neighbours gathered for butchering bees or schwienschlachte, as they were known in southern Manitoba Mennonite communities. The pigs were shot, then taken to a butchering trough where boiling water from a large pot, or miagrope, was poured over them to make it easier to scrape off the pig's bristles.[4] The pig was eviscerated while hanging from its hind legs. The carcass was cut in half, and all meat removed. Intestines were cleaned and used as sausage casings, meat from the head was used to make head cheese, fat was rendered in the miagrope to create lard. Spare ribs or rebspäa were cooked in the lard in the miagrope. Traces of meat remaining in the miagrope after the lard was removed were saved as jreewe or cracklings, to be eaten with toast for breakfast.[5]

The cooking and eating of rebspäa by the many Mennonite farmers working at a schwienschlachte is a parallel tradition to that of the pit barbecue in the southern United States. African American journalist and cookbook author Toni Tipton-Martin explains that the latter is "a tradition perfected by black men who have been cooking whole hogs over glowing coals to celebrate hog butcherings, summer holidays and family reunions since slavery days."[6] She says that barbecue's origins derive in part from the Taino, Indigenous peoples in the West Indies "who preserved food by smoke-drying it over a pit fire on a wooden grate called a barbacoa." The latter was an import by sixteenth-century Spanish colonizers. "By 1790," she says, "the word 'barbecue' was in use in America; it had taken on the implications of a social gathering by 1733."[7] Food historian Michael Twitty notes that the Black history of barbecue was subsequently erased:

"it was enslaved men and their descendants, not the Bubbas of today's Barbecue Pitmasters,[8] that innovated and refined regional barbecue traditions."[9]

Doubtless the first demonstration of barbecue-as-cooking-technique in what is now Manitoba was by Indigenous people tens of thousands of years ago. As barbecue scholar Adrian Miller reminds us, "any close scrutiny of barbecue's history bares its Native American roots."[10] But the earliest documented barbecue-as-social-gathering in Manitoba, which the *Manitoba Free Press* claimed was "the first ever held in the city" of Winnipeg, was hosted by the Foresters, a fraternal organization, at their first annual picnic. On 28 August 1890, the *Manitoba Daily Free Press* reported, "nine of the city butchers, under the direction of Mr. Taylor, who has had some experience in this line in the east," prepared a barbecue for the citizens of Winnipeg for the opening of Elm Park (a private park that existed in what is now Kingston Crescent along the Red River, five kilometres south of the Forks).[11] Tickets were fifty cents (twenty-five cents for children), and participants were asked to bring their own knives and forks.[12]

The event attracted a crowd of 2,200, many of whom arrived by trains that made several trips from Winnipeg to Elm Park that day.[13] The *Manitoba Free Press* deemed the barbecue "a howling success. The ox, which had been donated by members of the order who are butchers, was roasted whole on the grounds, the novel sight attracting the greatest interest, and the keen appetites of the hungry were soon appeased by plentiful supplies of the savory beef, which was artistically carved and served to all who had a knife and fork—and to lots who were satisfied to use their fingers in conveying the luscious food to their anticipating mouths."[14] The *Winnipeg Tribune* reported that the "roasted ox, or barbecue" was nothing but bones by six in the evening. "Hundreds could be seen going around with a chunk of roasted beef smacking their lips and declaring it excellent. The drummer having been delayed playing got the shank bone for his share."[15]

While ox was the featured animal at this "first" Manitoba barbecue, other popular meats included buffalo and beef. The highlight of the Manitoba Saskatchewan Inter-Provincial Picnic on Labour Day 1930, for example, was, the ad in the *Brandon Daily Sun* claimed, a "mammoth buffalo barbeque."[16] "As we go to press," the *Roblin Review* reported, "word has been received that two Buffalo are on their way from Wainwright National Park to Roblin [Manitoba] for the barbeque at the pic-nic [*sic*]."[17] Earlier that winter, buffalo was the featured meat at the annual winter carnival in The Pas (more than 600 kilometres northwest of Winnipeg). Local Ininew (Cree) people barbecued the buffalo downtown, reported the *Winnipeg Free Press,* drawing "hundreds of interested spectators, and buffalo meat sandwiches were distributed far and wide."[18] And 225 Dene in Churchill (on Hudson Bay) barbecued two quarters of beef on the day they received their treaty annuity payments in 1932.[19]

Forty years after the "first" Manitoba barbecue, the term was still so little known in Manitoba that newspapers commented on its novelty and took pains to explain it. University of Manitoba's Faculty of Arts and Law held a barbecue at the Fort Garry Hotel in downtown Winnipeg to celebrate homecoming in 1930; *The Manitoban* called it both a "novel" and a "perfect" dinner.[20] A serialized fictional story in the *Tribune,* with similarities to J.G. Kirby's Dallas Pig Stand discussed in Chapter 2, helped explain the new phenomenon of the barbecue restaurant to readers:

> "Why do they call it a barbecue?" Cherry wanted to know. "It looks just like any other place to eat." They had reached the lighted building. A dozen cars were parked by the road and there were more in an enclosed space at the other side of the structure. Pearson brought the roadster to a halt and the three stepped to the ground. "There's a theory," Max explained, "that these places actually barbecue their meat—cook it whole, you know, over a bed of coals. As a matter of fact I think their kitchens are just about like any other restaurant's. You get good food and not much service— which suits most folks when they're driving." . . . Cherry and Dan and Max found places at the counter. They gave their orders and were served almost immediately. The hot coffee was strong and delicious, the chicken delicately tender. Though the portions were huge Cherry finished every crumb.[21]

A year after this story was published, the first two barbecue restaurants in Manitoba had opened.

The Log Cabin Barbecue & Chicken Inn and the Raycroft Barbecue & Tea Gardens were operating in and near Winnipeg by 1931. The Log Cabin was located about half a kilometre north of the Lockport bridge,[22] while the Raycroft was at 2551 Portage Avenue. The latter advertised a seventy-five-cent chicken dinner, and both barbecue restaurants featured nightly dancing.[23] They were joined in 1933 by Duke's Barbecue at 2523 Portage Avenue. Operated by Alex and Florence LeDuke, and featuring chef Martin Free and pianist Earl Houston, Duke's was "open all night."[24] Duke's made the front page of the *Free Press* in 1954, when the LeDukes' daughter

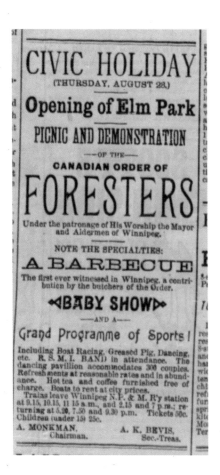

Figure 39. Advertisement for the Foresters' Picnic. *Winnipeg Tribune*, 26 August 1890, 4.

Ruth LaFlamme was charged with stabbing her husband (and the Duke's Barbecue pianist) Romeo at the restaurant.[25]

A number of other barbecue restaurants opened in Winnipeg in the 1930s. George Cochamas's Barbecue Café, also known as Barbecue Lunch, operated at 273½ Donald Street, opposite Eaton's department store, in 1935.[26] Erifily and James Nash became its proprietors in 1947; Elizabeth Hogenson was employed as cup reader.[27] Bill's Barbecue operated in the early 1930s on Henderson Highway between McIvor Avenue and Strood Avenue, beside the North Kildonan Exhibition Grounds. It was owned by John Woodhead Jr., and held a weekly "public dance frolic" with a live band.[28] Also serving barbecue in this decade was Joe's Barbecue at 769 Burrows Avenue, with Joseph Boychuk as proprietor.[29]

By the 1940s, two other barbecue restaurants had joined the crowd. Oden's Bar-B-Q at 1030 Main Street seems to have left little trace in the historical record.[30] But, according to the Manitoba Historical Society, DiCosimo's Chicken Inn, which opened in 1942, became notable as "one of the first fast-food restaurants in the city and an important youth hangout."[31] Its owner, Silvio Jack DiCosimo, also owned the Chick-N-Coop, at 614 Portage Avenue, which specialized in "southern style" barbecue spare ribs.[32] By 1947, the Chicken Inn, at 318 Main Street, was for sale for 15,500 dollars, inclusive of its "roasting ovens, [gas] Barbecue pits and gas range in kitchen." A year later, the price had been slashed to 12,500 dollars as the owner, according to a classified ad in the *Winnipeg Free Press*, was said to be "going abroad."[33]

Winnipeg's most famous barbecue restaurant, a landmark of Black history in Manitoba, opened in 1952. Haynes Chicken Shack served barbecue at 257 Lulu Street until 1998.[34] Sheila

Figure 40. Postcard of a buffalo with the text "We had this fellow for Lunch today, as guests of the Canadian Governm't who provided us with a Buffalo barbecue," 1919. Internet Archive, postcard by F.W. Bell, Wainwright National Park, Alberta, https://archive.org/details/PC005123 (accessed 24 May 2023).

Craig's review in the *Winnipeg Tribune* said the restaurant was "a tidy looking bungalow with its two main rooms sectioned off into smaller rooms and booths" and seats for forty.[35] Menu items included southern fried chicken, chicken tamales, barbecued spare ribs, chili, and Creole fried shrimp.[36] Owner Piercy Haynes[37] had been a champion basketball player and boxer, softball pitcher, carpenter, Canadian Pacific Railway sleeping car porter, Pilgrim Baptist Church member, and Mason, as well as the first Black man in the Royal Canadian Navy since 1852. His life has been understudied,[38] in part due to, as historian Barrington Walker explains, a long tradition of racism and national mythmaking by white scholars followed by a preferential focus on Black

Figure 41. Bison rib meal at Feast Café and Bistro, Winnipeg. Photograph by Janis Thiessen, 2022.

elites at the expense of the history of more ordinary Black Canadians.[39] Indeed, the building that housed Haynes Chicken Shack is vacant and derelict, despite pleas by local historians such as Christian Cassidy to protect it for its cultural and historical significance.[40]

While Black people have lived in what is now Manitoba since the eighteenth-century fur trade (often as enslaved people), a Black community emerged in the province only after changes to immigration policy allowed them to enter Canada in larger numbers in the 1960s.[41] The history of this community is still understudied: Robin Winks's *Blacks in Canada* briefly mentions Blacks in Manitoba in only two of its fifteen chapters, including reference to the migration of Oklahomans escaping Jim Crow legislation in the first decade of the twentieth century.[42] Pilgrim Baptist Church (41 Maple Street), a social hub for Black Manitobans since 1924, does not appear in a study of early Manitoba churches and neither is it on the Manitoba Historical Society's list of Manitoba's historic sites.[43] And yet Black Manitobans have a long and significant history. In 1917, Winnipeg became the birthplace of the Order of the Sleeping Car Porters, the first Black railway union in Canada, when existing railway unions (and their white members) were rejecting them.[44] At that time, the Black community in Winnipeg resided primarily in the North End and Point Douglas. As historian Saje Mathieu said, "There's a reason they're all living by the train station, and it's because no one will rent to them beyond the train station."[45] This racism, in its many forms, was documented in the local newspaper.[46] By 2016, some 30,000 Manitobans identified on the Canadian Census as Black, a consequence of the third-highest Black population growth rate in twenty-first-century Canada.[47] This increased immigration has seen the establishment of a new Black community around Central Park, where 28 percent of residents identify as Black (as compared with 3.9 percent in Winnipeg as a whole).[48] Despite their centuries-long presence, Black Manitobans were not elected to office until 2018.[49]

Haynes Chicken Shack, like many of the barbecue restaurants in Winnipeg of that era, was also a music venue, albeit one with a difference: it hosted Black entertainment legends such as Billy Daniels, Oscar Peterson, and Harry Belafonte. Haynes himself had "made his professional debut as a pianist" at Duke's Barbecue. Haynes played piano Saturday nights, when the Chicken Shack was open until 3:00 a.m.[50] The chefs were his wife Zena Bradshaw Haynes, and sister-in-law Alva Mayes.[51] When Haynes ran for the Liberal party in the Logan riding, he held a fundraiser at the restaurant, serving pork hocks, black-eyed peas, rice, fried chicken, and cornbread, accompanied by a Dixieland band.[52] After Haynes's death in 1992, employee Debbie Johnson and her husband Louis Brown purchased the restaurant and its recipes for barbecue sauce and fried chicken.[53] The coleslaw recipe, however, remained with its creator, former employee Olive Mae Berryman.[54] Johnson and Brown closed the restaurant in 1996.

Barbecue restaurants like Haynes Chicken Shack were slowly supplanted by backyard barbecuing, which became popular in Canada only in the 1950s. It was in that decade that war-related government import restrictions were lifted on domestic appliances like the portable charcoal barbecue.[55] Many Winnipeg barbecue restaurants were not pit barbecues (charcoal pits were a fire hazard in the city) but used gas. Pit barbecue was the exception, held occasionally at events such as the Manitoba Stock Growers Association's annual field day in 1960. The *Russell Banner* reported, "Firing the pit will start at 9 o'clock the night before and at 4 a.m. the 2000 pounds of beef will be carefully placed on the embers to come out in 12 hours' time fit for a king."[56] The growing availability of portable charcoal barbecues brought barbecue from the commercial and community realms to the domestic realm; they were advertised to Canadians as a "manly art."[57] An advertisement in the 1959 *Brandon Daily Sun* asked, for example, "How about a barbeque for dad? Eating outdoors can be so much fun and most fathers would really enjoy . . . the gift of a brazier."[58] In postwar Canada, the social expectation often was that men were the breadwinners, absent from the home during most of the day, and their wife's domain was the kitchen. The barbecue was where men could assert themselves domestically

Figure 42. Postcard showing interior of Oden's Bar-B-Q at the corner of William Avenue and Arlington Street in Winnipeg. Purchased from eBay.

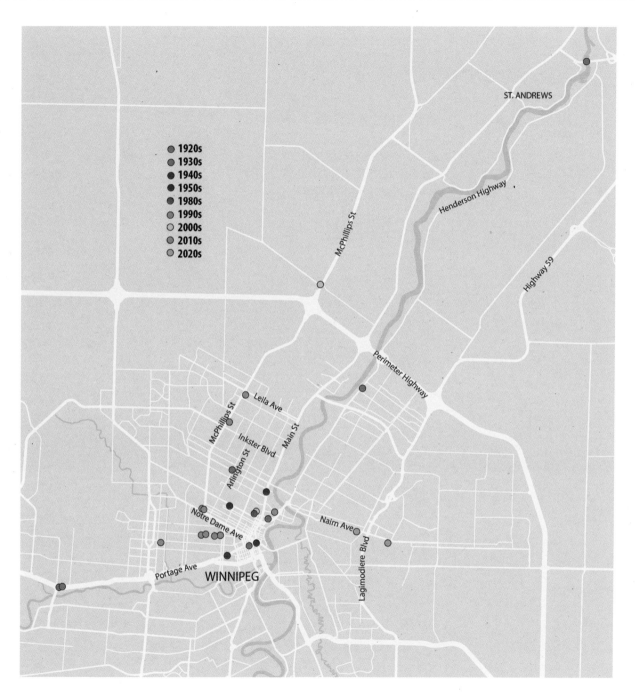

Map 6. Barbecue restaurants in Manitoba.

Figure 43. Former home of Haynes Chicken Shack. Photograph by Kimberley Moore, 2022.

without completely overthrowing the gendered division of labour.[59] Men came to identify meat eating as a "key element of masculinity."[60]

The gendered labour division between the professional male chef and the domestic female cook has a long history, even apart from barbecue. "Let the man of the house worry about the beverages for your cocktail party—your chief concern will be the food," advises a 1948 guide to hostessing produced by Winnipeg's Hudson's Bay Company downtown store.[61] Even today, according to food scholar Emily Contois, gender roles in the context of food "are often singular, fixed, heteronormative, and prescriptive."[62] Paid employment in a kitchen outside the home, particularly when performed in the prestigious role of chef, tends to be seen as a man's domain. Food scholar Jonatan Leer says, "Home cooking as a kind of care work performed by women"[63] has received less status (and no financial compensation).[64]

On the family farm, the definition of masculinity has similarly been connected to food production, but that definition changed over time, shaped by economic and social circumstances. Historian Cecilia Danysk's examination of European colonization and settlement of the western Canadian prairies from 1880 to 1930 focuses on this changing definition among the mostly unmarried men who became farmers. Newspapers warned bachelors that without wives, their ability to raise crops and livestock or even to feed themselves would be seriously compromised: hawks would eat their chickens, pigs would uproot their gardens, cattle would eat their crops, and calves would take all their mothers' milk.[65] They needed to find a wife quickly to avoid these catastrophes. In the 1880s, as Indigenous peoples were being dispossessed and land was being allocated to settlers, Danysk says, "bachelor farmers were expected eventually to settle down, own a farm, marry and raise a family. Those who had not yet done so were excused on the grounds that they were still economically unprepared to support a family, or there was a shortage of women."

By the 1920s, however, society's perceptions of prairie bachelors had shifted. There were more European women on the prairies so more farmers were married, and bachelors tended instead to be farmhands, a role that Danysk says was "perceived as evidence of an unambitious nature. Manitoba's Department of Agriculture began to characterize farm workers as men 'who have failed in pretty nearly every walk of life.'"[66] A "real man" was a married man with his own farm.

A century later, Mennonite historian and farmer Royden Loewen spoke with us about his own understandings of how societal perceptions shaped his work and masculine identity. He had been conventionally farming 1,700 acres (turkeys and grain) with his father and brother, but now is organically farming 320 acres (almost 130 hectares) with his son.[67] Loewen says his switch to organic farming was made in part due to "political" and "social" reasons, which he explained by sharing an exchange he had with the Richardson Pioneer agronomist who had sold him "the herbicides and the treated seed and the synthetic fertilizer" when he was a conventional farmer. When the agronomist learned that Loewen was becoming an organic farmer instead, he said, "Oh no! You're going over to the other side!"[68]

> And to placate him, I said, "Oh, no, no, Terry, it's entirely based on greed." And he said, "Oh, yeah, I can respect greed." I said, "There's two things; one is I'm tired of you making more money selling me herbicides than I make money selling grain, that's just greedy. I actually want more of the profit. But secondly," I said, "There's something called social capital." I said, "Where I work, the University of Winnipeg, my status will increase significantly if my colleagues find out that I'm an organic farmer." And he said, "Oh yeah, okay. I can respect that, too."[69]

Loewen's brother, by contrast, organically farms only a quarter-section of his many hectares of land. Loewen says his brother told him: "'I can't possibly do more, because I won't be respected, whereas you're a professor: people know you're weird to begin with, so that's fine.'"[70]

Figure 44. Close-up of the hands of Royden Loewen as he makes kjielkje noodles on board the Manitoba Food History Truck. Photograph by Kimberley Moore, 2019.

Figure 45. Royden Loewen slices kjielkje noodles with a large knife on board the Manitoba Food History Truck. Photograph by Kimberley Moore, 2019.

Figure 46. Royden Loewen passes kjielkje noodles through his fingers on board the Manitoba Food History Truck. Photograph by Kimberley Moore, 2019.

Who is a "good" or "real" farmer is defined in much the same ways as who is a "good" or "real" man. Royden Loewen explains:

> Farming is very much social. I mean, the farmers all look at one another. Every farmer knows . . . I mean, there's an informal pecking order as to who's a good farmer and who's not a good farmer. I mean, I learned that from my father. He would drive past land and say, "Oh yeah, that's *that* guy." Or worse, he says, "Oh, that's a schoolteacher trying to farm. Schoolteachers should not try to farm!" Or you know, I remember we interviewed a guy, an organic farmer from Altona, Joe Braun, who just told us how he remembered—and I absolutely resonate with this—that he detested his role as a conventional farmer in the '70s and '80s when they were using herbicides. Then he said, "And of course, you always had an overlap." Because it was much, much better to overlap and have a strip of stunted grain from too much chemical, than to allow wheat to have a strip of untreated land and there would be a bright strip of mustard or something. That is the biggest shame there was. So yeah, my father loved [the herbicides] 2,4-D and MCPA when they came out in the '50s and '60s because, for once, you could get rid of that embarrassing mustard plant! It's not that mustard necessarily reduced your yield a lot, it was just like, such an obvious weed that it was so embarrassing. And so, farmers are constantly looking at one another.[71]

Shaped by these social expectations, Loewen chooses to grow sunflowers, hemp, and corn as these crops are tall "and so they'll hide the weeds. So, we won't be embarrassed. So, this is a thing."[72]

University of Winnipeg safety and health manager Kevin Smith had to navigate similar social expectations regarding masculinity in rural Manitoba in the early years of his marriage. His wife had a teaching degree and more employment opportunities than he did, so he stayed home to look after their children. In doing so, he had to face the question Emily Contois raises in her scholarship: "What does it mean to be 'a real man' and a good father when our social world continues to shift beneath our feet?"[73] Smith explains, "I think I was in the advanced class. . . . We were unique. Certainly, I was the only stay-at-home dad in Roblin. . . . Yes, I was very much an oddball in rural Manitoba, being the guy that looked after the kid."[74]

> I made up for it because I—at the time that we moved to Roblin, I was in process to join the City of Winnipeg Fire Department. . . . I got my First Responders ticket and I started working on the ambulance [in Roblin, Manitoba]. . . . And eventually my opportunity came to join the fire department, so I had those two sides to me, where I was looking after kids but I was also an ambulance attendant and a fire fighter. [Imagining how others in Roblin would have thought about him:] "So that part, okay, we'll give him that. He's not such a weird guy after all."[75]

KJIELKJE AND SCHMAUNTFAT

KJIELKJE:

1 cup flour
2 eggs

Form flour into a small mound, and add eggs to a small divot in the centre. Combine until dough is formed. Roll out dough thinly, then roll up the sheet of dough and cut it into wide strips. Cook in boiling water for 2–3 minutes.

SCHMAUNTFAT:

1 cup heavy cream
1 tsp flour
½ cup butter
salt
pepper

In a separate saucepan, melt butter and a teaspoon or so of flour to make a roux. Add cream, salt, and pepper, and simmer until thick and creamy. Serve schmauntfat over kjielkje.

Royden Loewen

Interviewed by Arshdeep Kaur and Colin Rier, Manitoba Food History Truck, Winnipeg, MB, 14 May 2019.

COLIN RIER: So you learned this recipe from your mother?

ROYDEN LOEWEN: I did, and I inherited the rolling pin. Which has . . . green handles. I remember that. . . . I'm not a chef, this is about the only dish I know how to make, so if I come across clumsily here . . .

COLIN RIER: So what are the historical roots of the noodles . . . like is it a specifically Mennonite food?

ROYDEN LOEWEN: Well, I imagine that most European societies would have had some form of noodle; the word "kjielkje" itself is a Russian or Ukrainian term, and it's interesting that when I tell my students that Mennonites who are Dutch- and German-speaking, uh, settlers, they moved eastward from 500 years ago from the Netherlands, because of religious persecution. They found themselves in northern Poland, in a German-speaking province called West Prussia, and along the way they picked up different foods. And this particular word, kjielkje, is a Ukrainian or Russian

Figure 47. A plate of kjielkje noodles covered in schmauntfat sits on a table in front of the Manitoba Food History Truck. Photograph by Kimberley Moore, 2019.

Royden Loewen owns a small 320-acre (130-hectare) organic farm that he and his son work on. It used to be a conventional farm using herbicides and artificial fertilizers, but they switched to organic farming over a three-year process of becoming certified organic farmers. They grow wheat, alfalfa, and sunflowers.[76] Royden is very environmentally conscious, which was one of the driving factors that contributed to the switch from conventional to organic farming, in addition to the capitalistic aspects.[77] He considers agriculture as a hobby because he is also professor emeritus of history at the University of Winnipeg.[78] His research expertise is in Mennonite history, including immigration, farming practices, and community settlements.[79]

term, so it suggests that they picked up this food when they moved eastward. In 1789 they headed to present-day Ukraine to farm the open steppe that the Russians had conquered from the Turks. And so there were Indigenous people there, but they were not agriculturalists, so the Mennonites moved in there, but southern Ukraine is also a place where Mennonites learned wheat farming. Northern Poland and the Netherlands are high-humidity places, and to grow a good wheat you sort of need a low-humidity place. So, I don't know the exact origins, but just by circumstantial evidence, they would have picked up this dish after moving to the Ukraine . . . the Ukrainian steppe, which is a very fertile steppe, but it's semi-arid, and to grow good wheat you want less humidity.

COLIN RIER: And the kjielkje, is it traditionally served as part of a larger meal?

ROYDEN LOEWEN: Yes, so the Mennonites would have had very much a wheat- and vegetable- and meat-based diet. You would make the kjielkje as part of a couple dishes, that you serve the kjielkje with. Like farmer's sausage, or in a chicken noodle soup.

COLIN RIER: What do you need to get started with your noodles?

ROYDEN LOEWEN: Well, we need to start with flour, and then—it's actually a very simple recipe. Eggs—flour and eggs, actually. Believe it or not, that's it.

Figure 48. Close-up of Royden Loewen's folded hands behind a plate of kjielkje and schmauntfat. Photograph by Kimberley Moore, 2019.

Kevin Smith

PUFFED WHEAT CAKE

vanilla flavouring

6 cups toasted puffed wheat (Co-op brand preferred)

3 tbsp Fry's Cocoa powder

½ cup Roger's Beehive golden corn syrup

½ cup butter

½ cup brown sugar

Place saucepan on stove, on low heat. Melt ½ cup of butter in saucepan on low heat. Add brown sugar and corn syrup. Stir in cocoa powder. Get a cup of cold water, and test mixture by dropping a small amount into the water. If it forms a soft ball, it is ready. If it is hard, it will be too brittle. When mixture is ready, add a large splash of vanilla flavouring. Let cool for a few minutes. Grease sides of a cake pan with butter. In a mixing bowl, add cooled mixture to the puffed wheat and stir until everything is coated generously. Press mixture into cake pan. When cooled, cut into squares.

Kevin Smith was born in Winnipeg and met his wife at the University of Winnipeg. After his wife received her degree, the couple moved to Roblin and raised their family there.[80] Kevin enjoys cooking with his children and passing his recipes down. He had taken the role of the family cook due to his experience in a professional kitchen at various hotels and centres where he gained skillsets in cooking.[81] He still sends his dishes to his children, who now live across Canada.[82]

Kevin's other work experience involves health and safety. He has had the opportunity to obtain first aid training and has taught first aid courses.[83] He is now manager of safety and health at the University of Winnipeg.[84]

Interviewed by Janis Thiessen, Manitoba Food History Truck, Steinbach, MB, 29 June 2018.

JANIS THIESSEN: I'm Janis Thiessen with the Manitoba Food History Project.

KEVIN SMITH: I'm Kevin Smith, and I'm with the University of Winnipeg. I'm a safety specialist.

JANIS THIESSEN: And you have helped us out in making this truck happen, and we're super grateful, so we thought we would start it up and you can see our method.

KEVIN SMITH: Terrific. It's always great to see a project go from the idea stage into the practical stage.

JANIS THIESSEN: So, you are going to be making puffed wheat cake?

KEVIN SMITH: Parkland . . . puffed wheat cake. If there is a secret ingredient it is this: Caribbean flavours, vanilla essence.

SARAH STORY: And why is this key to your recipe?

KEVIN SMITH: Well, normally, you do require vanilla. I found this product by accident, and I started using it in place of vanilla.

SARAH STORY: Where did you get your recipe? I'm kind of curious.

KEVIN SMITH: Okay, so this is actually really important. I remember Kim working at the school. The school was going to do a celebration of Manitoba's 125th anniversary and so there was a committee that was struck at the school. . . . I wasn't working at the school at the time, but they sent home this yellow golden piece of paper that says "here it is, your very own Manitoba 125th anniversary puff wheat cake recipe," and the task was people were to make this puff wheat and send it to the school so the kids could have puffed wheat snacks during the field day and the activities they were doing there.

In rural Manitoba, Smith observed, "Dad's always on the barbecue. That kind of stuff. Or Dad would make chili. You know, Dad's making chili. Those kinds of things? Yeah, but in terms of packing lunches. . . ."[85] Packing lunches was seen as the mother's domain. But it was not only Smith's neighbours who questioned the role he played in his family; Smith had to fight his own internalization of sexist food-provisioning roles. "I'll be honest with you. I didn't expect, as I was brought up, that I was going to be a primary caregiver. And it was weird for me, even. When we had money crunches, I would start feeling like, as a man, I'm not doing what I'm supposed to be doing. And Kim [Smith's wife] would try to reassure me, 'No, your job is here.' So, it was even hard for *me* to wrap my mind around that what I'm doing isn't being lazy, it's actually very important and integral. Yeah, it was a struggle at times."[86]

Gendered understandings of food provisioning existed in newcomer communities in the province as well. We interviewed Krispin (Kris) and Peegy Ontong, who have lived in the southern Manitoba city of Steinbach since 2010. The Ontongs generously invited us to conduct the interview in their home while they cooked a dinner that we later shared. As they cooked, they described the centrality of food for the Filipinx Manitoban community. Separated from many family members left behind in the Philippines, Filipinx gather regularly with friends to build community via potlucks. Filipina Canadian scholar Glenda Tibe Bonifacio argues that these potlucks are particularly distinctive in the Pinoy[87] community: "Particularly for Filipinos in diaspora, food symbolizes the richness of coming together among friends. In the Prairies, sumptuous Filipino gatherings are quite distinct from the simplicity of 'Canadian' treats."[88] The Ontongs described the gendered dimension of these gatherings:

> SARAH STORY: Is it the women in your culture who do most of the cooking for these potlucks? Or do—
>
> PEEGY ONTONG: It depends.
>
> KRIS ONTONG: As you can see, I'm the one who's cooking right now!
>
> PEEGY ONTONG: It's not gender-exclusive. A lot of the men, Filipino men, are great cooks.
>
> KRIS ONTONG: It's usually the husband who teaches the wife to cook.
>
> PEEGY ONTONG: Not all the time, though! Not all the time.

KRIS ONTONG: Yeah. And then after we've transferred all of our knowledge, then it's their turn to just do the cooking the whole time [laughs].

PEEGY ONTONG: Oh yeah, right. But just to defend the Filipino woman, not—I mean, it's equal. It's great, though, that Filipino men really own up to the domestic side. Because a few years ago, maybe our fathers' generation, they'd be like, "No, I am the earner. I bring home the bacon. You cook. You clean up." I guess it's not just in *our* culture.

KRIS ONTONG: It's from the Spanish influence of being a predominantly Catholic country; it's patriarchal. That's where it comes from. And now it's gradually changing because of all the influences from other cultures, mass media, and all that.[89]

Historian Jon Malek notes that Spanish colonial influences persisted among Filipinx into at least the 1970s but that migration to Canada "allowed Filipinos to reevaluate their heritage and recraft their national identity in the diaspora."[90]

One such organization assisting Filipinx Canadians to recraft their identity in the diaspora is the Southeast Manitoba Filipino Association (SEMFA), to which the Ontongs belong (and which Kris chaired for a time). The SEMFA hosts activities for Filipinx Manitobans to connect with each other, and participates in cultural events to share Filipinx traditions with other Manitobans. We visited Steinbach during its Summer in the City festival in June 2018, shortly before our interview with the Ontongs. The SEMFA sponsored a food booth at the festival that provided inihaw na baboy, Filipinx barbecue pork skewers. When we asked if the Filipinx barbecuers would be interested in coming on board our food truck to share their recipe and their story, they laughed and declined. Their particular marinade for inihaw na baboy required days of preparation, we were told; best to enjoy Filipinx barbecue at the festival instead.

KRIS ONTONG: That was the best barbecue we've ever had over here, but that is not the best Philippine barbecue that you ever tasted.

JANIS THIESSEN: Really?!

KRIS ONTONG: Yes! There are some that are much better than that! Go to the Philippines, it's like ten times better than that.

JANIS THIESSEN: In North American mainstream—whatever—culture, everyone makes such a big noise about southern barbecue, southern United States barbecue.

KRIS ONTONG: Well, it's good, too. In its own way, it's good.

JANIS THIESSEN: It's a totally different thing. But I had not heard of Filipino barbecue until I was at Summer in the City.

KRIS ONTONG: But then again, if you tasted last year's Filipino barbecue, it was way different than the one we served this year. . . . And the one that we served this year is very close, very close to the one we are used to [in the Philippines], which is so great [laughs]. That's one of the things we miss there—because it's a street food over there.

JANIS THIESSEN: Oh, what??

KRIS ONTONG: Yeah! [laughs]

JANIS THIESSEN: [inhales deeply]

KRIS ONTONG: [laughs] Now you want to go the Philippines![91]

The largest Filipinx community in Canada (in per capita immigration) is in Winnipeg.[92] The Filipinx diaspora increased in size and expanded in range after the Philippines gained independence from the United States in 1946. Migration to Canada accelerated in the 1960s as a result of both changes to Canadian immigration policy in 1962 and declining employment prospects in the Philippines.[93] Filipinx newcomers in Canada work in health care, education, and garment manufacturing, among other fields.[94] Winnipeg's garment industry actively recruited women workers from the Philippines in the 1960s and 1970s, and existing Filipinx Winnipeggers sponsored their families for immigration.[95]

PEEGY ONTONG: It's just a part of our psyche, I guess, to really work hard. Because the Philippines in itself is a labour market. There's a lot of overseas Filipino workers. In every country, there are a lot of Filipinos.

KRIS ONTONG: Oh, we're known for that. We're known for exporting our labour.

PEEGY ONTONG: Yeah. That's our main export: labour.[96]

Filipina Canadian scholar Glenda Tibe Bonifacio echoes this claim: Filipinx "comprise the largest labour diaspora in the world, mostly as caregivers, domestic workers, nannies, nurses, and workers in other feminized occupations."[97]

Despite their global diaspora, Filipinx have yet to receive significant attention for their cuisine. Food journalist Anthony Bourdain described Filipinx food in 2017 as "ascendant" and "underrated."[98] In Manitoba, Filipinx food (such as chicken adobo, lumpia, barbecued pork, and pansit) has been showcased at Folklorama, Winnipeg's largest ethno-cultural festival, as early as 1978.[99] Thirty-five years later, there was still so little familiarity with Filipinx food in Winnipeg that the *Free Press* provided a glossary of Filipinx food.[100] Halo-halo is a "dessert mixture of palm fruit, young coconut, jackfruit, boiled beans and other fruit, topped with evaporated milk and shaved ice." Kalderata is a beef stew whose tomato sauce is accented with liver paste, while kare kare is an oxtail stew in a peanut sauce. Longganisa is a sweetened pork sausage popularly served at breakfast with rice and egg. Lumpia is a variation on spring rolls. Pancit, "the most accessible Philippine foodstuff," was described as a glass-noodle-based dish and sisig as a dish featuring pork jowl.

The reporter noted that these dishes could be tasted at any of the more than two dozen Filipinx food trucks and restaurants that existed in Winnipeg at the time. Many of these restaurants were located in the West End and North End, where Filipinx Winnipeggers tended to settle—traditional neighbourhoods for newcomers to the city due to the areas' lower cost of housing. McPhillips Street (in the North End and east of Main Street) is the home of many Filipinx-related businesses, leading to the Filipinx nickname for the street as "McPhilippines."[101] Ellice Avenue in the West End saw the opening of the first Jollibee in Canada, a popular fast-food chain from the Philippines. While Jollibee is franchised, other Filipinx restaurants in Winnipeg are independently owned; many have come and gone over the years.

Casa Bueno's Maynila Room (349 Henry) advertised their all-you-can-eat "Filipino cuisine" in 1989; they eventually were replaced at that address by Pampanga Restaurant, also featuring Filipinx food. The Maynila Room buffet featured a different diverse menu every day, ranging from tuna fettucine, clam chowder soup, and adobong pusit sa agata (squid in coconut milk) on Mondays to lasagna, cream of mushroom soup, and lengua estofada (ox tongue in tomato sauce) on Saturdays.[102] Manabat Filipino Take-out, owned by Ruben and Teresita Manabat, operated on Sargent Avenue between Toronto Street and Beverly Street in 1999; they had closed by 2022.[103] Rice Bowl Restaurant (641 Sargent Avenue) has served

Chinese, Vietnamese, and Filipinx food since at least 2010, including barbecued pork, lumpia, and kare kare.[104]

While Angelina, Kim's neighbour in the West End, serves Kim her barbecued pork skewers and turon over the fence, several specialty grocery stores and food trucks in Winnipeg provided Filipinx food to Manitobans who weren't so lucky. The steam table at Lucky Supermarket (1051 Winnipeg Avenue) included Filipinx food for takeout and was featured in a local restaurant review in 2010.[105] Similarly, Tindahan Food Market (906 Sargent Avenue) has offered Filipinx food for takeout since at least 2014, including barbecued pork, lumpia, kaldereta beef stew, kare kare beef stew, and chicken adobo.[106] Seafood City, a popular grocery chain in the Philippines, opened a store in Winnipeg in 2019. The store has three takeout counters: Crispy Town (serving Filipinx fried foods like bagnet or deep-fried pork belly), Grill City (featuring Filipinx barbecue), and Noodle Street (offering Filipinx soups).[107] Chef Roddy Seradilla launched the Filipinx food truck Pimp My Rice in 2012, serving Filipinx barbecue. This was followed by his Corydon Avenue restaurant Bisita (Tagalog for "guest"). Corydon is the main street of Winnipeg's Little Italy, far from the Filipinx hubs in the West End and North End; Bisita restaurant is no longer in existence.[108] Despite such closures, in 2022 there were still more than two dozen places in Winnipeg selling Filipinx food. While names like Pampanga Restaurant, Jenmuels Lechon Cebu & Grill, and Manila Bites make the nature of their cuisine clear, others are less obviously identified with names like Grassmere Family Restaurant and Myrna's Café.

The Ontongs view chicken adobo rather than barbecued pork as the unofficial Filipinx national dish: "It's very simple and uniquely Pinoy or Filipino."[109] The word "adobo" comes from the Spanish word *adobar*, meaning "marinade." Adobo meat (whether chicken or pork or beef) was at first marinaded in coconut vinegar; more recently, cooks prefer to use Filipinx soy sauce (a less salty version of Chinese soy sauce, and a reflection of the Philippines' history of trade with the Chinese). The choice of marinade ingredients depends on the meat: chicken is fastest and easiest to prepare as the meat does not require as long to marinade as pork or beef. Pork cuts in Canada are bigger than in the Philippines because the breeds of pigs are larger here, but Filipinx use more parts of the pig: the head, tail, heart, and lungs are used in dishes such as

CHICKEN ADOBO

chicken thighs

soy sauce (Silver Swan or Marca Pina or No Name brand; *not* Kikkoman)

lemon juice

white vinegar (Datu Puti or other brand)

peppercorns

ground pepper

salt

bay leaves

dash of sugar

½ clove of garlic

cooking oil (sunflower or canola oil)

Marinate the chicken thighs in soy sauce and lemon juice. Sauté garlic in cooking oil until brown in pan. Add peppercorns to taste. Take chicken out of marinade and fry in pan. Pour in a splash of marinade and add an equal amount of vinegar. Add bay leaves and an optional dash of sugar. Plate and serve with rice seasoned with salt and ground pepper.

Krispin and Peegy Ontong

Interviewed by Sarah Story, Ontong residence, Steinbach, MB, 6 July 2018.

KRISPIN ONTONG: Today I'm going to share how we prepare our unofficial national dish in the Philippines. It's called chicken adobo. . . . We have our version of this chicken adobo. "Adobo Tagalog" as they call it so that's what we're going to prepare. It differs, depending on what kind of meat you put in there. So, you have choices between chicken, pork, or beef. Now, the easiest would be chicken because it's easy to soften, to tenderize the meat compared to pork or beef so that's why it's always chicken adobo.

SARAH STORY: Why did you choose to cook chicken adobo?

KRISPIN ONTONG: Okay. So, like I said, it's actually a very easy dish to prepare. You can buy all the ingredients from your local supermarket. It can be any kind of soy sauce, any kind of vinegar. You can use any combination of peppercorn and ground pepper and of course bay leaves if you want to make it really fragrant and then that's it basically. . . .

SARAH STORY: Do you write down some of your recipes?

KRISPIN ONTONG: Most of it is passed on from parent to son or daughter. In this case I'm just trying to emulate what my mom used to make.

Krispin and Peegy Ontong moved to Steinbach, Manitoba, in 2010 from the Luzon region of the Philippines after a devastating hurricane there.[110] They are always proud to represent the Filipinx community and are still deeply connected to their heritage. Peegy used to help her parents with their popcorn concession stand in the Philippines, and both of her parents had a business background.[111] Krispin's family came from a government background.[112] The couple met during their training at their workplace. They also attended the same university and found they had much in common.[113] The Ontongs enjoy cooking and gathering regularly with friends and family to enjoy Filipinx food made from local Canadian ingredients.[114] Krispin Ontong is the former president of the SouthEastMan Filipino Association.[115]

FILIPINX PORK INIHAW

1 ⅓ cups white vinegar
¼ cup plus 1 tablespoon crushed minced garlic
1 tablespoon freshly ground black pepper
8 pork chops
1 tablespoon fish sauce

Combine 1 cup vinegar, ¼ cup garlic, and pepper. Flatten pork chops slightly by pounding with mallet or side of cleaver. Marinate pork chops in vinegar mixture 1 hour. Combine remaining vinegar and garlic with fish sauce. Drain pork chops and grill about 5 minutes on each side, or until done. Serve at once with vinegar-garlic dip on side.

Barbara Hansen, "Grilling, Asian style," *Winnipeg Free Press*, 24 January 1996, C1.

Figure 49. Chicken adobo from Max's Restaurant, Winnipeg. Photograph by Janis Thiessen, 2022.

Figure 50. Filipinx barbecued pork from Max's Restaurant, Winnipeg. Photograph by Janis Thiessen, 2022.

lechon, sisig, and kare kare.[116] Adobo also has the advantage of making tasty leftovers, Krispin Ontong says, "because the longer it stands, the more delicious it becomes. Because it's basically marinade. So, if you taste this again tomorrow, it's going to be a lot better."[117] The marinade for Filipinx barbecue is similar to that for adobo, in that both are vinegar-based. A *Winnipeg Free Press* article said that the barbecued pork at Folklorama's Filipinx pavilion in 2001, for example, was "marinated in vinegar, garlic, soy sauce, pepper, 7-Up, and sugar."[118]

As we have seen, barbecue can be difficult to define. It is an event and a place, but also a food. It is often gendered. And it exists in various forms in all kinds of ethnic and cultural contexts. For Black people and for Filipinx in diaspora, food—and especially barbecue—is meaningful. Whether procured from Haynes Chicken Shack, a Pinoy food truck, or made at home, barbecue is both ubiquitous and essential.

KRIS ONTONG: All of this food, that's what keeps us sane, being so far away from our friends and family. That's what got us through, actually.

PEEGY ONTONG: Yeah. Taste of home, every time.[119]

CHAPTER FIVE

The Warm North

Long frustrated by academic histories that purport to be national while focusing solely on southern Ontario, our team was determined that the Manitoba Food History Project should avoid the Manitoba equivalent: "Perimeteritis" or treating the capital city of Winnipeg (much of which lies within the circumference of the Perimeter Highway) as representative of the entirety of the province. For that reason, we decided early on that we wanted to visit Churchill, Manitoba's northernmost town, located on the shores of Hudson Bay. We spent ten days in Churchill, not nearly long enough to establish relationships with the Indigenous peoples who make up the majority of the region's population.[1] Churchill is accessible only by train or plane, and we opted to travel by land to better experience both the unique terrain and the vast distance between Winnipeg and Hudson Bay.

We took the VIA Rail train from Winnipeg to Churchill in early June 2019, after the tracks had been repaired from floods two years earlier.[2] We travelled economy class, sleeping

Figure 51. Close-up of hands preparing bannock-wrapped wieners, Churchill. Photograph by Janis Thiessen, 2019.

in one- to three-hour stretches in our seats for two nights. They turned off the heat in coach at night, so it was very cold and difficult to sleep, even with the fifteen-dollar VIA sleep kit of blanket, ear plugs, neck pillow, and eye mask. The seats reclined forty-five degrees, and if you were lucky and the cars were not full, you could secure two pairs of seats facing each other. That allowed you to recline all the seats and prop up the large footrests, making an almost flat bed if you were not too tall and slept diagonally.

VIA is known for the quality of their food on this route, but the tourist season had not arrived yet, so there was no dining car but only a double-decker observation car with a bar area on the lower level. The bar served prepackaged food such as ham-and-cheese croissants, Jimmy Dean breakfast sandwiches, and microwaveable potato curries. The train stopped for a few hours in Thompson, northern Manitoba's largest city, 765 kilometres north of Winnipeg and 400 kilometres southwest of Churchill. Here, train staff encouraged us to pool together to take taxis to the Thompson City Centre Mall to buy food at either Safeway or Walmart. They assured us that the prices there would be lower than what we would find in Churchill, so it would be wise to provision ourselves in Thompson for our Churchill stay.

The train's economy seats filled between Thompson and Churchill; a one-way ticket was seventy dollars for that distance. But not all those who got on the train during that stretch were headed for Churchill—many were locals travelling to other northern communities such as Ilford and Gillam. They had come prepared, with bags of food, pillows, and duvets or blankets. Some of those who boarded said they boated from Thicket Portage to Mile Six to catch the train there rather than at Thicket Portage itself, because doing so shaved twenty minutes off the slow train journey. The slowness of the train in the northern part of the province is because of the muskeg: the peat bogs here are affected by permafrost and their stability changes with the weather and the seasons, causing railway tracks to heave. The train slowed to only about thirty kilometres per hour at times, and stopped every sixty kilometres so workers could walk the length of the train to look for potential problems. Train travel in the North, we learned through experience, was very different from that in the South.

Though its existence is often omitted when provincial histories are written, "The North" occupies considerable space in the settler Canadian imagination. It's an imagination that is shaped by colonialism; an imagination that is, in the words of Unangax̂ scholar Eve Tuck, "saturated in the fantasies of outsiders."[3] One of those fantasies, Anishinaabe historian Brittany Luby reminds us, is of the North as a vast barren wasteland, empty and thus ready for settler acquisition. "I beseech you," Luby exhorts, "to create a framework that rejects not only *wild* Indians and *wild*erness, but *wild* foods. I ask you to acknowledge a people with purpose and intention in the material world."[4] What that requires, in part, is a refusal to impose our settler understandings of what is necessary for a good life (or good food) on those who have lived differently—and well—for tens, if not hundreds, of thousands of years.[5] "Hunters up north don't need lettuce," dietician Teri Morrow observes. "There's roots and tubers, there's lichen—a ton of things."[6] Caribou consumption, for example, provides all the nutrients humans need except vitamin D. As Fisher River Cree Nation member Dorothy Crate observes, "Wild meats are very healthy foods because they eat all the natural medicines from the water in the bush, and all that medicine we absorb into our bodies."[7] Caribou, for example, fits well with the Canada Food Guide: intestines, stomach contents, and the soft ends of bones met the milk and milk products guide requirements; the bread and cereals category was met by consuming the heart, liver, kidneys, bone marrow, intestines, and stomach webbing; and fruits and vegetables were covered by partially digested stomach contents (called nerukka), eyes, and the liver.[8]

Although we had travelled from a balmy plus sixteen Celsius in Winnipeg to freezing temperatures in Churchill, our experience of the warm North began on the train. We discovered shared musical and photographic interests with Jason Ransom, a guide returning to Churchill for the tourist season; he subsequently introduced us to his employer, Wally Daudrich, from whom we learned about his greenhouse efforts in Churchill. Ransom took us on a Zodiac inflatable boat one evening on a tour from the mouth of the Churchill River into Hudson Bay, landing us on a large ice floe in the waters of Nunavut—an extraordinary experience that left us in awe. He harvested a few pieces of iceberg on our way back, placing them in glasses to share some whiskey with us once we were back on dry land. We met Mayor Michael Spence on more than one occasion at events in town, including the Churchill Marine Observatory Open House, a local art show, and a community barbecue. Spence introduced us to Helen McEwan, a peer educator at the Marlborough School, who shared much of her knowledge of food in the region. We met curator Lorraine Brandson and became acquainted with her research at the Itsanitaq Museum,[9] and explored the community archives housed in the local library. Our hotelier, John Hrominchuk, loaned us his truck so we could explore the area, take photos at Cape Merry, and audio record the ice breakup on the Churchill River.[10] Locals encouraged us to branch out from the town's tourist-oriented restaurants and eat where they ate: at the hospital cafeteria in the Town Centre, a large community complex on the shores of Hudson Bay. We tried cloud jelly, bannock, Arctic char, and other local "country foods." While on the train, we had met some Inuit tour guides from Arviat who joked with us that we should try muktaaq, the frozen raw whale skin and blubber that is a traditional Inuit food high in vitamins C and D. But muktaaq, like snow geese and caribou, is not readily available commercially: you have to harvest it yourself or know someone who is willing to share with you. We did not taste muktaaq, but Helen Webber, the prolific northern cookbook author and co-founder of Webber's Lodges, generously invited us into her home and prepared snow geese for us.

And on our last day in Churchill, we tasted caribou. Local archivist Louise Lawrie invited us to join a centenarian's birthday party she planned with some Sayisi Dene and Dene-Cree elders and their families from Tes-He-Olie Twe (Tadoule Lake), as well as an Inuk elder from Arviat, Nunavut. Together, on the beach behind Churchill's Town Centre, we collected driftwood to fill a metal drum that had been converted into a hearth and fitted on top with a metal grill for cooking. Chunks of caribou meat and chopped onions were fried with some canola oil in a cast-iron pan. One elder made bannock to wrap around hot dog wieners. Over a few cups of flour in a bowl, she sprinkled some baking powder, enough to cover the flour's surface. She added some salt and mixed the dry ingredients by hand. Then she added two eggs and some water, kneading the mixture into a dough. After shaping the bannock dough around the wieners, she deep-fried them in canola oil in the cast-iron pan over the fire, turning them once. We ate these with tea, prepared in a kettle over the same fire. The kettle was constantly monitored so the spout would always face the wind—otherwise, the tea would taste of smoke, the elders explained. Afterward, we drove one of the elders and her family home to their apartment nearby.

Figure 52. The port of Churchill. Photograph by Janis Thiessen, 2019.

One meal is not enough to establish a relationship with anyone. Ten days is not enough to understand Churchill. Cree historian Winona Wheeler observes that "most historians lack the understanding and skill to 'do' Indigenous oral history within its own context."[11] As settlers and academics from the southern part of the province, we do not have (and may never develop) the kinds of community connections that Wheeler describes as necessary for the sharing of Indigenous oral history. Our team did not want to produce the kind of provincial history that avoids encounters with the North because of the time and expense of travel, and so we chose to visit Churchill. But we also did not want to replicate the offensive practice of generations of historians: "racing into Indian country with tape recorder in hand and taking data," as Wheeler describes it.[12] We were strangers and outsiders in a small town. As our university's "Guidance for Research with Indigenous Communities and Participants" states, "Indigenous peoples and communities have long been subject to historical exploitation by non-Indigenous researchers which has left a lasting legacy of mistrust of research relationships and created a barrier between the Indigenous community and the research community. Breaking this barrier requires fostering meaningful relationships through conducting research in a culturally sensitive manner. Ideally, researchers will be invited to do research, rather than offer to do research."[13] We count ourselves very fortunate indeed to have been invited to an Indigenous centenarian's birthday party! We were not invited by locals to do research in Churchill. But again, as Manitoban scholars seeking to write a representative history of the province, we felt we couldn't *not* go to Churchill. Oral history is not the only way to study northern or Indigenous history. And settler academics should not presume that their primary method for studying Indigenous history is oral histories they conduct themselves—that

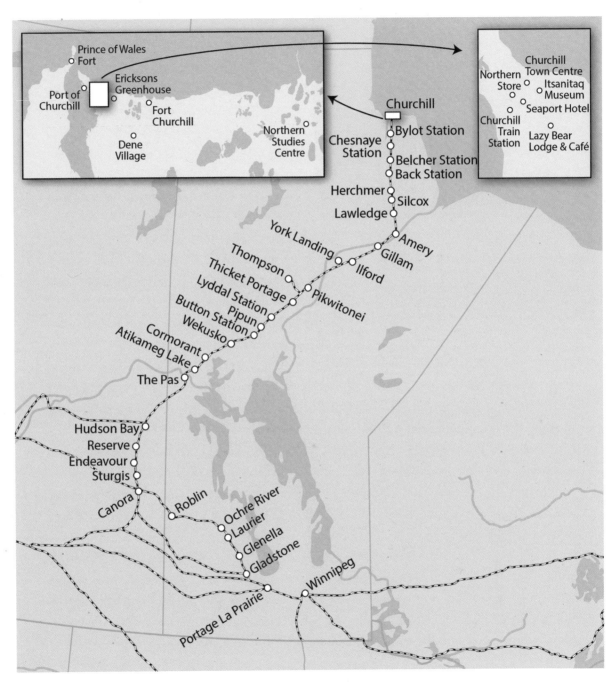

Map 7. VIA rail route and stops from Winnipeg to Churchill, and Churchill and environs, 2019.

would be the extractive and colonial process that Wheeler and our employer warn against. Indeed, we as historians would do well to remember that the ability to do oral history interviews with *anyone* is not only up to us! As settler academics, we should not presume that anyone *wants* to build meaningful relationships with us . . . particularly if the primary goal of that process is a recorded and archived oral history. We understand that to assume otherwise is to perpetuate a colonial method of doing history that undermines the oral history principle of informed consent.

Kimberley Moore always reminds those who take her Introduction to Oral History workshop series at the University of Winnipeg's Oral History Centre that one of the first questions oral historians should ask themselves is: What do you hope to learn through interviews that you cannot learn through existing sources—including archived interviews? The Archives of Manitoba contain interviews with Hudson's Bay Company employees and others who moved to Churchill for work, as well as interviews with Inuit students in Churchill, but we could not locate archival interviews with Churchill Dene.[14] At most, there is a brief depiction of trapper Battice Plakoti's wife making pine needle tea in outtakes of a 1919 video prepared for the Hudson's Bay Company's centenary celebrations.[15] The Manitoba Museum, however, has a collection of interviews conducted in 1973 with Dene elders in Churchill by Allan and Mary Code (Mary Code was Dene and had lived in Dene Village outside of Churchill). We were granted permission to access this collection. All but five of the eighteen recordings (primarily in Chipewyan, but some in English) have English summaries or transcripts; those thirteen recordings, unfortunately for us, do not include discussion of food or foodways. Their focus is on drumming and songs, trapping and sale of furs, and employment and training. While the odd mention is made of fishing and hunting caribou and moose for food, no further detail is provided.[16]

As non-Indigenous scholars from Winnipeg on a short journey to northern Manitoba, we talked and dined with Indigenous people on our trip, but were not granted permission to record and archive oral histories with any, though we did ask. We were not in Churchill long enough to establish the kinds of meaningful relationships needed to record formal interviews. We were not permitted to do field recording (much less record an oral history) with the Dene

Figure 53. Evening landscape near Gillam, taken from the VIA train. Photograph by Kimberley Moore, 2019.

Figure 54. Exterior of the VIA train on arrival in Churchill. Photograph by Kimberley Moore, 2019.

Figure 55. Interior of the VIA train's observation car. Photograph by Kimberley Moore, 2019.

Figure 56. Janis Thiessen and Kimberley Moore on the shore of Hudson Bay. Photograph by Kent Davies, 2019.

Figure 57. Landscape at Cape Merry. Photograph by Janis Thiessen, 2019.

Figure 58. Kent Davies with recording equipment on the shore of Hudson Bay. Photograph by Kimberley Moore, 2019.

Figure 59. Kimberley Moore and Janis Thiessen in Parks Canada Adirondack chairs at Prince of Wales Fort. Photograph by Kent Davies, 2019.

elders we met. The Inuit guides we met on the train declined our requests for interviews. Some Indigenous people we talked to in town named specific non-Indigenous people in the community that we should interview rather than themselves. We respect these people's choices not to record an interview with us.

The population of Churchill (870 in 2021) is a varied one, composed of many people who have migrated to the North over generations. Many arrived in response to the historical presence of Fort Churchill and the American Strategic Air Command and Rocket Range, Churchill's strategic position as a shipping port, and a variety of economic opportunities in the region including tourism.

In light of this, we did leave Churchill with half a dozen interviews that reflected varied experiences of the North. We were not even off the train before striking up a conversation with Glenn Wingie, an employee of the Arctic Gateway Group. We interviewed him as we travelled between Thicket Portage and Thompson.[17] He explained how important the railway was for Churchill residents. Railway freight was shipped out of The Pas, destined for Churchill, with some dropped at communities en route. Once at Churchill, remaining freight was loaded from the train onto barges and distributed around Hudson Bay. More recently, freight was loaded at Thompson rather than The Pas. The train also transported anything south for Manitoba Hydro; this happened twice weekly before the rails were washed out, water from floods having eroded the railway lines' roadbeds, leaving the tracks in several locations either collapsed into holes or suspended in mid-air. Truck trailers placed on train cars (known as piggybacks) headed to Churchill for the Northern Store, Home Hardware, and contractors; some freight was then put on planes to go further north. VIA hauled freight on piggybacks behind their passenger trains because CN did not want the business; piggybacks were more efficient than refrigerated cars. In the past, Wingie said, there used to be six to eight such piggybacks per train, but much of that transport has been replaced by a barge ship from Montreal that does three circuits per summer instead. When the American company OmniTRAX took over the railway, they took the freight business from VIA. Gardewine (a trucking company with origins in Flin Flon, Manitoba) had been shipping the majority of freight, but with the recent explosion of freight companies, Wingie said, they no longer have a monopoly on loading and unloading. He used to make

Figure 60. A barrel converted into a wood stove, with a kettle on top, along the shoreline of Hudson Bay. Photograph by Kimberley Moore, 2019.

purchases of food for Churchill residents in Thompson or Gillam, where prices were lower, and deliver it in a freight container. Passenger service had been three times weekly and freight service twice weekly to Thompson, so this was a convenient way for some Churchill residents to shop for food.[18]

The town of Churchill traces its origins to the construction of a Hudson's Bay Company post on the west bank of the Churchill River in 1717. Prince of Wales Fort was subsequently constructed from 1733 to 1773.[19] The Hudson Bay Railway on which we had travelled had its beginnings in 1911 as a more direct route than the St. Lawrence River for shipping grain from Canada to Europe; it was completed in Churchill in 1929.[20] The grain elevator and harbour were built in Churchill at that same time; with a storage capacity of five million bushels and four deep-sea berths for loading ships, regular grain shipments from the port began in 1931.[21] The port and railway were sold to OmniTRAX in 1997, and the ending of the Wheat Board monopoly in 2016 prompted the closing of the port. Flooding in 2017 damaged the rail line, shutting it down for a few years; air travel was the only way to deliver goods to the community during that time, increasing the price of food in Churchill.[22] A year later, the port and railway were purchased by Arctic Gateway Group, a partnership between AGT/Fairfax and OneNorth, the latter composed of local and Indigenous investors. Rail repairs resulted in the port's reopening in 2019, and two years later, AGT and Fairfax transferred their 50 percent ownership to OneNorth.[23]

ETHNIC ORIGIN	TOTAL
French, not otherwise specified	50
German	60
Ukrainian	65
Dutch	15
Polish	25
British Isles, not otherwise specified	10
Filipino	15
Caucasian, not otherwise specified	15
First Nations, not otherwise specified	15
Métis	60
European, not otherwise specified	10
Russian	15
Norwegian	25
Swedish	15
Hungarian	15
Greek	10
Romanian	10
Icelandic	25
Ojibway	10
Inuit, not otherwise specified	30
Dene, not otherwise specified	30

Table 2. Ethnic origins of Churchill residents, 2021. Source: Statistics Canada, Census Profile, 2021 Census of Population. Statistics Canada Catalogue no. 98-316-X2021001. Ottawa. Released 29 March 2023. https://www12.statcan.gc.ca/census-recensement/2021/dp-pd/prof/index.cfm?Lang=E (accessed 18 July 2023).

While tourism and grain shipment are major economic drivers in Churchill these days, at one time whaling was also a major industry. Canada's North was not settled in the same way as the South, historian Allan Greer observes, but it was nonetheless subjected to colonialism via "imperial/commercial penetration" and resource "extractivism."[24] An example of such is the history of whale processing in Churchill. In 1948, the Adanac Whale and Fish Products Company was founded.[25] They processed 500 beluga whales annually, resulting in 36,300 kilograms of meat and 6,800 kilograms of oil.[26]

Forbes Powell recalled that his father and several other farmers from Grandview had owned shares in the whaling plant. Powell, together with half a dozen other Grandview young people, went to Churchill one summer in the 1950s to work there.

> JANIS THIESSEN: I'm sorry, but how did folks from Grandview [more than 900 kilometres south of Churchill] become involved in Churchill?
>
> FORBES POWELL: Beats the hell out of me! I don't know. I really don't.[27]

Powell took a thirty-six-hour train ride from Dauphin, and was provided room and board in Churchill by the whaling plant. He said, "We sort of had a bunkhouse where we stayed. Not much for washing facilities or anything like that."[28] Powell's job was to bring the whales up a ramp onto the plant floor and then remove the blubber. "The plant was run by steam. And old Ed Belmore, he had one arm but he had a ticket for steam, so he was our steam guy. So probably forty, fifty feet up into the plant. So just run by cable and a winch, and up they'd come. And we had a freezer. And the whale oil—they'd render it down into oil, and the *stink*."[29] Removing the blubber and rendering it down "wasn't hard," Powell recalled. "You had a long handle with a curved knife on the end of it. And you just went down and slit them open and peeled it off."[30] He lasted only six weeks on the job, though, as he seriously burned himself while cleaning the plant with the steam hose at the end of his shift one day.[31]

The whales averaged twelve to fifteen feet (3.5 to 4.5 metres) in length, and the Indigenous hunters who caught them were paid a dollar per foot.[32] Inuk Elder John Arnalukjuaq recalled his time catching whales for Adanac:

It is hard to get a beluga whale right away, because the waters of the bay [at the mouth of the Churchill River] are murky. But we would follow the ripples on the water from the whale's tail. We would follow the ripples when we couldn't see the whale itself because of the muddy water. You couldn't see when they were in deeper water. You can see them when they come up for air. They are barely visible when they are in deep water. Sometimes the whales would end up in deep water and, the waters being murky, we would lose them. . . . When they came up for air and when they were close we would watch which way the whale was swimming. . . . The whales we caught we would bring to the whaling station where they were hauled in by the Qablunaat [non-Inuit people].[33]

Two or three whalers would travel in each motor-driven six-metre freighter canoe for the hunt. Whales, some up to 545 kilograms and over five metres long, were harpooned by hand (in later years, they would be caught by net) and towed to the Adanac plant at the mouth of the Churchill River for processing. Whale oil was sold to Canada Packers for margarine and shortening production (though Powell recalls adding it to chicken feed), and the meat was sold as steaks and ground for feed for poultry and mink.[34] Canned whale meatballs make an appearance as an ingredient in a Churchill cookbook; it's unknown whether Adanac produced them.[35] Adanac was later purchased by George Dowler of Morris, Manitoba; it subsequently reopened as Churchill Whale Products.[36] Whale processing ended by the 1970s, as Manitoba mink farming collapsed (destroying the market for mink feed) and whale harvesting quotas were drastically lowered from 1,300 to 265.[37] The last commercial whaling business in the area, Churchill Whalers Cooperative, closed in 1968.[38]

Churchill's history has been shaped by multiple intrusions of outsiders over the years, particularly scientists and the military. The town itself was created in 1933. The United States established a military tent camp at Hudson Square; it was succeeded by the Akudlik Marsh camp and then Fort Churchill, a military base a few kilometres outside of town. Fort Churchill came under Canadian military control in 1946. A rocket facility was built at Fort Churchill in 1957–58, which remained in use until 1984. American forces left in 1964, and the base was demolished in 1981; it later became the Churchill airport. The subsequent drop in area residents had a significant impact on local business and society.[39]

One such affected business was the S&M Grocery Market, also known as Sigurdson & Martin. The store was opened in 1947 and closed sometime around the year 2000.[40] Located behind the current Northern Store, its offerings were both diverse and limited. The store had a lunch bar that served coffee, sandwiches, and soup. Fresh fruit was usually restricted to apples and oranges, but strawberries were occasionally available and Japanese oranges were on the shelves at Christmas. The store shipped to communities further north that did not have their own grocery stores. Helen Webber, who is related to the store's founders, observed that food provision had changed by the twenty-first century: "I was in Rankin [Rankin Inlet, Nunavut, 470 kilometres north of Churchill] the other week and I couldn't believe their grocery store. It's huge! And it's got a Tim Hortons in it."[41]

We spoke with Patti McIntyre and Maureen Martin Osland, daughters of the founders of S&M. Their parents were traders and trappers who migrated to Churchill from Arborg, Manitoba, and Montreal, Quebec, in the 1930s. They vividly described the difficulties of feeding their family in Churchill, even as owners of a grocery store.

> MAUREEN MARTIN OSLAND: We got to eat the dented cans, the squished butter, the old bread, and the old meat, that nobody else bought. . . .
>
> PATRICIA MCINTYRE: Groceries—you know, you couldn't get decent salad and lettuce. By the time they got to Churchill, they had been on the train for a week. And who knows how long they've been in a warehouse. So, we'd have milk, and at that time it wasn't dated, and so . . .
>
> MAUREEN MARTIN OSLAND: You never took a drink until you smelled it.
>
> PATRICIA MCINTYRE: It was a common occurrence: you get up in the morning and the milk is sour, so you'd have to have toast. You know, that was the reality of it.
>
> MAUREEN MARTIN OSLAND: It was very common to have sour milk.[42]

Osland explained the role of the store in the community: "You have to remember that there was five thousand people living there at the time; there's now eight hundred. There was five thousand people, and there was the fort five miles away, which was the army base. There was a lot of people. . . . And there was, you know, the ships were coming in all summer and the scientists were coming in and the rocket range people. It was a pretty bustling place as compared to now."

MAUREEN MARTIN OSLAND: But you know, it was a very unique community and very— You know, we had the whole world coming there when we were young. We had ships from England. We had—

PATRICIA MCINTYRE: China, Russia.

MAUREEN MARTIN OSLAND: —ships from Spain and China. We had the army. We had the navy. We had the locals. We had the trappers. You know, it was a town full of characters.[43]

Helen Webber similarly commented on the number and diversity of Churchill visitors and residents.

JANIS THIESSEN: I think one of the things that has surprised me—again, Southerner bias, right?—to think of Churchill as remote. But this rotation of people—

HELEN WEBBER: People—

JANIS THIESSEN: —from around the globe that come here.

HELEN WEBBER: —that come here, yes.

JANIS THIESSEN: It's not insular, for sure.

HELEN WEBBER: No, no! Yeah, that's kind of what I was saying. There's just been so many people here that, I mean. . . . Some you want and some you don't [laughs] but interesting characters all of them. Farley Mowat. David Suzuki. People, some of them that we don't even know. I mean, private jets come in out there and we don't always know who's wandering around or what their agenda is, or whatever.[44]

Unfortunately, as their agendas changed, many people would leave Churchill permanently, transforming the community in the process. Osland described how the closure of the army base affected the town and her family's business: "The population gradually declined and so it's harder to find workers. You know, in the early days when Dad and Mom had the store, they had two or three butchers, they had cashiers, they had a floor manager."[45] S&M grocery would eventually close.

Grocery stores were not the only food provisioners in Churchill; there is also a long tradition of gardening in the region, by both settlers and Indigenous peoples. Ben Larson, Thicket Portage elder, recalled, "All the people around here used to have a garden. There are

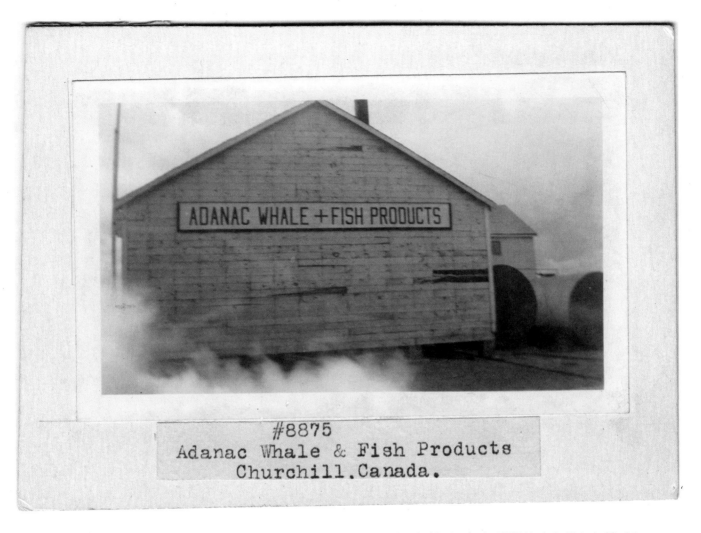

#8875
Adanac Whale & Fish Products
Churchill.Canada.

Figure 61. Exterior of Adanac Whale and Fish Products Company. Carver County Historical Society fonds #8875, Manitoba Historical Society.

different types of soil. Some good for tilling potatoes. You put fish in it for fertilizer."[46] And yet by 1975, journalist Bob Lowery observed, "In remote communities gardening once flourished but has dwindled to a lost art."[47] What Larson and Lowery left unsaid is *why* fewer Indigenous peoples in the region gardened by the 1970s: Indian residential schools and the Sixties Scoop—both designed by the state to eliminate Indigenous identity—disrupted the generational transmission of food production knowledge.[48]

The first garden created by Europeans in the Churchill area was that of English explorer Samuel Hearne in 1784; only turnips produced consistent yields.[49] By the twentieth century, some settlers had small-scale gardening success by importing soil or blending muskeg with sand and other amendments. The aunt of Osland and McIntyre was one such gardener.

> MAUREEN MARTIN OSLAND: Our aunt Helga probably had the nicest garden in town. . . . A lot of people didn't have running water, and so you would do your dishes in a tub. And the dish tub [water] would get thrown on the garden, along with your eggshells and your coffee grinds. And she grew carrots and lettuce and tomatoes and—
>
> PATRICIA MCINTYRE: But they also—the grapefruit skins, because they ate grapefruits [laughs]. We didn't eat grapefruits at our house. I just remember them being—
>
> MAUREEN MARTIN OSLAND: She'd just spread them out.
>
> PATRICIA MCINTYRE: Yeah, just put them on there and then rototill it in.
>
> MAUREEN MARTIN OSLAND: And she had the best little garden, and hers just grew like crazy.[50]

Others made efforts to warm the soil in various ways to improve their odds of gardening success. Helen Webber explained, "The season is short. I mean, there are only certain things you can grow outside in the ground and with the community garden they'd done the tire thing and . . . which helps because it warms the ground and I think they are starting to get some decent stuff from it."[51]

Helen McEwan described the difficulties of teaching gardening to children in a region with significant environmental limits.

> We tried growing radishes into little pots to show the kids how easy it was: they didn't grow [laughs]. I tried to transplant. We tried to do the Three Sisters planting: we had squash, corn, and beans growing. Put it out in the Danica's flower bin there [a memorial to former Churchill resident Danica deLaroque]. They all died. It was too cold. My hands were freezing as I was trying to water and arrange things. So, the season? You have two months, basically. . . . Potatoes are really successful. Things that you can plant into the ground. . . . I'm still trying to do things. I'm going to try to transplant those beans into my little greenhouse area. I've got squash coming up and things like that. I've been trying to grow tomatoes for ten

years [laughs]. I still haven't mastered them. How to start them and not go spindly by the time you get them into your greenhouse, and then produce in August: I haven't been able to do that. It's a work in progress.[52]

Greenhouses are the most successful gardening effort in Churchill; the largest was built by Bill and Diane Erickson (cousins of Helen Webber) in the 1970s at their home just outside of town. They grew tomatoes primarily, later adding a 6,000-square-foot (560 square metres) greenhouse tunnel to grow a wide variety of vegetables as well as strawberries; they sold their surplus at the Northern Store. Their soil was a mix of local muskeg, peat, and seaweed.[53] Without a greenhouse for warmth and protection, gardens are at the mercy of the highly variable weather in the region.

HELEN MCEWAN: [laughs] They tease us, the weather people [laughs]. They give us a little bit of hope and then they take that away, and then the hail! That one day! Were you here that one day?

JANIS THIESSEN: Yes!

KENT DAVIES: Yeah! That's when we got here.

KIMBERLEY MOORE: Yes.

HELEN MCEWAN: There. You had a perfect example of what's possible in Churchill.

KENT DAVIES: Yeah, and that was only for a few minutes.

HELEN MCEWAN: Yeah. There was sunshine, beautifully warm in the morning, and then came the hail and then came the rain and then came the wind and then the sun came out in the evening [laughs]!

KIMBERLEY MOORE: Yeah, all in ten hours.

HELEN MCEWAN: All in ten hours, yes! And that's typical. And that's the challenges we have with the gardening.[54]

Despite the fact that traditional Indigenous diets in the region are not dependent on gardens, governments and universities launched programs to expand northern gardening efforts. These initiatives were not always well planned. A case in point is the story of George Ponask, an Indigenous fisherman, trapper, and entrepreneur in Thicket Portage. Beginning in 1974, he was part of the Thompson Research Greenhouse project, which established polyethylene greenhouses to grow tomatoes, peppers, cucumbers, beans, and cantaloupe at Thicket Portage, Lynn Lake, Leaf Rapids, South Indian Lake, Ilford, The Pas, and Flin Flon.[55] The project was the initiative of Manitoba's Department of Northern Affairs, the University of Manitoba's agriculture and plant science departments, and the City of Thompson.[56] Its intention was to encourage northerners to grow food for their own consumption.

A year later, the Thompson Research Greenhouse project had expanded to forty-one greenhouses in twenty northern communities, despite such challenges as damage to the polyethylene greenhouses by wind, dogs, and polar bears.[57] George Ponask decided to purchase additional greenhouses in 1977 and turn them into a commercial business, named Kistigan Enterprises (Ininímowin for "garden"). He found a market for his vegetables with wholesalers in Thompson.[58] A year later, his vegetables (including two tonnes of tomatoes and ten tonnes of potatoes) were also marketed in Gillam, Churchill, and Wabowden.[59] Ponask described his business:

> Kistigan began about four years back as an experiment with greenhouse tunnels. We started out with six people. The first year and the second year, a LEAP grant created employment. I had in mind a farm garden because there wasn't much going on around here. During the third year, we started raising bedding plants in addition to an outdoor garden. This is nothing new really. . . . Woolworth and Canadian Tire handle some of our bedding plants and flowers. We grow 6,000 bedding plants, nine plants to a pack, and 15,000 vegetables. Several varieties are transplanted outside to a field. . . . The soil is fair, but it takes awhile to develop it.[60]

In 1980, as part of a Katimavik project, Ponask began experimenting with solar-heated greenhouses.[61] But the company failed shortly thereafter.

Though the *Winnipeg Free Press* had run numerous stories about the success of this Indigenous-owned business in its early years, there was no newspaper story about its closure. Decades later, however, a columnist in a local newspaper speculated on the reasons for Kistigan's demise: "There have been greenhouse efforts in our north in the past; at Thicket Portage and Churchill to mention just two I recall. I'm not sure why these pioneering efforts didn't work out, but it could be they were just ahead of their time . . . I don't recall exactly why the Thicket Portage greenhouse project failed, but it seems to me one telling factor was it was based on

Aug 1954

Figure 62. Exterior of Adanac Whale and Fish Products Company. University of Winnipeg Archives, Western Canada Pictorial Index, Miscellaneous Collection (A2410-71768).

selling to the Thompson market [rather than limiting the focus to the local community]."[62] The real problem was not overambition on the part of a local Indigenous entrepreneur, however, but the failure of the provincial government to provide consistent and reliable rail service in the North. Kistigan Enterprises "will be in serious trouble," Thompson MLA Ken Dillen warned in 1977, "because the [Canadian National] railway has not agreed to transport its produce to markets at Thompson."[63] CN railway service continued to deteriorate throughout the 1970s, culminating in the removal of station agents at Thicket Portage and four other northern communities, which locals accurately predicted would negatively impact Kistigan Enterprises.[64]

There have been more recent efforts to establish greenhouses in the North, but they are often the initiative of White residents (like the Ericksons) and scientific or government visitors to the North, and their primary focus is not local food security. Churchill Northern Studies Centre (CNSC) researcher Carley Basler began a Growcer greenhouse, a type of C-can (or large shipping container) hydroponic garden that CNSC calls "Rocket Greens" in recognition of the history of rocket research at the CNSC site.[65] The project began when the rail line to Churchill washed out.[66] Vegetables and herbs grown included butterhead lettuce, leaf lettuce, four kinds of Asian greens, mustard greens, collard greens, kale, spinach, basil, cilantro, dill, parsley, and mint.[67] Rocket Greens' first harvest was Christmas 2018, when they donated 200 heads of lettuce to the local community feast. A year later, fifty people purchased eighty-dollar weekly Rocket Greens subscriptions.[68] Store prices for fresh vegetables fluctuate dramatically in Churchill—cauliflower can be six dollars one week and eleven dollars the next—so the subscription is a boon for those craving produce.[69] The CNSC believes that Rocket Greens has "an instant and immediate impact on our food security here in Churchill. There's never been something producing this amount of quantity of produce year-round in Churchill ever before."[70] Though Rocket Greens provides occasional produce to two grocers, the hospital cafeteria, and a few restaurants,[71] it is difficult to argue that Rocket Greens has a significant impact on food security in a town of 900 people.

Another recent greenhouse effort in Churchill is the revival of the Ericksons' greenhouse after its purchase by Lazy Bear Lodge owner Wally Daudrich.[72] He has repaired and expanded it, using loamy soil from river and pond bottoms, mineral soil from the local forest with

Figure 63. Entrance to Churchill Northern Studies Centre. Photograph by Kimberley Moore, 2019.

Figure 64. Growcer at Churchill Northern Studies Centre. Photograph by Kimberley Moore, 2019.

Figure 65. Rocket Greens poster inside Churchill Northern Studies Centre. Photograph by Kimberley Moore, 2019.

Figure 66. Carley Basler inside the Growcer. Photograph by Kimberley Moore, 2019.

Figure 67. Carley Basler, Kimberley Moore, and Kent Davies inside the Growcer. Photograph by Janis Thiessen, 2019.

Figure 68. Plants growing inside the Growcer. Photograph by Kimberley Moore, 2019.

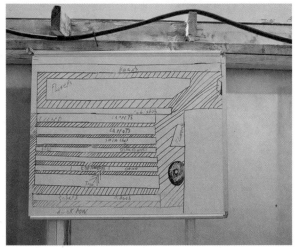

added clay for nutrients, and sea kelp as natural fertilizer.[73] He has successfully grown apples, pumpkin, zucchini, tomatoes, Chinese gooseberry, beans, peas, carrots, Swiss chard, lettuce, onions, rhubarb, and saskatoons, and is planning to add cherries and apricots. The 560 square metres of greenhouses provide produce for the restaurant at Lazy Bear Lodge, which also offers elk, Arctic char, and bison on their menu.[74]

Provincial regulations require that meat served in Manitoba restaurants is inspected, so the elk and bison at Lazy Bear are probably farmed rather than locally hunted. It is illegal to purchase wild meat directly from hunters, even for home consumption. Kivalliq Arctic Foods in nearby Rankin Inlet sells processed caribou, musk ox, and Arctic char; such commercial offerings are rare, however.[75] And harvesting country foods oneself is challenging, as Carley Basler explained to us:

> We hunt ourselves so we do moose and caribou and geese. We are not fisher people so we like to do trades with people that fish. . . . We are only entitled to a moose each per year and a caribou each per year . . . unlimited snow geese. . . . We used to trap on a man's trapline. . . . He signed my boyfriend on as his help on his trapline; in exchange, we gave him Arctic hares and ptarmigan. . . . It costs money to do that here, too. The gas is expensive. . . . You need equipment, and it's cold and demanding conditions, so you need good equipment. . . . It requires maintenance ability.[76]

Many Churchill residents hunt, fish, and forage: we interviewed Port of Churchill and airport worker Joe Stover, for example, who described hunting moose and caribou, harvesting mussels, and fishing for Arctic char.[77] Helen Webber recalled, "When we started with the goose hunting

Figure 69. Jason Ransom, Wally Daudrich, and Kent Davies inside a greenhouse, Churchill. Photograph by Kimberley Moore, 2019.

Figure 70. Temperature gauge inside greenhouse, reading 40°C. Photograph by Kimberley Moore, 2019.

Figure 71. Whiteboard diagram showing what is growing in the greenhouse, Churchill. Photograph by Kimberley Moore, 2019.

Figure 72. Jason Ransom and Wally Daudrich behind a boom microphone inside a greenhouse, Churchill. Photograph by Kimberley Moore, 2019.

Figure 73. Interior of a greenhouse, Churchill. Photograph by Kimberley Moore, 2019.

[at her lodge fifty years ago], it was five a day and fifteen in possession [i.e., you could hunt five every day, and keep up to fifteen in storage]. And now, it's eighty a day and there's no possession [limit] on it."[78] She said, "I prefer the snow goose to the Canada goose. One of our signature recipes [at her hunting lodge] is the goose pie that we make. We use Canadas and snow in that because we just use the legs and thighs and we boil it until it all falls off the, right off the bone. So, it's very tender. . . . If we have caribou or moose, mix them together and it makes a great chili and great burgers."[79] Webber harvests local cloudberries, which are like raspberries in appearance but they grow on ground-level bushes and produce only one berry per stem: "The third week of July, normally they start to ripen enough to be picked, and by the second week of August, it'll be done. . . . You're on your hands and knees all the time for them."[80] Helen McEwan explained the harvesting of cranberries and blueberries: "Cranberries are best after a frost. So, we wait for the, kind of the cold weather, the end of September. . . . We have to get to the blueberries before the geese do, so [laughs]. We have about three days, so [laughs]. And then there's all kinds of other different kinds of berries and stuff. But blueberries, cranberries, different currants. Black and red currants are kind of the norm and standard here."[81]

Country foods are of particular significance for Indigenous people in the Churchill region. Itsanitaq Museum curator Lorraine Brandson explains that "blood from country food is considered by many as highly important whereas store-bought food is described as bloodless food with little nutritive value."[82] For almost forty years, Indigenous people have been able to maintain their diet of country food even if they were staying in the Churchill hospital. This provision required some legal arrangements, however.

KIMBERLEY MOORE: Before we turned on the recorder, you were saying about the native diet in hospitals. So, do you know—I don't imagine this is your area of expertise, but do you know when this started?

MAUREEN MARTIN OSLAND: Well, I worked at the Churchill Health Centre for a lot of years. And they did a lot of lobbying to get permission to do that because it was making people sick to come from a northern diet and eat a Churchill diet.

PATRICIA MCINTYRE: But it's—you're not allowed to serve wild meat, right?

MAUREEN MARTIN OSLAND: Unless it's inspected somehow. So, they made arrangements and I can't recall the details, but they made arrangements to actually have seal and that kind of thing available.

KIMBERLEY MOORE: Do you know approximately when that started happening?

MAUREEN MARTIN OSLAND: Well, I left in 1989 and it was just maybe a couple of years before that. So, I'd say '87, '86, maybe around there. And the Churchill Health Centre lobbied for it.[83]

This respect for Indigenous foodways is a marked contrast to governments' earlier actions. The forcible relocation of the Sayisi Dene by the Canadian government, ostensibly to protect their most important country food (caribou), instead interfered in terrible and lethal ways with their food security. Traditionally, the Dene trapped and hunted caribou, ptarmigan, duck, geese, and fish in their territories in what is now northern Manitoba and the southern portion of the Northwest Territories. With the arrival of the Hudson's Bay Company in the 1700s, they engaged in trade at the posts established at Prince of Wales Fort, Caribou Lake, and Little Duck Lake. The Dene way of life was threatened by the decline of the fur trade, which led to the closure of the Little Duck post in the 1950s, by the assimilationist policies of the 1951 amendments to the Indian Act, and by the publication of a provocative article in the *Beaver*, the Hudson's Bay Company magazine. The article, by the "chief mammalogist of the Canadian Wildlife Service," incorrectly stated that the caribou population was being overhunted by local Indigenous people, based in part on a misinterpretation of a photograph of a Dene winter caribou cache.[84] The government response was to forcibly relocate the Dene to a tent community on the outskirts of Churchill in 1956; they had to leave behind their boats and traps. Denied access to their traditional hunting grounds, they also had to deal with local game wardens in Churchill who restricted their ammunition to protect (unnecessarily) the caribou population, and local RCMP who viewed their hunting dogs as an annoyance and shot them.[85]

Government interference in Dene life continued for many years, leading to the death of a third of the population.[86] In 1957, the Churchill Dene were moved to Camp 10, a former army camp, described by Churchill museum curator Lorraine Brandson as "located on the cold and windy [Hudson] Bay side of the townsite . . . adjacent to the cemetery."[87] Dene Elder Eva Anderson described the impact of this government decision:

It was very disturbing to our people because we were now to live a few steps away from a mass burial ground. If our people were in charge and if someone had listened to our voices, a different site may have been selected instead of next to a graveyard. Our people the Sayisi Dene had always respected the spirits of the dead. A burial ground is a sacred place, not to be disturbed. It's a resting place for our relatives who are gone to the spirit world. The white people who made the decisions for our people did not acknowledge our culture and traditions.[88]

In 1966, the government moved the Dene yet again to an inadequate segregated housing project called Dene Village, southwest of Churchill.

Finally, in 1973, a group of Dene decided to return to Tes-He-Olie Twe (Tadoule Lake), successfully resisting the government control of their lives that had led to so many deaths.[89] Phil Dickman, who had been a Community Development Officer in Churchill and supported the Dene's return, later reflected: "There's not a band of Indigenous people in Canada who were abused to the extent they were, for nothing else but to save caribou herds. To save the herds, the government decided to destroy the Sayisi Dene. The experts later agreed there was no caribou crisis. It was the only tribe [in Canada that was] taken and dumped in a hellhole. And they died. They were all going to die if they didn't leave Churchill."[90] It was not until 2016 that the government of Canada apologized for their actions and provided compensation to the survivors and their descendants. Dene community leader Jim Clipping was circumspect about the government apology: "I asked, 'What's in the apology? That you're sorry, you killed over 100 of my people? You expect me to forgive you?' I would sooner have my friend back, my family back to go out hunting. But that's long gone."[91]

Not all Dene left Churchill; those who remained had their transmission of traditional knowledge (including of foodways) disrupted by their multiple forcible relocations. Helen McEwan, known at Duke of Marlborough School as Grandma Helen, is a peer educator working to help local Indigenous families recover those foodways. She lived in Churchill as a child, moved away as an adult, and then returned. "I came here as a vegetarian in '99 [laughs] and then, I lasted about a year and then I started [eating meat]. And this is a story of all the vegetarians that come here that I've connected with. You crave meat, and we started eating the wild meat, the caribou. Caribou is awesome; it's organic [laughs]. And moose meat and fish and stuff like that.

Helen Webber

Interviewed by Janis Thiessen, Churchill, MB, 14 June 2019.
Recipe copyright Helen Webber, used with permission.

JANIS THIESSEN: So, thank you very much for making this possible. We are pretty excited and we've heard from a lot of people [that] your cookbooks are the cookbooks for the region, and to find that you're also willing to do a little sample cooking, it's really exciting.

HELEN WEBBER: Good! I'm glad you're looking forward to it.

JANIS THIESSEN: Very much so. So, we'll let you get started, however you want, and then we'll just ask you questions as you go along, if that's okay?

HELEN WEBBER: Okay, well what I'm doing right here are—we just call them goose tidbits in the cookbook, and it's something that we've served to our guests at Diamond Lake for I don't know, probably fifty years, somewhere in that span and it usually goes over quite well. As well as the goose tidbits, I've also baked up a little bit of French bread for you to eat them on or to try—we make cloudberry, black currant, different jellies and jams for the lodges, so I've got samples of those there for you to taste. And then, I don't know whether you heard about it, talking to other people, but we're kind of known for our

Helen Webber was born in Churchill, Manitoba. Her great-grandfather immigrated to Canada in the 1930s; he subsequently owned a store in Arborg.[92] Helen first started experimenting in the kitchen and creating new dishes when she joined the Churchill Ladies Club, which made meals for the Lions Club's meetings.[93]

Helen's husband purchased a hunting lodge; she worked as its cook. The couple has owned numerous lodges in northern Manitoba including a hunting lodge, a fishing lodge, and a couple of lodges in Churchill.[94] At the request of lodge patrons, Helen became the co-author of many unique cookbooks that feature the dishes that she served in the lodges.[95] The Blueberries and Polar Bears cookbooks series includes *Blueberries & Polar Bears*, *Cranberries & Canada Geese*, *Black Currants & Caribou*, and *Icebergs & Belugas*. They all feature traditional northern Manitoba dishes.[96]

Figure 74. Helen Webber seated at her table with food she has prepared before her, Churchill. Photograph by Kimberley Moore, 2019.

Figure 75. Snow goose tidbits and sliced bread. Photograph by Janis Thiessen, 2019.

cranberry cake with butter sauce, so I've got that for you to taste after we're done. So, um, I'll start with the goose tidbits and if you have any questions, just let me know.

JANIS THIESSEN: Yeah, tidbits because they are the remains of the goose after you take out the breast and that? Or—

HELEN WEBBER: No, this is the breast. This is snow goose breast that we're cooking up here. And I've just taken it and sliced it very—quite thinly sliced, it kind of falls apart. This is nice, tender.

JANIS THIESSEN: It's awfully dark.

HELEN WEBBER: Yes. It's very much like beef, in fact a lot of people will think of beef. In fact, that reminds me of a story—we had goose hunters at the lodge one year and one fellow was kind of on his own, and we served goose pie for dinner. And I don't know what he heard when whoever took the food out told him what we were eating, but after dinner he came to me quietly in the kitchen and he said, "I know I'm at a goose hunting lodge, but I just wanted to let you know that I don't eat goose." And I said "Okay," and then I thought, well I better ask him what he thought of supper, and I said, "Well, how did you enjoy the supper?" "Oh, that beef pie, that was just delicious!" So, I didn't say a word, I didn't tell him that he'd eaten goose for dinner and quite enjoyed it. Of course, that's a lot of people's reaction to goose. So, this is probably going to make it a little smoky in here, my vent has died, so we're just going to have to live with it.

JANIS THIESSEN: So, did you hunt these yourself?

HELEN WEBBER: Um, no. We have a goose hunting lodge, not far from town, and actually this is friends of ours— my . . . the co-author for the cookbook, she and her son and grandson came up for goose hunting in May, and so this is stuff that we harvested in May.

SNOW GOOSE TIDBITS

2–3 snow goose breasts
3 tbsp butter
Dymond Lake seasoning
½ cup vermouth

Slice snow goose breasts thinly into bite-sized pieces, and brown in pan with butter. Sprinkle liberally with seasoning on both sides. Add vermouth and simmer 1–2 minutes. Reserve pan juices to pour over bread when serving.

Figure 76. Snow goose tidbits and cloudberry jelly on a table in the foreground, with Helen Webber at her kitchen stove in the background. Photograph by Kimberley Moore, 2019.

Now, I'm not a vegetarian [laughs]."[97] She explained the informal economy that exists in Churchill to share knowledge and food.

> JANIS THIESSEN: So, I was just wondering, if you were [to] move here or just [were] born here but are not necessarily skilled. If you aren't catching these things yourself, how do you get into that meat economy that exists?
>
> HELEN MCEWAN: You try to connect with other people. And other people are very open and take you along with them and stuff. They'll introduce you to the places and take you out hunting and stuff like that. There's a lot of hunters in Churchill. Indigenous and not. Experienced people who are very kind and will show people. They're happy to show you where to go and go hunting together and things like that. . . . You make do with what you've got, you have. And, you share that with other people, too. Like when you bake, you share that with other elders or other people that are struggling. You share your berries—I'm sharing mine right now; I still have some frozen ones [laughs]—by baking and things like that. Flour is a huge expense. It's probably three times the amount that you would pay down south. If you buy it down south and ship it here, it's equal to the price that you would pay here. . . . So, you find ways to get stuff, like from Thompson, now. If somebody's coming back from Thompson, you ask them to bring you forty pounds of flour or whatever.[98]

The openness and kindness that McEwan describes here were also what we as historians experienced during our week and a half in Churchill.

Our return trip to Winnipeg was again by rail. The remoteness of vast stretches of Manitoba was highlighted by the absence of cell phone signals shortly after leaving Churchill. When cell service was reacquired just outside of Thompson, many passengers phoned the Thompson pizzeria and placed orders, which were delivered by taxi to the Thompson railway station for pickup.[99] The coach cars quickly filled with the smell of hot pizza, leaving us regretting that we were not familiar enough with the region to have planned ahead in this way. The number of the train's occupants rapidly decreased from Thompson to Winnipeg, as the train made its long loop through Saskatchewan and back into the southern half of Manitoba. Our ten-day visit to Churchill was the beginning of more than three years of research for this chapter, which we offer as a gesture of solidarity to those in the North together with thanks for the warm welcome we were extended. Eve Tuck and K. Wayne Yang remind us, however, that "solidarity is an uneasy, reserved, and unsettled matter that neither reconciles present grievances nor forecloses future conflict."[100] Like many settler scholars from the South, there is still much we do not know about foodways in the North, but we respect that no one (Indigenous people in particular) owes us their stories or knowledge.

CHAPTER SIX

Manomin

Scholars of western Canadian agricultural history used to focus on the role of settler farmers in the South, largely ignoring the long agricultural histories of Indigenous nations throughout the prairie provinces.[1] Settler Manitobans in thrall to stereotypes of Indigenous hunting and gathering remain unaware of the intricate knowledge of and careful management of the landscape by Indigenous peoples for the cultivation of food for millennia.[2] Scholars Courtney W. Mason and Michael A. Robidoux point out that Indigenous nations have "engaged in diverse land-based practices that made use of local or regional ecosystems, fluctuating climates, and varying access to resources, including seasonal patterns of mammal and fish migrations."[3] In recent years, scholars have given greater attention to these Indigenous agricultural practices.[4]

Perhaps the most familiar Indigenous farming practice for settler Canadians is the "Three Sisters": the interplanting of corn, beans, and squash. Beans and corn were domesticated several thousand years ago by Central American Indigenous peoples; squash was domesticated by Indigenous groups in the southeastern United States. Through transcontinental trade among Indigenous peoples, the Three Sisters were brought to Manitoba some 2,000 to 3,000 years ago. Corn was selectively bred by the Anishinaabeg (Ojibwe) to mature within 100 days for the local climate in what is now Canada.[5] Planting the Three Sisters together provided weed suppression and tall cornstalk support for climbing beans.[6] But the Three Sisters were not the only involvement by Indigenous people in farming in present-day Manitoba.

There is extensive historical evidence of agriculture by Indigenous peoples throughout the province (though archaeological research has tended to concentrate on southern Manitoba). Archaeological finds at Netley Creek, Lockport, and Melita, including hoes, corn plants, and crop storage pits, reveal evidence of Anishinaabe agriculture in present-day Manitoba at least 400 years before arrival of the first European settlers.[7] Indigenous people in what became Manitoba had both "communally cultivated land" as well as individual farms before the creation of the province in 1870.[8] The H.Y. Hind Red River Exploring Expedition in 1857, for example, found Indigenous farmers all over the region, growing fields of corn at Garden Island; potatoes, onions, and turnips at Fairford; wheat, barley, and potatoes at Fort Alexander; and other crops at St. Peter's, north of the Forks.[9] The agricultural landscape was also managed by Indigenous peoples through seasonal setting of controlled fires.[10] These fires were deliberately used to improve biodiversity, reduce acorn weevils (thus yielding a more abundant acorn crop), improve root crop yields, increase forage for deer, maintain berry patches, stimulate regrowth of willow and aspen for beavers (who were used to manage the production of manomin), and direct the movement of buffalo.[11] Scholars Robin Wall Kimmerer and Frank Kanawha Lake note, "The most important outcome of fire use was the intentional creation of a mosaic of habitat patches that promoted food security by ensuring a diverse and productive landscape. . . . In contrast, fire was often used by the colonists with a different intent—uniformity, such as production of pastures, cropland, and plantations."[12]

Settler prejudices against Indigenous peoples, historian Sarah Carter tells us, affected their ability to continue to prosper as farmers. "It was believed that the sustained labour required of them was alien to their culture and that the transformation of hunters into farmers was a process that historically took place over centuries."[13] But government policy rather than Indigenous culture was what impeded the agricultural success of Indigenous people in post-1870 Manitoba, including the reserve system and restrictions on access to technology. Carter points out that the 1876 Indian Act, for example, prevented Indigenous people from acquiring homesteads in

Manitoba, "thereby preventing the Indian farmer from seeking better railway, market, or soil advantages."[14] Carter quotes missionary John McDougall:

> He cannot visit a friend on a neighboring reserve without a permit. He cannot go to the nearest market town unless provided with a permit. In what was his own country and on his own land he cannot travel in peace without a permit. He cannot buy and sell without a permit. He may raise cattle but he cannot sell them unless the government official allows. He may cultivate the soil but he is not the owner of his own produce. He cannot sell firewood or hay from the land that is his by Divine and citizen right, and thus reap the result of his own industry unless subject to the caprice or whim of one who often becomes an autocrat. Said an Indian to me a few days since, "I raise cattle, they are not mine, my wood I cannot sell—my own hay I cannot do what I would with—I cannot even do as I like with the fish I may catch."[15]

Settlers nonetheless complained to local Indian agents that Indigenous farmers were "unfairly" competing with them in the marketplace.[16] Eric Tang notes that some Indigenous farmers, using "newly developed dry land farming techniques and acting as a collective . . . won local prizes and awards for their crops."[17] And yet at the same time as Indigenous farmers were criticized as competitors and winning agricultural competitions, they were also disparaged as "perfectly worthless" in a *Manitoba Free Press* article in 1889.[18] The Indian Act was amended in 1881 to prevent Indigenous people from selling their produce: the Royal Commission on Aboriginal Peoples (RCAP) notes that purchasers were "subject to summary conviction and a fine or imprisonment for up to three months."[19] This section of the Act was repealed only in 2014, far too late to be of any help.[20] Historian Jean Friesen says that by the 1890s, Indigenous peoples in Manitoba were "subject to an agricultural policy that effectively discouraged any development of a commercial agriculture that might have put them on an equal economic footing with whites."[21]

Denial of the history of Indigenous agricultural practices was necessary for the settlement of western Canada by Europeans. Sarah Carter notes that the creation of homesteads in what became western Canada "covered and smothered Indigenous ways of living in the West, and it was intended to do so; those defined as 'Indian' were denied the homestead land grant and instead relegated to reserves."[22] She says that "it was vital to the enterprise of establishing colonial rule in western Canada to cast First Nations as the antithesis of agriculturalists—as hunters, incapable and ignorant of farming, and thus having no concept of true land owner-ship."[23] This denial, suppression, and restriction of Indigenous farmers was not limited to the settlement years of the 1870s to the 1890s. The 1935 Prairie Farm Rehabilitation Act resulted in the dispossession and relocation of Métis from Ste. Madeleine when their farmland was redes-ignated as pasture. The RCAP notes, "Under the act, people were entitled to full compensation provided their tax payments on their land were up to date—a problem for many Métis people who eked out a living working for other farmers. . . . Their houses were burned, their church was dismantled, and by 1938, the once vital community of Ste. Madeleine had virtually vanished."[24] The Manitoba Indian Agricultural Program (MIAP) from 1975 to 1993 was also problematic. Though the ostensible intention was to increase the number of Indigenous farmers in Manitoba, the legacies of colonialism and the Indian Act worked against this goal.[25] Indigenous farmers had outdated agricultural equipment because they did not have sufficient credit and could not use reserve property to secure loans.[26] The MIAP was discontinued when the federal government (which provided funding and support) deemed the number of viable farm units created and farm productivity unsatisfactory.[27] As a consequence, many Indigenous farmers who participated in MIAP had their credit ratings drop or lost their equipment in bankruptcy.[28]

Manomin, also known as "wild rice," is a crop that has been cultivated and harvested for centuries by Indigenous people but was not recognized as an agricultural commodity by settlers until the mid-twentieth century.[29] Manomin is grown throughout Manitoba, including the Whiteshell and at Berens River, Cormorant, Herb Lake Landing, Little Grand Rapids, Norway House, Pikwitonei, Sherridon, The Pas, and Thicket Portage.[30] Manomin,[31] a type of grass, is described by scholar Kathi Avery Kinew as the "only cereal grain native to North America."[32] It's a popular side dish served in restaurants in Churchill (the promotion of a generalized Indigenous culture is a common advertising strategy for Churchill tourism).[33] Such conflation of multiple Indigenous nations' cultures into one generic "Indigenous" culture is not uncommon among settler Canadians.

Manomin is not a wild crop that is harvested without being sown or managed, as the English name "wild rice" implies.[34] Its range was expanded by Indigenous people who sowed it in new regions, and so varieties are found from northern Manitoba to southern Florida. The blog post of Margaret Lehman with Niisaachewan Anishinaabe Nation notes that manomin "contains three times the amount of fiber as white rice and is up to 30 times higher in anti-oxidants."[35] It takes on the flavour of the lake from which it was harvested, and so is a very regional dish.[36] A quarter of Canada's manomin is produced in Manitoba.[37]

Manomin came to present-day Manitoba with the Anishinaabeg, who planted it after their arrival here in the late eighteenth century.[38] They viewed manomin as both a spiritual gift from the Creator[39] and, as Lehman says, itself "a spirited being capable of entering into reciprocal relationships with human and other-than-human entities."[40] According to Anishinaabeg scholar Winona LaDuke, manomin is "a food that is uniquely Anishinaabeg, the centerpiece of our community's nutrition and sustenance, our ceremonies, and our thanksgiving feasts."[41] The Anishinaabeg developed a number of agricultural practices to plant, tend, and harvest manomin, and to increase its production.[42] These included seeding (both to improve yields and to create new fields), weeding, and, as Wayne Moodie notes, "bundling, or the tying of wild rice stalks in sheaves."[43] Bundling improved yields and reduced losses to pests, wind, and rain.[44] The Anishinaabeg also trapped muskrats along lakeshores to prevent them from eating the crop, and created perches for hawks who decreased the blackbird population that also fed on manomin.[45]

Although our project did not include interviews about the manomin production processes,[46] fortunately, others have already done so, including Kathi Avery Kinew for her doctoral dissertation and scholar Ranald Thurgood for the Indian History Film Project.[47] Iskatewizaagegan (Shoal Lake #39) Elder Azawashkwagoneb (also known as Fred Greene) described how manomin was managed on Crowduck Lake in Manitoba from the 1920s through to the 1960s. Kinew says Elders would decide "when to pick, when to rest the rice. . . . We had a beaver dam at the opening of Crowduck Lake. We would open it up and regulate the water levels for the rice to grow."[48] Onigaming Elder Shuniaagoneb (also known as Stuart Jack) recalled, "We trapped around the fields to prevent muskrats from eating the roots. We shooed away blackbirds (who love to eat the premature grains). We checked the rice constantly and would not allow picking too early. We taught our children how to pick so that the grain came smoothly off the stalk into the canoe and no stems were broken. We developed all sorts of ways of harvesting the rice. In years of low water, a picker would walk the shoreline on snowshoes and hold a sack as an apron for the rice to fall into as they picked."[49]

Anishinaabe (Ojibwe) Elder Alvin Hagar elaborated:

> I never harvested it myself. But when they harvested there's two in the boat—one is in front paddling and the other one is in behind. And they have two sticks about forty inches long and one leans over the bow and then he hits the top of the rice—it falls into the boat and then [he] goes on the other side, brings it down, and he hits it again. They get a rhythm going. And just, as they pull the paddles along he can knock this off. . . . One fellow is doing the paddling and the other one is doing the harvesting. . . . And then he has a rhythm just going, you know, and then they harvest that at one spot and then they don't get all the rice. It doesn't ripen at the same time, and you can get over the same area maybe three or four times. But I think the harvest is the last two weeks in October.[50]

Hand harvesting of manomin was skilled labour. Scholar Yngve Georg Lithman describes, "The harvester must pull the straw (which often extends several feet over his head) into exactly the proper angle over the canoe in order that the rice should not fall on either side of the canoe. Furthermore, the blow has to be struck at the proper angle with a delicately balanced force; otherwise the straw will either break (thereby ruining the possibility of the stalk restoring itself to an upright position to allow for a subsequent harvest) or the blow will be too light to cause the ripe seed to fall into the canoe."[51] For the Anishinaabeg, manomin's value is not just as a food source; as Kinew states, it has "cultural and religious significance . . . economic and nutritional importance . . . and . . . political symbolism."[52]

Government intervention in the production and sale of manomin negatively affected Anishinaabeg in the 1950s and 1960s. Leases were used by the Manitoba government to regulate manomin harvesting in the 1960s; most of them went to non-Indigenous people.[53] In the 1950s, buyers began to purchase manomin directly at lakeside immediately after harvest rather than after processing by Anishinaabeg. A consequence was that Anishinaabeg were less able to negotiate prices, as unprocessed (or green) manomin is liable to spoilage and so must be immediately sold.[54] Processing had been an exclusively Indigenous task until the 1950s: it

Figure 77. Manomin harvesting machine developed by H.B. Williams and Holliday, and bagged rice on dock for transfer to the parching and dancing grounds, Lac du Bois, 1 October 1938. © Ducks Unlimited Canada. Photograph reproduced courtesy of UMASC, Mac Runciman fonds, CA UMASC MSS SC 86, PC 93 (A.92-72).

Figure 78. Two unnamed men in a canoe, harvesting manomin with two short sticks, Lac du Bois, 2 October 1938. © Ducks Unlimited Canada. Photograph reproduced courtesy of the University of Manitoba Archives & Special Collections (hereafter UMASC), Mac Runciman fonds, MSS SC 86, PC 93 (A.92-72).

involved heating manomin on a willow rack and then agitating it and winnowing it by tossing it in the air to remove the husks.[55] Alvin Hagar explained the process in detail:

> And then when they harvest the rice they put it in a bag and then soak it in the water for maybe a half hour, forty-five minutes to get the bugs and that out. Then they'd spread it on the blankets to let it dry, and then they'd get a cast iron pot around and then they have a fire in there. And then they put the rice in there, and then they stir that rice. Some man would sit on the side and he'd stir that rice all continuously to get the hull away from the rice. And then when that was finished they would put it into another smaller bucket and then the man would what he called "dance the rice." He'd have on a pair of moccasins that would be a light color, and he would what they call "dance the rice." And that would get the hulls away from the rice. And then when they winnow it they just hold it up in the air and then just press it down, and then the wind would blow all the chaff away—they do that three or four times. And then they would get all the hull away from the rice.[56]

By the early 1980s, 80 percent of Manitoba manomin was exported to the United States for processing.[57]

Government intervention in water levels through hydro projects had a similarly adverse impact on manomin, as well as on other Anishinaabe food sources. Water levels on the Winnipeg River were changed by the 1893 construction of the Norman Dam and by the completion in 1958 of the Whitedog Falls Generating Station. These projects drowned Winnipeg River manomin, disrupting Anishinaabe food security and increasing their reliance on wage labour.[58] The Churchill River Diversion in 1960 similarly affected food practices of the O-Pipon-Na-Piwin Cree Nation (OPCN). South Indian Lake, where OPCN is situated, was raised three metres by this hydroelectric project, and water levels in Lake Winnipeg, Nelson River, and Churchill River were also altered, resulting in changes to animal migration patterns, loss of fish habitat, and damage to berry patches.[59] Some 213,700 hectares of land were flooded, destroying traplines.[60] North America's second-largest whitefish fishery, producing a million pounds (453,600 kilograms) of whitefish annually from South Indian Lake, was decimated.[61]

As manomin became marketable as a delicacy in 1980s, selling for fourteen to sixteen dollars per pound, what had been an Indigenous agricultural practice became beset by

Figure 79. Manomin harvest, Pauingassi, 1977. Mennonite Heritage Archives (hereafter MHA), Conference of Mennonites in Canada Native Ministries Photograph Collection, CA MHC 721-57-229.

competition from non-Indigenous people.[62] Commercial harvesters Cliff Zarecki and Steve Richardson, for example, purchased a one-dollar permit in 1981 from the Ontario Ministry of Natural Resources to harvest manomin on Mud Lake, Ontario, over the objections of local Indigenous and Métis people and in violation of the province's moratorium on commercial permits. The Métis ancestors of Harold Perry were those who had established manomin in Mud Lake, using seed they brought from Rice Lake, Ontario. Perry explained the difference between Indigenous and commercial harvesting: "We gather the rice in canoes and just take enough to get us through the tough times. . . . They'll come in with a mechanical harvester that will clean out the lake in hours."[63] Alvin Hagar elaborated: "When the commercial harvester goes through it takes all the rice and there's no rice to fall off or seed. In three or four years there would be no more wild rice."[64] Mechanical harvesting at Mud Lake was prevented when it was determined that there was, in fact, no public access to the lake and non-Indigenous residents subsequently refused to allow mechanical harvesters onto their property.[65]

There are several companies in Manitoba that sell branded manomin; none are Indigenous-owned. The oldest of these is Du Bois brand, whose lake-grown manomin has been harvested by the Williams family since 1915. Fourth-generation owner Judy Williams Skrzenta's ancestors were Dominion surveyors who "learned to gather and cure the wild grain working alongside the local Indigenous people."[66] This somewhat contentious Indigenous connection (the confrontation between Indigenous people and land surveyors is partly what led to the creation of the province)[67] was played up in a promotional photo for the company's products in 1970. In addition to manomin, Du Bois packages and sells manomin-containing products such as lentil pilaf, fettucine, flour, and pancake mix. Wild Man Ricing, owned by Richard Atkins, has operated for a decade, harvesting manomin from seven northern Manitoba lakes near The Pas. The company sells manomin, manomin flour, and manomin soup mixes.[68] Naosap Harvest, owned by Tracy Wheeler-Anderson, is based in Cranberry Portage, and has sold manomin and manomin flour since 2009.[69] Far North Wild Rice, owned by Richard Russell, is based in Flin Flon. With the exception of Du Bois, there appear to be no commercial processors of manomin in Manitoba, so some of these companies send their harvest to Saskatchewan or the United States for processing before packaging it themselves.[70]

Indigenous-owned manomin companies exist, however, in the neighbouring provinces of Saskatchewan and Ontario. NWC Wild Rice Company, which describes itself as "authentic Indigenous," is owned and operated by Métis, Dene, and Ininew manomin harvesters in Saskatchewan. Established in 2019, they sell various grades of manomin.[71] Kagiwiosa Manomin began in 1985 as a worker cooperative of Waabigoniiw Saaga'iganiiw Anishinaabeg near Dryden, Ontario.[72] Their manomin advertising highlights the differences between Indigenous-produced manomin and the commercial paddy-grown rice that dominates the market: "Paddy rice is shorter than Manomin and is produced using chemical fertilizers, herbicides and insecticides. Non-Native processing of paddy rice differs drastically from the traditional wood fire method

Figure 80. Unnamed Anishinaabe (Ojibwe) girl with winnowing tray made of birchbark, Lac du Bois, 1 October 1938. © Ducks Unlimited Canada. Photograph reproduced courtesy of UMASC, Mac Runciman fonds, CA UMASC MSS SC 86, PC 93 (A.92-72).

Figure 81. Parching the manomin, Lac du Bois, 2 October 1938. © Ducks Unlimited Canada. Photograph reproduced courtesy of UMASC, Mac Runciman fonds, CA UMASC MSS SC 86, PC 93 (A.92-72).

Figure 82. Jacob Owen parching manomin while two of his children watch, Pauingassi, 1977. MHA, Conference of Mennonites in Canada Native Ministries Photograph Collection, CA MHC 721-57-219.

Figure 83. Unnamed Anishinaabe (Ojibwe) woman stirring up manomin during parching process to prevent burning, Lac du Bois, 2 October 1938. © Ducks Unlimited Canada. Photograph reproduced courtesy of UMASC, Mac Runciman fonds, CA UMASC MSS SC 86, PC 93 (A.92-72).

Figure 84. Dancing and winnowing manomin, Lac du Bois, 1 October 1938. © Ducks Unlimited Canada. Photograph reproduced courtesy of UMASC, Mac Runciman fonds, CA UMASC MSS SC 86, PC 93 (A.92-72).

Figure 85. Close-up of concrete pots in which the manomin is danced, Lac du Bois, 1 October 1938. © Ducks Unlimited Canada. Photograph reproduced courtesy of UMASC, Mac Runciman fonds, CA UMASC MSS SC 86, PC 93 (A.92-72).

HARVEST CASSEROLE WITH WILD RICE

HARVEST CASSEROLE

1 cup wild rice

1 medium green pepper, chopped

1 can cream of chicken soup

1 can mushrooms

1 medium onion, chopped

1 cup grated Canadian cheese

1 can cream of mushroom soup

Brown sausage in a large skillet. Add onion and green pepper and continue cooking until vegetables are limp. Drain off excess fat. Add uncooked wild rice, cheese, both soups, mushrooms, and mix well. Pour into a 3-quart casserole and bake 1¾ hours at 325° F.

From *Manomin Wild Rice Recipes* (Toronto: Ontario Ministry of Northern Development and Mines, c. 1980), 17.

FRIED WILD RICE

1 cup cooked wild rice

bacon drippings or butter

Cook one cup of wild rice in water. After it has been drained, while it is still hot, pack tightly into a well-greased container. Refrigerate overnight. Cut into thick slices and fry in bacon drippings or butter. Serve with plenty of butter, maple syrup, and bacon or fresh fried fish.

From *Old Time Recipes of Manitoba Indians* (Winnipeg: Indian Ladies Club, Winnipeg Indian and Métis Friendship Centre, 1963), 9, https://digital.scaa.sk.ca/ourlegacy/permalink/24770 (accessed 28 May 2023).

of Kagiwiosa Manomin. Paddy rice processors and non-native wild rice processors ferment freshly harvested green rice and then parch it using natural gas or propane. The resulting rice (identified by its narrow-shafted, shiny black appearance) loses much of its nutty smell and flavour, is less nutritious, less digestible and takes substantially longer to cook."[73] In Manitoba, a similar Indigenous-owned manomin cooperative, Manominekay, was established much earlier, but it was also much shorter lived.

In 1964, twelve bands formed Manominekay, the Manitoba Indian Wild Rice Producers' Co-operative, with resources from the Manitoba Indian Brotherhood (now the Assembly of Manitoba Chiefs). By 1973, they had expanded to include sixteen bands as members.[74] By the 1970s, they had made plans to plant manomin at Swan Lake, received a loan and a grant to build a processing plant, and had provincial leases to harvest manomin in the Whiteshell.[75] They comprised a thousand harvesters, earning forty-five cents to a dollar per pound; the manomin retailed for seven dollars per pound.[76] By the time Manominekay folded in 1981, it included eighteen bands. Their failure was attributed at the time to either band competition for leases or lack of government support.[77] Indigenous harvester Allan Anderson explained, "All those huge Canadian corporations get government subsidies and outright grants. This corporation got no help. The government couldn't wait to jump on it just because it was Indian-run."[78]

According to articles in the *Indian News*, Manominekay's collapse resulted in "a one-man commission into the province's wild rice industry" led by Manitoba's Minister of Natural Resources Harry Enns, despite Indigenous peoples' insistence that manomin was "their property to manage in their own way."[79] Manomin harvesting and sales had changed dramatically by the early 1980s, involving "cash-at-shore deals between pickers and buyers" with pickers earning "up to $600 a day," the *Indian News* reported.[80] Provincial royalties on manomin were cancelled in 1981 because, Minister Enns explained, "the royalty payments were geared to penalize those few companies which honestly reported the amount of rice they gathered . . . and we have no way of policing it."[81] An additional problem was the competition between hand pickers in canoes and mechanical harvesters in airboats; the latter "go through and take 25 per cent of the harvest for a few people and leave the rest damaged."[82] In 1981, Manitoba decided to allow only hand pickers in the Whiteshell (this had been one of the recommendations of the 1981

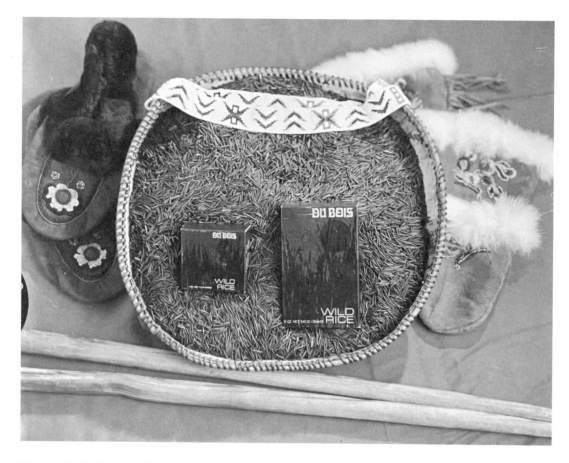

Figure 86. Du Bois manomin promotional photo, 1970. Photo 70-295, Archives of Manitoba, Wild Rice set up, Government photographs, CH0267, GR 3552.

commission); by 2016, however, mechanical harvesting was permitted in the Whiteshell lakes of Heart, Echo, Little Echo, South Cross, Jessica, Betula, and White.[83]

The 1981 Wild Rice Industry Commission had claimed that manomin was not covered by any treaties.[84] "Since all production of natural wild rice occurs on Crown lands, it is only fair that the people of Manitoba benefit from this natural resource," the commission argued. "Proper revenue should be forthcoming from the wild rice resource."[85] But the Paypom Document,

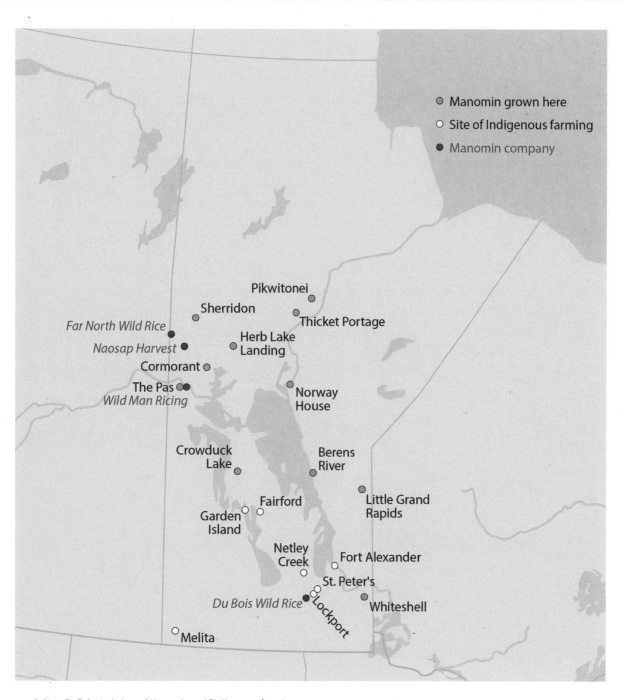

Map 8. Selected sites of Manomin and Indigenous farming.

Legend:

- ◎ Manomin grown here
- ○ Site of Indigenous farming
- ● Manomin company

Pikwitonei

Sherridon

Thicket Portage

Far North Wild Rice

Herb Lake
Landing

Naosap Harvest

Cormorant

The Pas
Wild Man Ricing

Norway
House

Crowduck
Lake

Berens
River

Fairford

Little Grand
Rapids

Garden
Island

Netley
Creek

Fort Alexander

St. Peter's

Du Bois Wild Rice

Lockport

Whiteshell

Melita

"a record of oral negotiations between a representative of the Crown and Chief Paypom, transcribed in 1873," provides a different perspective. It states that the Indigenous signatories of Treaty 3, which includes the Whiteshell, "will be free as by the past for their hunting and rice harvest."[86]

Manitoba subsequently passed the Wild Rice Act in 1983, which reserved some areas for harvesting exclusively by Indigenous people but required all harvesters to obtain permits.[87] But a revision of the Act in 1984 recognized Indigenous peoples' exclusive rights to harvesting manomin in certain geographic areas. A 1990s court challenge to this aspect of the Wild Rice Act by non-Indigenous rice growers resulted in proposals to support the Indigenous manomin industry.[88] The Aboriginal Justice Inquiry, reviewing these events in 1991, concluded that harvesting manomin is an Indigenous right, and manomin is not a natural resource under control of the Crown: "Aboriginal people see the harvesting of wild rice as a traditional occupation which their ancestors never would have given up intentionally at the signing of the treaties. While the provincial legislation has recognized an Aboriginal role in the industry, the *Wild Rice Act* gives no assurance that this role will continue as a matter of right in the future."[89] The Aboriginal Justice Inquiry recommended that the province recognize manomin harvesting as an Aboriginal right, and "negotiate co-management agreements" with Indigenous people for any off-reserve regulation of manomin.[90] A subsequent revision of Manitoba's Wild Rice Act in 2015 permitted "registered Indians" to harvest manomin "for household purposes" without a permit; transportation and sales of manomin still required permits, however.[91]

Indigenous harvesting and processing of manomin in Manitoba was threatened not only by commercial harvesters in the province but by commercial production in Minnesota and California. Canada provided 42 percent of the global supply of manomin before 1978. After that date, several domesticated strains of manomin that had been developed in Minnesota were sown in paddies for mass production. California also began commercial production of domesticated manomin within existing white-rice paddies, even patenting a particular strain. Paddy cultivation allows the use of mechanical harvesters instead of the more environmentally sensitive (but time-consuming) "two stick" process traditionally used by the Anishinaabeg. By the 1980s, 94 percent of the world's manomin was paddy-grown domesticated varieties grown in California and Minnesota; prices for lake-harvested manomin dropped as a result.[92] The Anishinaabeg in Minnesota have fought back. They took Busch Agricultural Resources (a division of the beer company) to court for false advertising: their manomin packaging "had two Indians on a canoe who appeared to be picking wild rice. They were taking a California-grown product, trucking it to Minnesota, where it was packaged and designated as a Minnesota product."[93] And the Anishinaabeg have long asked that the University of Minnesota cease its genetic research on manomin, arguing that it threatens the lake-grown manomin that is their treaty right to harvest.[94] In northwestern Ontario, the Manomin Project is similarly working to preserve Indigenous rights to manomin.

The Manomin Project is a joint venture of the Niisaachewan Anishinaabe Nation and the University of Guelph. It thus differs tremendously from the relationship between Anishinaabeg nations and the flagship university in Minnesota. Describing itself as "a community restoration initiative focused on manomin research, culture revitalization, and treaty living,"[95] the Manomin Project's long-term goals are to "co-develop culturally appropriate crop management techniques responsive to settler-imposed changes" as well as to "stimulate agricultural expansion in northwestern Ontario while contributing to cultural revitalization, economic and food security in Anishinaabe communities, and scholarly discussions of interdisciplinary research."[96] The project's work has brought into question some long-standing practices within the academy, drawing attention to the insufficient ways in which nationwide approaches to university ethics are at odds with Indigenous ways of being and knowing.

In Canada, university research ethics is governed by the 2018 revision of the *Tri-Council Policy Statement: Ethical Conduct for Research Involving Humans*, known as TCPS2.[97] The Manomin Project observes that TCPS2 "has failed to ask researchers to respect Indigenous worldviews and other-than-human relationships when working in aquatic environments and with Indigenous foodstuffs."[98] They explain that the Anishinaabeg did not "*discover* or *unlock* the secrets of aquatic plant production. Instead, Manomin (which translates most accurately into English as 'spirit berry' or 'gift from the Creator') offered itself to Nanaboozhoo . . . a half-spirit and half-human trickster figure. . . . Stories featuring Nanaboozhoo and Manomin reinforce the importance of humility in interspecies relationships. . . . Manomin is an animate, spirit being, capable of expressing its desire to support human life and activities. Like Nanaboozhoo, who fasted and requested aid, ethical researchers must create pathways through which Manomin can express its will."[99] Drawing on their work with manomin, the Manomin Research Project argues that Indigenous nations should control research and determine research ethics within their own territories.

The history of manomin in Manitoba is symbolic of the differing world views of Indigenous and non-Indigenous peoples in North America with respect to both food and property. A lack of familiarity with Indigenous agricultural practices, together with racist assumptions about Indigenous peoples' farming abilities, led to the definition of manomin as "wild" rice. This attribution of wildness to manomin allowed its commercialization by non-Indigenous people, much like the definition of Indigenous territory as "vacant" land made the settlement of western Canada by Europeans and others possible. A century of government intervention, including through legislation and hydro projects, further hampered Anishinaabeg control of their traditional food resource. A full embrace of the Aboriginal Justice Inquiry's recommendations regarding manomin, as well as of the ethics advocated by the Manomin Project, would transform the production, sale, and study of manomin in Manitoba. It remains to be seen whether Manitobans have the willingness to do so.

CHAPTER SEVEN

1491

Indigenous chefs and restaurateurs are a rarity in Canada.[1] Steven Watson, a member of Peguis First Nation, is one such chef. Combatting culinary colonialism, he has created a remarkable initiative in Manitoba to recover Indigenous cuisine for the twenty-first century: a work of both culinary and historical imagination that he calls 1491.[2] Bannock is a popular (and meaningful) food for Indigenous peoples in Manitoba, but it uses ingredients like white flour, white sugar, salt, and baking powder that were introduced after European contact. "It's the stuff that we were given when we had our rights taken away, to hunt, to fish, to live off the land," Algonquin chef Marie-Cecile (Cezin) Kakgoosh Nottaway-Wawatie explains.[3] But what would Indigenous food look like today, Watson asks, if its development hadn't been disrupted by colonialism?

Food, as historian L. Sasha Gora reminds us, has been "a tool of colonial control and resistance" in Canada.[4] Bison and beaver were deliberately overhunted by non-Indigenous people as part of the state's effort to remove Indigenous people from their lands and make way for the settlement of the West by non-Indigenous farmers.[5] Treaty-mandated food rations were withheld by government and local Indian agents to facilitate the process of moving Indigenous people onto reserves and their children into residential schools. These schools functioned as labour camps where many Indigenous children were subjected to hunger and starvation, as well as to nutrition experiments conducted without their knowledge or consent.[6]

According to scholars Tabitha Robin (Martens), Mary Kate Dennis, and Michael Anthony Hart, Indigenous chefs and restaurateurs in Canada are returning to an earlier history of Indigenous engagement with the land, one that recognizes food as "spiritual, ceremonial, and medicinal."[7] A number of Indigenous-owned restaurants have opened in Manitoba and across the country in the last several years. Manoomin Restaurant opened in 2022 in the Wyndham Garden hotel on Long Plain Madison Reserve, Manitoba's first urban reserve, with Opaskwayak Cree Nation executive chef Jennifer Ballantyne. The restaurant is smudged every morning, and serves pickerel, bison, and manomin.[8] Christa Bruneau-Guenther, a member of Peguis First Nation, is the chef-owner of Feast Café Bistro in Winnipeg's West End.[9] Nooaitch First Nation member Sharon Bond-Hogg owns Kekuli Café, which has franchises throughout British Columbia in Kelowna, Merritt, West Kelowna, and Kamloops.[10] Anishinaabe chef-owner Gerry Brandon's L'Autochtone Taverne Americaine is in Haileybury, Ontario.[11] The Mr. Bannock food truck in North Vancouver is owned and operated by Paul Natrall of the Squamish Nation.[12] Inez Cook is the Nuxalk chef-owner of Vancouver's Salmon n' Bannock, which also will open the first Indigenous-owned eatery in a Canadian airport.[13] Toronto's Kū-kŭm Kitchen, noted for once serving seal meat, is owned by Odawa chef Joseph Shawana.[14] Nk'Mip Cellars in Osoyoos, British Columbia, states that they are the first Indigenous-owned winery in North America, while Indigenous World Winery in Kelowna, British Columbia, is Syilx-owned.[15] These restaurants, food trucks, and wineries build in new ways on the legacies of La Toundra, the restaurant in the Canada pavilion at Montreal's Expo '67 that served Indigenous foods including beaver, and the Gik'san-owned Liliget Feast House that existed in Vancouver, British Columbia, from 1995 to 2007.[16]

The establishment of Indigenous restaurants like these has been beset by many difficulties, both financial and legislative. Access to capital has proved a challenge for Indigenous entrepreneurs.[17] In Victoria, British Columbia, the Confederated Native Authority proposed the creation of an Indigenous restaurant with government assistance in the 1970s but was turned down.[18] The use of wild meat in restaurants, desired by many Indigenous chefs, brings traditional practices into conflict with provincial legislation. In the 1960s, for example, Manitoba Resources Minister

Figure 87. Steven Watson before roasted parsnips and turnips, plated bison, and a bowl of fresh sage, Winnipeg. Photograph by Kimberley Moore, 2019.

Sterling Lyon introduced amendments to the Wildlife Act to permit consumption of wild meat at club meetings in churches and restaurants but not as regular restaurant menu items. These amendments were objected to by other Members of the Legislative Assembly like Michael Hryhorczuk from Ethelbert Plains, who argued that "wildlife should not be sold for profit."[19]

The earliest attempt to create an Indigenous restaurant in Manitoba was in the 1970s. Winnipeg's Indian and Métis Friendship Centre (IMFC) began offering cooking classes in 1973, which, according to correspondence of the Communities Economic Development Fund (CEDF), focused on the preparation of "rabbit stew, duck soup, bannock, deer, moose and possibly pemmican" in the hope of "eventually opening an [Indigenous] restaurant" that "*would not be* a social service effort."[20] The provincial government got involved, investigating whether wild meat could be served in the proposed restaurant despite existing legislative restrictions: in 1975, the Renewable Resources Trapper Education Department "designed a hypothetical project collecting beaver and muskrat from the Duck Mountains and Summerberry marsh areas, bringing them to Swan River and The Pas respectively" for meat processing.[21] There was also government consideration of the possible creation of a pilot wild meat processing project as part of the Wild Fur Development Program, but it seemingly went nowhere.[22] Provincial government support was obtained in 1977 for funding a study by the CEDF of the feasibility of the creation of an Indigenous restaurant in Winnipeg. The government's reasons for doing so were not solely to support Indigenous peoples' creativity or economic development, however, but also a consequence of their racist assumptions about Indigenous people: the *Winnipeg Free Press* reported that "Corrections Minister Bud Boyce said Thursday the restaurant would be a 'crime prevention' project, designed to help people who need to learn how to work."[23] By 1979, however, CEDF remained supportive of the idea but was not offering funds.[24] Support from other government entities was similarly capricious: the City of Winnipeg owned the Exchange Building on Princess Street and initially considered renovating and leasing it for this purpose, but later suggested the province purchase the building instead.[25] The CEDF general manager H.J. Jones observed, "Frankly, I am really beginning to wonder what the City is up to here. If we are to get moving on this project after all this time, I am getting to the conclusion that we should be looking for somewhere else."[26] A feasibility study was finally conducted in 1980, and 236 Edmonton Street was ultimately the location chosen.[27]

Figure 88. Exterior of Bungees restaurant in Winnipeg, 1983. MHA, Jacob M. Unrau fonds, CA MHC PP08.

Bungees was selected as the name of the proposed Indigenous restaurant because, CEDF correspondence with Bungees reports, it was "a name of respect, for a respectable historical contribution (and catchy besides)."[28] The name was registered as a business in 1977 by Mary Richard, director IMFC; Yvonne Monkman, principal Little Ones' School; and Joy Fedorick, assistant director Youth Action Project Inc.[29] The IMFC correspondence with the Communities Economic Development Fund indicates it envisioned "a native restaurant that would combine a free and easy atmosphere with native décor, with Indian and traditional dishes being served by native people in traditional dress," including dandelion salad, fresh fish, and Bungee burgers (a beefalo—bison hybrid—bannock burger).[30] The business would be operated for profit and "would provide incentive for other native people to attempt such economic endeavours, and any profits would go towards a development fund for future ideas."[31] The proposed design for the restaurant was reminiscent of the theatricality of Ichi Ban and its companion restaurant, the Grande Canal of Venice.[32] According to CEDF correspondence, "Diners would be greeted by an Indian hostess standing by a kettle and fire, they would be offered a drink in a cocktail lounge that is designed as a teepee with native artifacts on the walls, and then could proceed to dinner. Tables would be located on the shore of the 'Red River' and would be designed as Red River oxcarts carrying furs and wares to a York Boat. More tables would be located in the York Boat. Murals arounds the diners would create an open-type setting, as would astro-turf and shrubbery throughout."[33] Don Marks of the IMFC said Bungees restaurant was imagined as the first step in the creation of an Indigenous "business and manufacturing complex," including eventually "2 manufacturing sites, for knitting and handicrafts . . . a boutique, hairdresser ('The Scalp Shop') and Bookstore" as well as "two theatres for plays and pow-wows," all within one downtown building.[34]

Bungees tested its menu with diners at Red River College on 4 and 18 March 1977, four years before it officially opened at 236 Edmonton Street on 28 September 1981.[35] The feedback from the trial dinners was generally favourable, though some diners' comments were more reflective of Indigenous–settler relations in Winnipeg at the time than of the food:

> The food is unique. I'd question a regular clientele like Hy's however—it strikes me like the Ichi Ban—I go once a year. Make sure staff *well* trained & smooth. You'll be exposing the native community so be prepared for dumb questions.
>
> As we have many types of restaurants from other countries it is now time we have some of our own native people (*Canadians!*).
>
> A comment that just couldn't go unnoticed: The girl in the blue dress is very attractive. And she added to the atmosphere!
>
> I think a restaurant of this nature would do well in a large city i.e. Toronto. I think I would eat there as a novel idea but I would not make it a frequent eating place. I don't think it would make it in Winnipeg.[36]

Despite the lack of government support or bank loans, co-owners Mary Margaret Richard and Patricia Yvonne Monkman had succeeded in creating Canada's first Indigenous-owned restaurant.[37]

Mary Margaret Richard

BUNGEES BANNOCK

5 cups flour	1¼ tbsp baking powder
1 tsp salt	¼ lb lard
1 cup milk	1 cup water

Preheat oven to 400° Fahrenheit. Mix flour, salt, and baking powder. Mix in the lard until dough is crumb-like. Pour in water and milk. Mix with spoon until thick. Knead with hands until dough does not stick to hands. Roll out, place on cookie sheet. Bake at 400° Fahrenheit for 20 minutes. Yields one bannock, which may be sliced and toasted.

Jerry Bass, *Restaurant Menu Guide & Cook Book* (Winnipeg, MB: Welmar-Case, 1981), 19.

Born in Camperville, Manitoba, in 1940, Mary Richard became a leader in Winnipeg's Indigenous community. A Métis woman who was an Akokaochise (Groundhog) of the Mahkwa (Bear) Clan, she moved to Winnipeg to train and work as a hairdresser. She was president of the Aboriginal Council of Winnipeg, president of Circle of Life Thunderbird House, president of the Indigenous Women's Collective, executive director of the Indian and Métis Friendship Centre of Winnipeg, senator for the Association of Friendship Centres, and executive director of Manitoba Association of Native Languages. Among other board appointments, she was a board member of Ma Mawi Wi Chi Itata Centre, Neeginan Centre, Median Credit Union, North Main Task Force, Indian Business Development Group, and Native Women's Transition Group. She was a recipient of the Order of the Buffalo Hunt, the Order of Manitoba, a National Aboriginal Achievement Award, and the YM-YWCA Woman of Distinction Award. She was co-owner of Bungees restaurant, later renamed the Teepee Restaurant and Lounge, which was the first Indigenous-owned and -operated restaurant in Canada. She died in 2010.[38]

As Richard noted, "There were a lot of feasibility studies but no one did anything to make it happen."[39] In its final form, Bungees's menu highlighted Indigenous cuisine and local ingredients, including char, pickerel, sturgeon, smoked goldeye, buffalo (including the heart and tongue), pheasant, rabbit, pemmican (served in strips, as a spread, and as a paté), wild mushrooms, and bannock.[40] The restaurant's décor was more restrained and conventional than the initial vision, featuring regular tables with white tablecloths and an accent wall of cross-sections of logs surmounted by a pair of wooden snowshoes.[41] The restaurant was remodelled in 1984 and renamed the Teepee Restaurant and Lounge; live music by Tom Jackson and K.C. "Kansas City Dave" Cramer was introduced.[42] By 1985, the private loan that Richard and Monkman had obtained to create the restaurant was repaid, but the restaurant closed permanently two years later.[43]

Since Bungees's closure, Indigenous chefs like Stephen Watson of Peguis First Nation have been taking the lead in the development of the growing Indigenous culinary scene in Canada. Watson has worked professionally as a chef at some of Winnipeg's most popular restaurants, including Hu's On First, 529 Wellington, and Brazen Hall, as well as at the famous American restaurants Per Se and French Laundry. He was a finalist for the CBC Manitoba Future 40 award in 2016, and his grandmother is related to retired Senator Murray Sinclair, who chaired the Truth and Reconciliation Commission.[44]

The Forks in Winnipeg (the juncture of the Red and Assiniboine rivers) has served for millennia as a significant food-trade site in the Americas, as people stopped here to stock up on locally made foods like pemmican.[45] With twentieth-century technological innovations in refrigeration and transportation, Manitobans are able to eat an increasing variety of foods from all over the world, both in season and out.[46] That culinary bounty can blunt our awareness of the diversity and deliciousness of the many local ingredients available to us here in the province. Restricting ingredients to those available before European contact presents some culinary challenges for Chef Watson:

> Basically, everything in bannock is something we cannot use [if we want to limit
> ingredients to those available before European contact]. . . . What we did though is
> because there's bannock and it's so tied to native food, we wanted some kind of bread,
> and this is where it came from. This took a while. . . . This one here is still fairly

ANCIENT BREAD

500 g ground barley

500 g ground amaranth

500 g ground wild rice

500 g cooked wild rice

2 duck eggs

200 g toasted walnuts

300 g dried unsweetened cranberries

1 L cold water

100 ml cold duck fat

200 ml maple syrup

Mix barley, amaranth, ground wild rice. Add in duck fat and mix to break up the fat into tiny pieces about the size of oats. Whisk eggs, maple syrup, and 750 ml of the water together, add into dry ingredients and mix well, you may need to add more water, as the grains may absorb differently depending on coarseness. Once mixed and slightly sticky, mix in cranberries, cooked wild rice, and walnuts until evenly distributed. Portion into 12 even pieces, roll into 2-inch wide logs. Preheat oven to 400°, and bake bread for 25 to 30 minutes. Serve while still warm, or reheat in the oven for a few minutes before serving later. As the bread is dense and without preservatives, it gets hard to eat after about 12 hours.

While this recipe is mine, one could easily switch things up, using blueberries instead of cranberries, or pecans instead of walnuts, or honey instead of maple syrup. Have some fun with it!

Recipe copyright Steven Watson, used with permission.

dense. There's no leaveners, no eggs, baking powder, or yeast or anything we can add, but what we do is we load it with stuff. So, it's loaded with hazelnuts and wild rice and cranberries so it's almost like eating a soft cracker as opposed to a piece of bread. . . . For the basic one, it's just cylinders because we just cut it into slices, and it works out well. And the one good thing is we shape it as it is and that's the way it's going to stay because there's no leaveners in there whatsoever.[47]

Another example is no canola oil, as it didn't exist in 1491. Instead, Watson uses fat from ducks and bison. Duck fat, in particular, has a delicious flavour—unlike bear fat, which he dislikes. The sauce he served us alongside the bison was not thickened with flour or cornstarch. Instead, he took his time reducing it, transforming two litres of stock into a quarter-litre of intense flavour. But other contemporary ingredients are not so easily replaced with pre-contact equivalents. Watson explained: "The main challenge—what we're finding—is not so much the ingredients, what was used, what can we do with it, but lack of salt. That's the big one. No processed sugar, no processed white flour, no processed fats like lard or anything like that, no baking powders, baking soda, that kind of stuff, but those we can find ways around. We can't find a way around salt yet."[48] One potential salt substitute is ashes, but using ash not only adds saltiness but bitterness. But is salt really necessary?

JANIS THIESSEN: Is the desire to find a salt replacement because that's a way of trying to make this food palatable to folks who have for centuries grown up with that taste?

STEVEN WATSON: It is, yeah. And at times, it's a battle, because there are things . . . One of the pros of this, what we do, is that it actually fits a lot of modern diets—and I mean diets as in, like to lose weight, to get fitter. The keto diet it fits, because a lot of meats; it fits the paleo diet, because, well [laughs], it is paleo, right? It fits a lot of those things. Generally, a lot of stuff we do is low carb, high protein, all those things. So, it fits a lot of trendy diets, it fits a lot of old-school diets. It fits with the elders who can't eat salt. There's a lot of heart disease on reserve and whatnot, so it fits there well.[49]

At the time of our interview, Watson taught in the Culinary Arts program at Commonwealth College. Founded as Patal Vocational School, the school serves students whose

Figure 89. Steven Watson's ancient bread shaped like the Métis symbol. Photograph by Kimberley Moore, 2019.

life circumstances can make it difficult for them to conform to the structural demands of more traditional universities or colleges.

> We have an Indigenous student base, we also have some international students, so part of our program here is Indigenous food research and development with what's around and what can we do. . . . The other part of it is that we try to do the next step. What that means is, 1491 they did it one way. Then over the next few decades it slowed down, and then it really basically stopped with the European influence. When it comes to Italian food, or French food, or Japanese, or Chinese, they've had hundreds of years since then to develop their food culture. Indigenous people have not. It basically stopped. So we're not necessarily saying we only do what they did [and] we only use the ingredients they used, but what would they have done in 500 years? What would they have developed, what would they have tried out in different ways?[50]

Sourcing some of these ingredients can be difficult. Some animals, like bison, are now farmed—these undergo health inspection prior to sale to the public. Other, wilder, ingredients are much harder to obtain. Watson says, "So bison, elk, we can get, certain types of venison we can get. But there are times when . . . Like, moose, can't [usually] get moose. Like, we've used it! We just did it last week; we did a moose stew with fried wild rice. We fried it in cranberries and onions and duck fat."[51] These sorts of experiments with uninspected but traditional meats are not done for public consumption, due to provincial health regulations. Watson is unable to offer moose as he cannot find any that have been inspected. And moose are too big and require too much land to graze to ever become a viably farmed animal. Watson recalled:

> I can't remember his name, but it was hilarious: I was walking out of the school to go get something from my car, and I saw him walking by with a big garbage bag on his shoulder. And he was like, "Hey, Steve! How's it going?" And I was like, "Oh, yeah, it's going good," whatever. And I go to my car and come back in, and he's in the kitchen, the garbage bag is on the table, and he opens it up and it's a caribou leg—and it's still got leaves on it! And it's like, "That's definitely not federally inspected!" [All laugh.] But still, you know, we made some sauces and stuff for it, and showed the students some things, and whatnot.[52]

Historically, the Canadian state played an active role in restricting the ability of Indigenous peoples to earn a living from food production, as discussed in Chapter 6. They did so in order to prevent economic competition with the European settlers they brought by the thousands to western Canada to farm. The construction of the Canadian Pacific Railway devastated the bison population, leading to mass starvation.[53] Legislation was passed in 1881 that regulated how, when, and if Indigenous peoples could sell agricultural products.[54] Indigenous peoples in western Canada, many of whom had farmed for centuries, were denied access to farming equipment under the Peasant Farming Policy of Assistant Indian Commissioner Hayter Reed.[55] Indigenous peoples on the Pacific coast had their salmon fisheries legally captured by federal fisheries officers to prevent them from competing with sport anglers and commercial canneries.[56] The move away from such regulation of Indigenous food production has been very slow.

Watson explained how regulation continues in the present day and affects his sourcing of ingredients, such as with the planned development of a fish-processing plant near St. Laurent on Lake Manitoba: "But they were opening a fish plant there, and we were actually going to get involved with that. But then it got delayed and whatnot. But there was going to be a fish plant where the Indigenous population could bring the fish they caught to this plant and actually sell it legally."[57] The fish-processing plant would have created 100 jobs, but its success was contingent on the opening up of the federal single-desk (i.e., monopoly) marketing system, allowing fishers the option of selling to buyers other than the Freshwater Fish Marketing Corporation.[58] Some Indigenous fishers, like those of the Norway House Fishermen's Co-operative, feared that the end of a marketing board would also end their ability to earn a living from fishing.[59] Gimli fisher Robert Kristjanson explained: "There are more people that have benefited from the [Freshwater Fish Marketing] corporation, much more. This will only benefit a few people who want to line their own pocket. Who is going to run up north and buy fish up there and transport it in? Here in Gimli, there are a lot of old fisher families and we will survive. But there are an awful lot of people north of Lake Manitoba (who won't)."[60] Indigenous people involved in food production continue to be affected by larger economic and political forces.

Steven Watson said:

> As hard as somebody might fight, we're going to need a push from somebody else who has power, maybe money, maybe demand. Maybe if Costco came out and said, "Hey, we want to sell a million dollars' worth of moose in a year," they might have the

Steven Watson

Interviewed by Janis Thiessen, Kent Davies, and Kimberley Moore,
Commonwealth College, Winnipeg, Manitoba, 16 January 2019.

JANIS THIESSEN: So, what are you making for us today?

STEVEN WATSON: So, we have two things going on. I think I wrote down the bison that we do, but I got some bread here too, we've been doing some testing on it. We're going to try it out today. So, what we are doing is we call it 1491, also known as pre-contact or time immemorial. But what it is, is basically any ingredients found only here, in this part of the world, 500 years ago—1491 or prior. That said, within reason. We're not necessarily going to get salmon from the west coast or up north and getting some seal or whale or anything like that, right? So within reason. . . . Basically, what we deal with here, a lot of bison, a lot of deer and a lot of elk. Catfish, pickerel, grains and fruits and different vegetation that was here 500 or more years ago. Here we have a bread made of whole grains, some wild rice, dried berries and hazelnuts, a little bit of honey, and some duck fat. . . . As for the bison, we slow cook it with some berries, some onions, and a little bit of tobacco. We then reduce it down to a sauce.

Steven Watson is a chef and former instructor at Commonwealth College. He dedicates much time to Indigenous food research and recipe development. Many of his students identify as Indigenous.[61] His research explores the possibilities of how Indigenous food might have developed over 500 years without colonialism.[62] Steven is from Peguis First Nation and grew up in Thompson, Manitoba.[63] Commonwealth College started as an institution that helped people in need in the local area who wanted to advance their skills.[64] Steven has extensive experience as a chef in various kitchens across Winnipeg, such as 529 Wellington and Brazen Hall, as well as famous international restaurants such as French Laundry and Per Se. His wide experience enables him to teach a variety of dishes to his students and share his knowledge.[65]

Figure 90. Steven Watson standing beside a frying pan containing duck fat smashed potatoes. Photograph by Kimberley Moore, 2019.

Figure 91. Close-up of Steven Watson's hands spooning reduction over slow-roasted bison, Winnipeg. Photograph by Kimberley Moore, 2019.

Figure 92. Plate of slow-roasted bison on smashed duck fat potatoes with burned sage. Photograph by Kimberley Moore, 2019.

SLOW-ROASTED BISON WITH BURNED SAGE

2 kg bison chuck, inside round, or similar

500 g yellow onions

4 L bison stock

1 kg turnips

2 tbsp crushed tobacco leaves

200 mL duck fat

500 g local blueberries

50 g sage

1 kg parsnips

Coat bison with tobacco leaves. Pick all leaves off the sage, keep the stems. Heat a heavy-bottom pot big enough to hold bison, stock, onions, and berries. Heat 100 ml of the duck fat in the pot, sear the tobacco-coated bison on all sides. Remove bison, add onions, berries, and sage stems. Cook for just a few minutes while stirring. Add stock, place bison back into the pot, bring to a simmer, not a boil, for about 2 hours or until the bison is tender. It might take more time depending on the cut of bison or its shape. Once bison is tender, let rest in the liquid for at least one hour (preferably overnight) to cool in the liquid, then gently reheat the next day.

Cut parsnips and turnips into half-inch cubes, toss with the rest of the duck fat, roast at 425° Fahrenheit for about 20 minutes or until tender but not mushy. Once removed from the oven, I like to char the edges with a torch or under a boiler. Fire is a great way to bring in ancient Indigenous flavours and methods.

To serve, strain half of the liquid into another pot, and simmer to reduce into a near syrup consistency, takes about 30 minutes, but as we do not use salt as it is not Indigenous to the region, reducing brings out flavours that salt would otherwise bring. Once reduced, take the bison, reheat in reserved liquid, then place roasted vegetables on a platter, remove bison from the liquid, place on the platter, pour reduction over the bison. With the sage leaves, carefully torch them until red and smoking, place around the bison immediately and serve right away so the room fills with ancient aromas.

Recipe copyright Steven Watson, used with permission.

DUCK FAT SMASHED POTATOES

Duck Fat Smashed Potatoes
1 kg baby yellow potatoes
100 mL duck fat
5 large sage leaves

In a pot, cover the potatoes in cold water, bring to a boil, and cook until the potatoes are just cooked, but not yet splitting. Pour the water out, cover in more cold water just to cool the potatoes enough to handle. Take each potato and gently flatten with flat utensil, like a measuring cup or can. Heat duck fat in a heavy-bottom pan over medium heat, drop in sage, and if sage sizzles, gently place potatoes in the fat to brown. Do not overcrowd the pan, ensure there is about half an inch in-between each potato. Once browned, transfer potatoes to a platter, top with the fried sage.

Recipe copyright Steven Watson, used with permission.

funds and the resources to push that through and get something done there. But I don't see that happening much because even bison has taken a long time. Like bison itself is close to beef; it is not super gamey. You can actually make a bison prime rib roast and cut that like beef and it's fantastic, and bison tenderloin is fantastic. But even that's been . . . I think it just started to get kind of popular when I was at a place called Green Gates [now known as The Gates on Roblin restaurant in Headingley, Manitoba], and that was twenty years ago.[66]

The various regulations that control how and where Indigenous food can be produced for public consumption occasionally work in Watson's favour, however. "We've done events at other places like CanadInns and whatnot. Technically, that's not allowed. You can't bring in 529 [529 Wellington Steakhouse] to do catering at CanadInns—health reasons plus business reasons. But because there's exemptions for 'ethnic' foods. So we fall under 'ethnic' food. I know, it's kind of funny. So we fall under the 'ethnic' regulations. So we can go in there and do the food legally, because we're 'ethnic.' And meanwhile, we're actually far more local than CanadInns is, right."[67]

Indigenous peoples on this continent had developed complex agricultural systems prior to European contact. They were building clam gardens more than 3,500 years ago on the western coast.[68] In fact, Indigenous farming techniques were more productive than those of either settler grain farmers or Europeans in the seventeenth and eighteenth centuries.[69] The Three Sisters yielded more energy and protein from the land than did monoculture planting.[70] As Watson describes it:

Quite sophisticated for thousands of years ago. So we figure that they would have done certain things like maybe what we're doing here, like taking potatoes and squishing them and frying them in duck fat. You know, reducing sauces for more flavour, or adding certain herbs and different things to foods—like we're going to burn some sage and that's going to be a garnish for our stew. Because burned sage is traditional in smudging, so we take that and apply it to actual food and we add a bit of an emotional side, a bit of a spiritual side as well.[71]

Chef Watson consults regularly with Indigenous Elders about whether it's appropriate for him to use sage and other traditional plants in these ways. For Indigenous students, this culinary usage can be very meaningful because of the connection to smudging.

JANIS THIESSEN: So I find this very interesting, that your approach is part creative, part historical research, and part consultations with community Elders. And particularly what you were mentioning about sage. So are there other aspects of cooking that have a spiritual component for you or for those in your community?

STEVEN WATSON: Tobacco is another one, and we use that often. There's actually a little bit in there [in the bison]. What we do is the same idea, for smudgings and whatnot. And actually the Three Sisters I mentioned used to be the Four Sisters, because tobacco was part of it. But tobacco is more of a spiritual side, not really a food, right? So it was often, not ignored, but pushed to the wayside in terms of food. So it became the Three Sisters. So what we'll do often is actually make things with the Four Sisters.[72]

Sage has significance in many Indigenous cultures in present-day Canada. In Anishinaabe stories, sage is the sacred plant that Nanabozho was given to address his fears, and it is a traditional medicine burned in smudging ceremonies.[73] It can be particularly emotional. Watson explains, "So part of this, again, is to bring another aspect of what cultures have done, is they bring emotion into food. . . . Emotion is tied to food, food is tied to emotion. Smells. You smell something, and it reminds you of your grandmother forty years ago. Or you smell something that reminds you of a dinner you had somewhere else. Whatever. And it's tied to that. So, if we can burn some sage, and it brings somebody back to something, we're doing something that people love."[74]

Modern techniques, modern presentation, but pre-contact ingredients. Watson notes that the recent culinary trend of molecular gastronomy plays with scents. He mentions that the famous Chicago restaurant Alinea, for example, uses specific scents to evoke particular times and locations while also adding a subtle taste. As a final step before serving us his tasting menu, Watson burned sage and wafted its smoke over the slow-roasted bison. "It's funny, because I was doing this before I read about that. And I was like, 'Hey! That's kind of like what we do, too!' Right, so it adds flavour by adding something that you don't even really eat. So a smell is more tied to flavour, and what we love, than taste is."[75]

Smells evoke memories. Reimagining Indigenous cuisine, reconnecting with pre-contact ingredients, can be a way of sharing memories, of recovering history that was disrupted by colonialism. Watson explained:

I am Native myself. Peguis First Nation. My grandmother is a Sinclair, or was a Sinclair. So she's—and I didn't know it, at all. She was raised Catholic, just before the Sixties Scoop.[76] So residential school and all kinds of things there. She was never one of the sad, sad stories. There's a lot of terrible stories, but she was— She was taken away from her family, and that's a bad part. But the school was fine; they treated her nicely and all that kind of stuff, so she was okay, in that sense. But I knew more about Catholicism. . . . I grew up in Thompson—didn't grow up in Thompson, but lived in Thompson for a big chunk of my life—and that's where we went to church every Sunday, went to midnight Mass on Christmas Eve. And even the city here, when she moved to the city [of Winnipeg], years after my parents did, we'd go to her place for Christmas Eve, and then she'd take us all to midnight Mass and whatnot. And then I realized just the past few years ago that there's a reason why, that I don't know that Indigenous side. It's because she didn't. It was taken. So what can we do to give that back a little bit? And this is part of it. Because I'm not in politics, I'm not . . . I am a teacher, but in food; I'm not a college professor or anything like that. What can we do? And this is part of it, that we can give back, we can do more, and we can give some education about this that is sorely lacking.[77]

The impact of colonialism on Indigenous people in Canada is ongoing. Canada's first Indian residential school took in students in 1834. By the 1960s, there were more than ninety such schools across Canada. Thousands of Indigenous children who were compelled by the state to attend these schools never made it out alive. As noted earlier, many children suffered physical or sexual abuse at these schools, while some were subjected to nutritional experiments without their consent or knowledge.[78] These children were separated from their families, their languages, their spiritual practices, and their culture—with significant consequences for subsequent generations. These impacts persist long after the closure of the last residential school in the 1990s, the federal government's apology in 2008, and the release of the final report of the Truth and Reconciliation Commission in 2015.[79] Watson reflected, "Kind of giving back to, I guess, my grandmother. I'm not even a spiritual person myself, but I feel like I owe something because she lost that part. . . . It's not like she led a bad life because of it, but she missed something that she might have wanted a piece of her, right? And my whole family lost that, too."[80]

Through his cooking, Watson is not trying to revive a pre-contact cuisine but to imagine how it would have developed in a modern context if the process of its development had not been disrupted by the settler colonial state. The goal is not to produce food that is of interest solely to historians but food that people will enjoy eating.

> JANIS THIESSEN: So much historical cooking, the focus is on authenticity—whatever the heck that means—and not so much on "Does anyone now actually want to eat this stuff?" And so the way that you are combining these two is really very interesting.
>
> STEVEN WATSON: And I had a fascination with that, in the historical side, and doing things that way. I bought a book, I think it's *Historical Heston Blumenthal*, it's called.[81] And he would do the dish, he would do it both ways. And that's kind of what I applied here. He would take a steak and kidney pie, and literally do it from a seventeenth-century recipe, the exact same way, in the exact same style of oven and pan and all that kind of stuff. And then he would do it the way he would do it in his restaurant.[82]

Watson has many menu ideas, and many dreams: pickerel with sumac and wild chives, served on a wild rice cake with potato and duck fat and onion; cooking modern Indigenous cuisine over open fires at Niizhoziibean, the south point of The Forks in Winnipeg that is dedicated to Indigenous themes; growing native plants in Winnipeg's Assiniboine Park; serving his 1491 menu as a guest chef at Raw Almond, the winter pop-up restaurant located on the ice of the frozen junction of the Red and Assiniboine rivers at The Forks. His creativity and ambition match that of some of the world's most celebrated chefs, like René Redzepi at Noma in Copenhagen. But Watson also has a mission.

> JANIS THIESSEN: There are a lot of parallels here between you and someplace like Noma [the Copenhagen restaurant], except that this is better [laughs] in that Noma's trying to experiment and recover local foods, but there isn't also an historical and a justice component in quite the same way.
>
> STEVEN WATSON: No, and when I was saying that a lot of kitchens have the strict research centre, that's one of them. For six months out of the year, they do nothing but test. And I follow them on Instagram and stuff, and they often will just show stuff from the testing kitchen. But yeah, and it's kind of similar in that way. They very much are local. They'll use foods that people didn't know were foods.[83]

Figure 93. Close-up of Steven Watson igniting some sage. Photograph by Kimberley Moore, 2019.

A key difference, of course, is that Noma's chef, René Redzepi, has no problem finding financial backers willing to fund such experimentation. Watson explained:

> René Redzepi, he has basically unlimited . . . He can go to anybody with money and say "Give me money," and they'll give it to him. I would if I had money. If I won a Super Seven lottery or whatever it's called now—LottoMax—I'd probably fund something like that myself, just for the ability to go and actually do it with them, or try it out, or whatever. So hopefully there's somebody like that here. Not necessarily one really rich guy, but a band, or a subsidy. Or even if we could . . . Like somebody in the government could subsidize so that it becomes the same price as regular foods or whatever. So that bison costs the same as beef, or whatever. If we can get something there, whether it's government or individual or a group of people or a band—just to spread that information. Because like I said, it's not a . . . I wouldn't be starting this to make money. I'd easily make more money just by opening a restaurant that sells burgers [laughs]. I can do pretty good burgers. I was there, I did the burger at Brazen Hall that won Burger Week, not this past year but the year before. So I mean, I can do those things, right? And this is not going to fly like a burger. This is not going to do a . . . We're not going to have a week like they have Fried Chicken Week or Burger Week. We're not going to do that in the next twenty, thirty years.[84]

It may take decades, but Watson is in this for the long haul. As part of Commonwealth College's Culinary Arts program, he opened teaching kitchens on reserves in Sioux Lookout, St. Theresa Point, and Wasagamack to train Indigenous youth. These young chefs will teach people the histories of Indigenous food and join Watson in reimagining it for the future. "We want to tie some emotion into there, too, because that's a big part of Indigenous food—emotion and spiritual. So if we can do that, we will. At the same time, something that people would want to eat. Not something that: 'Oh, that's good for 500 years old' but 'No, that's really good,' regardless of if they know the story behind it."[85] Watson teaches his students those stories, and they in turn will expand the growing Indigenous restaurant scene in Canada.

CONCLUSION

Beyond Manitoba Food History

Having perused these stories of food in Manitoba, readers might reasonably ask, "What then, if anything, is Manitoban food?" It is an echo of a question that Canadians sometimes ask more generally: "What exactly is Canadian food?" One way historians have attempted to gain a sense of how the idea of local food intersects with identity is through the analysis of Canadian cookbooks.

The documentation of Canadian cuisine has a long history. The first cookbook published in present-day Canada, Menon's *La cuisinière bourgeoise,* was printed in 1825; the first in Manitoba was in 1896 by the Ladies' Aid Society of Winnipeg's Grace Church.[1] A community cookbook like the latter, oral historian Rebecca Sharpless explains, was "an ingenious idea that allowed women to raise money for causes they cared about while staying well within the gender conventions of the day."[2] Manitoba's many ethnicized groups were particularly prolific in generating such community cookbooks. "In no other province," declares Elizabeth Driver, former president of the Culinary Historians of Ontario, "was the variety of immigrant cultures expressed so clearly through cookbooks as in Manitoba before 1950, where one finds Icelandic, Jewish, Scottish, Ukrainian, and German recipe collections."[3] Manitoba was also the home of significant food businesses like Blue Ribbon Limited, Codville and Company, Western Pure Foods, McKenzie Seeds, and McFayden Seed Company, all of which produced cookbooks; Blue Ribbon's became particularly popular.[4]

The recording of recipes predates the invention of published cookbooks, of course. People wrote down recipes (in various forms) for their own domestic use long before the first cookbook was published, and they continue to do so today. Food historian Jane Busch says, "Manuscript recipe books and printed cookbooks are fundamentally different. Manuscript recipe books are repositories of family recipes kept by the female head of the household. Often these recipe books were inherited."[5] These handwritten recipe collections "tend to contain more complex recipes requiring greater precision, such as desserts and preserves, rather than everyday dishes that did not follow specific recipes."[6]

A number of Canadian cookbooks were published during the centennial of Confederation in 1967. These cookbooks further contributed to historians' debates over what constitutes Canadian food, and have been described by food writer Sara Wilmshurst as exercises in "citizenship performance through cookery."[7] By the 1970s, according to writer Rhona Richman Kenneally, "'Canadian cuisine' was a very open concept, comprised, ultimately, of any foods prepared in any region of the country, by members of any of its different ethnic communities, during any period of its history. . . . Characteristics of this formulation of a national cuisine of Canada were consistent with other indicators of active musing about what it meant to be Canadian, particularly as regards impulses toward multiculturalism, modernity and nationalism."[8] Readers may wonder which Manitobans are considered to be "ethnic," as well as where Indigenous peoples fit (if they do) in such definitions of Canadian cuisine. Mary Maushard, in the *Winnipeg Free Press* in 1982, for example, observed: "To experience Canadian cuisine is to taste foods from a mixing, but not a melting, pot of ethnic diversities; foods that make the

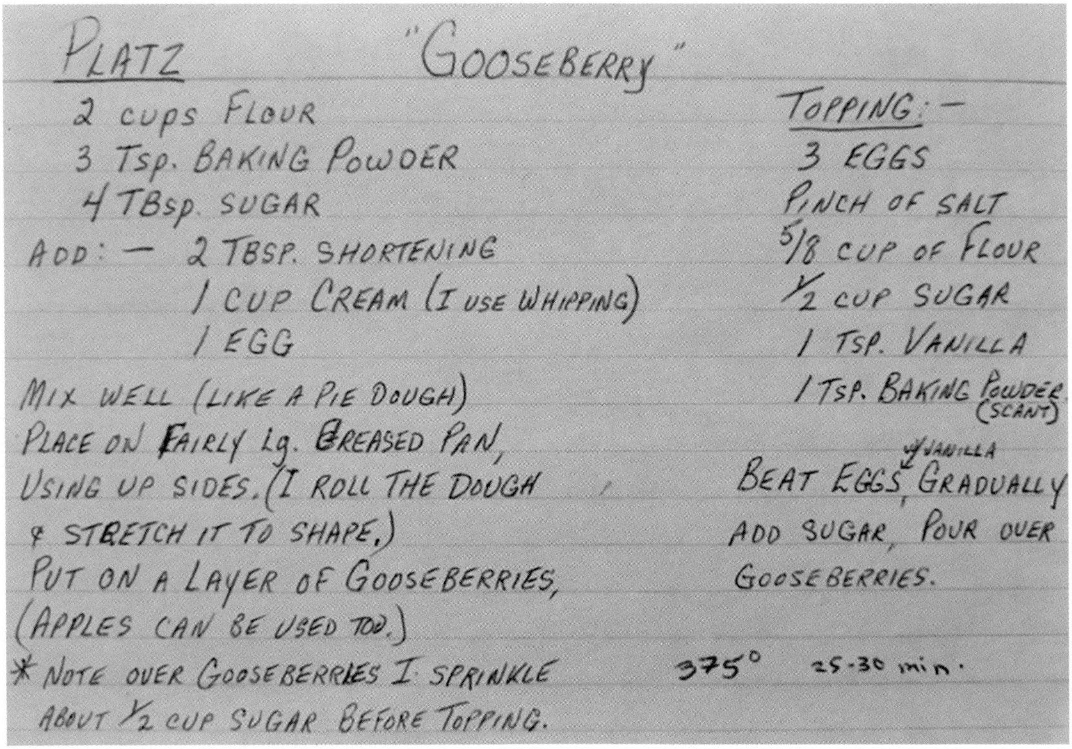

PLATZ "GOOSEBERRY"

2 cups FLOUR
3 Tsp. BAKING POWDER
4 TBsp. SUGAR
ADD: — 2 TBSP. SHORTENING
1 CUP CREAM (I USE WHIPPING)
1 EGG
MIX WELL (LIKE A PIE DOUGH)
PLACE ON FAIRLY Lg. GREASED PAN,
USING UP SIDES. (I ROLL THE DOUGH
& STRETCH IT TO SHAPE.)
PUT ON A LAYER OF GOOSEBERRIES,
(APPLES CAN BE USED TOO.)
* NOTE OVER GOOSEBERRIES I SPRINKLE
ABOUT 1/2 CUP SUGAR BEFORE TOPPING.

TOPPING: —
3 EGGS
PINCH OF SALT
5/8 CUP OF FLOUR
1/2 CUP SUGAR
1 TSP. VANILLA
1 TSP. BAKING POWDER (SCANT)

BEAT EGGS & VANILLA, GRADUALLY
ADD SUGAR, POUR OVER
GOOSEBERRIES.

375° 25-30 min.

Figure 94. Recipe card for gooseberry platz written by Margret Thiessen, Janis's mother. Courtesy of Janis's sister Tanis Thiessen, 2023.

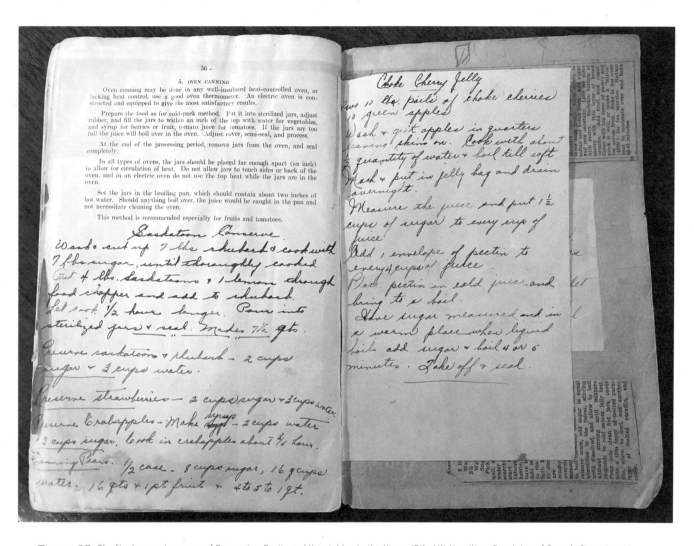

Figure 95. The final pages in a copy of Preserving Fruits and Vegetables in the Home (Ethel W. Hamilton, Dominion of Canada Department of Agriculture Bulletin No. 77, 1933) belonging to Clementina Cherlet, Kim's great-grandmother, with annotations and additions written and pasted in by Marcella Ledoyen, proprietor of Adolphe and Sally's Diner (see Chapter 2). Photograph by Kimberley Moore, 2023.

most of what an inhospitable climate has to offer; foods that are at once as old as the first white settlers, the French Canadians, and as young as the wave of 1960s immigrants."[9]

Such questions about ethnicity and Indigeneity in connection with cuisine have been raised only in recent decades. Food studies scholar Krishnendu Ray, for example, reminds us, "Ethnicity is not a thing. It is a relationship of domination and the very grounds on which the dominated have successfully pushed back."[10] And food reporter Corey Mintz has argued, "If there is such a thing as 'Canadian food,' it belongs to Indigenous peoples, communities that farmed, hunted, fished, preserved, and cooked long before the French showed up with their mother sauces and names for different-sized cubed vegetables."[11]

But Indigenous peoples' cuisines (there are many!)[12] should not be viewed as just another kind of "ethnic" food[13]—or co-opted as part of Canadian cuisine, as food writers and scholars Eric Ritskes, Natalie Doonan, Sam Grey, and Lenore Newman explain. Eric Ritskes notes that Canadian food is increasingly identified as food produced from particular local ingredients.

> So, in Canada, saskatoon berries and salmon and moose and wild ginger and cedar and fiddleheads and maple syrup and bison and wild rice and Arctic char become representative Canadian foods. But, to put it bluntly: this is a culinary invention born of settler colonialism. These foods are not Canadian foods. Or, at the very least, they did not begin as Canadian foods. They are Indigenous foods. They are Skwxwú7mesh foods, Gwich'in foods, Nehiyaw foods, Anishinaabe foods, Inuk foods, Mi'kmaq foods. These ingredients, methods, and dishes belong to nations that existed long before Canada did and nations that continue to exist. How they came to be called 'Canadian' is part and parcel of the larger invention of Canada, part and parcel of the settler colonial legacy that permeates Canada to the present day.[14]

Natalie Doonan agrees: attempts to define Canadian food by particular ingredients "cannot be disentangled" from Canada's colonial history.[15]

Sam Grey and Lenore Newman elaborate on this interaction of colonialism and cuisine within Canada. "Because multicultural inclusion is the means by which Indigenous Peoples' gastronomies are commodified and alienated, they experience not *gastronomic multiculturalism* but *culinary colonialism*," they observe.[16] They define "culinary colonialism" as "the extension of Settler jurisdiction over, and exploitation of, Indigenous gastronomy . . . initially the destruction of Indigenous food systems as a tool of war (*conquest*), followed by forced conversion to a Settler diet (*assimilation*), before the revalorization of Indigenous gastronomy for Settler consumption (*appropriation*). Indigenous cuisines are thus gentrified, reoriented toward the demographic that originally sought their eradication."[17] The assimilation phase described by Grey and Newman is elaborated on by historian Travis Hay, who explains that settler scientists' racist assumptions that Indigenous people were "genetically predisposed to diabetes, obesity, and other metabolic syndromes because of the foodways of their ancestors" allowed them to blame the victims rather than the "embodied and structural violence of federal Indian policies."[18] The appropriation phase described by Grey and Newman can be seen in menus that promote culinary tourism to Manitoba's North: "Indigenous foods such as Braised Peppered Elk, Arctic Char and Manitoba Bison grace the tables" at the Lazy Bear Lodge in Churchill, for example.[19] Indigenous cuisines are thus either ignored or are "de-Indigenized through reclassification as a national heritage and reinterpretation by non-Indigenous chefs and restauranteurs."[20] Cuisine, Grey and Newman remind us, is *political* as well as cultural—and the former is particularly important to keep in mind regarding Indigenous food sovereignty. It is precisely this political nature of cuisine that we highlight in Chapter 5 in our discussion of greenhouses in northern Manitoba; in Chapter 6 on manomin; in our discussions of ethnicity, identity, and authenticity in Chapters 1 and 4; and our discussion of government regulation of food in Chapters 2 and 3.

If cuisine is as much political as it is cultural, then perhaps the response to the question "What is Manitoban/Canadian food?" should be "Why are you asking that question?" Folklorist Doreen Klassen shares a story about her experience of being served tortillas and beans while visiting a Mennonite colony in Mexico: "Is this Mennonite food?" she asked. "Yes," she was told. "We eat this all the time, and we are Mennonites."[21] Manitoban food, then, is whatever foods Manitobans are eating. So is "What is Manitoban/Canadian food?" a question historians should even be asking anymore? Given that the result historically has been to ethnicize and racialize certain cultures or to engage in culinary colonialism—either a culinary "othering" of some (typically, non-white) peoples or the culinary dispossession of Indigenous nations—the answer must be no. New lines of inquiry into the relationship between food and place are instead necessary.

Our project team was not interested in defining Manitoba food; we asked different research questions. Ours is the "Manitoba" Food History Project only insofar as restricting our research to current provincial boundaries allowed us to put affordable limits on our travel. Our project has been driven to ask what we believe to be more interesting, more meaningful questions: What are various people(s) living here eating? What meaning do those foods hold for them? How and why have those foods and foodways changed over time? And what do those food histories teach us about the history of the lands in which we live? Or, as our project website asks: How has food been produced, sold, and consumed in Manitoba, and how have those processes changed over time? We need to stop asking nationalist questions about food identity, just as we need to stop asking questions about food authenticity. And when others ask those questions, we need to challenge them: Why are you asking? What is the end goal of such a question?

Knowing the stories behind the foods we eat may not enhance their taste. But a greater understanding of the food history of the places we call home has other benefits, as we hope this book has shown. Food history is not an entertaining distraction from "real" history, and, as historian Jeffrey Pilcher says, neither is it a "mere condiment to tempt students and the public toward other, presumably more substantial, fare."[22] Rather, as Pilcher explains, "deeper engagements with the past" are made possible through food history's exploration of "the gendering of food, its embodied experiences, and the ways that mundane acts of provisioning create social and cultural meanings."[23] The editors of the Canadian food history collection *Edible Histories, Cultural Politics* make a similar argument: "Food history offers a new vantage point on long-standing history questions about cultural politics and power, gender relations, ethnic and racialized histories of inclusion and exclusion, imperial designs and nation building, sexual and gendered performances, class struggles and cultural identities, regional diversity, and the role of the state or corporation in shaping daily practice."[24] Recognizing the importance of documenting the history of change in food production and consumption, National Life Stories at the British Library began a collection of oral histories in 1998 titled *Food: From Source to Salespoint.* It now contains more than 300 interviews.[25]

In the same way, the Manitoba Food History Project exists to document the changes in the history of the production, retail, and consumption of food in this province. We have recorded oral histories in restaurants and food production facilities, at festivals and farmers' markets, in person in cooking classes and remotely via the Internet, as well as in our food truck/mobile oral history lab. While recording oral histories is a method of filling gaps in archival records, we view it also as a methodology that is uniquely capable of prompting researchers to ask new questions; as oral historian Alessandro Portelli reminds us, "open-endedness at all levels is one of its distinctive, formal characteristics."[26] We honour that open-endedness by refusing to view this book as the culminating summary of our research. As we noted in the Introduction, this book is a complement to the oral history archive and project website created during the course of our research. That archive and website cannot be effectively summarized, and neither should it be. Here we rely on lesser quoted words of oft-quoted Portelli: "What do we, as historians, do with the aesthetic project of many narrators, with the beauty incorporated in so many of the stories we hear? Do we, as purveyors of truth, expunge these features from our work (thus, of course, maiming the authenticity of the document) or do we recognize them as facts in their own right, to be acknowledged and used?"[27] A book as the culmination of a research project such as this cannot do justice to the beauty of the stories we heard and read and were told, through the occasions by which they were imparted, through culinary labours of love. And the project will continue, with ongoing additions to the oral history archive and project website.

Oral history is only one tool in our methodological store, albeit an essential one. We also believe strongly that food photography is not merely decorative but has the ability to capture "subjective, multi-sensory, time-based experiences," as food writer Yael Raviv notes,[28] and that the soundscapes of cooking, and of the places in which we cook, hold evidentiary value beyond words. We share Raviv's conviction that recipes are "embodied narratives" that "provide insights into memories and identities that are not represented at all in written narratives and other archival evidence."[29] The chapters, photos, recipes, maps, and biographies in this book highlight only a small portion of the food history knowledge we have documented on our website and archived at the University of Winnipeg Oral History Centre with the participation and consent of those we have interviewed. Together, they contribute to our understanding of the history of (for example) settler colonialism, ethnicity, migration, gender, and state regulation. Food history is about resistance and persistence, as well as cultural and economic (and physical!) survival.

Turning a final time to the question we posed at the beginning of this chapter, "What is Manitoban or Canadian food?," we have learned, through the ethnically, culturally, and geographically diverse interviews and the other records accumulated over the course of the project, that it is not a useful question to ask. The answer is too often a debatable and ever-changing list of foods or ingredients. Neither does it tend to acknowledge the long history of Indigenous nations in shaping food production and consumption or the ongoing impacts of settler colonialism. Focusing instead, as our project does, on the question of how food has been produced, sold, and consumed in Manitoba has led us to realize that food is in tension between those who use it to maintain their identities, and those who use it to regulate the "other" (whether they be Indigenous peoples through settler colonialism, or Asian Manitobans through displacement and legislation, or urban caterers to "mass eaters" through the increased regulation of a sanitized city). As Natalie Doonan observes, "Canadian identity is disputed, and respecting its unresolved status, rather than trying to define it once and for all, including through its cuisine, is part of maintaining a commitment to creating alliances between Indigenous and non-Indigenous populations in this country."[30] What we need, then, is not a definition of Manitoban food but the reimagining of history to include the disparate stories of the many people who make it. The Manitoba Food History Project is a step in that direction.

Manitoban Cookbooks 1884-1949

COOKBOOK TITLE	DATE	CITY	AUTHOR /EDITOR	PUBLISHER
The Modern Home Cook Book and Family Physician	1894	Winnipeg MB	Frank M. Lupton	Royal Crown Soap Co.
Unknown	1895	Winnipeg MB	J.H. Rose	
The Souvenir Cook Book	1896	Winnipeg MB	Ladies' Aid Society of Grace Church, Winnipeg	The Consolidated Stationery Co. Ltd.
The Home Cook Book	1901	Winnipeg MB		
The Wheat City Cook-Book	1901	Brandon MB	Ladies of the Methodist Church	Record Printing House
One Hundred Selected Recipes	1902	Winnipeg MB	St. Stephen's Church (Presbyterian) Ladies Association	
Good Recipes	1903	Neepawa MB	Ladies of Neepawa	Neepawa Register Print
Taylor's 1904 Calendar Cook Book	1904	Portage la Prairie MB		Red Cross Pharmacy
Blue Ribbon Cook Book	1905	Winnipeg MB		Blue Ribbon Manufacturing Co.

Title	Year	Place	Organization	Publisher/Sponsor
The New Cook Book	1906	Winnipeg MB	Grace Elizabeth Denison	
The Red Cross Almanac and Cook Book	1906	Portage la Prairie MB		Red Cross Pharmacy
Tried, Tested and True Recipes for the Practical Everyday Use of Gold Standard Goods	1906	Winnipeg MB		Gold Standard Baking Powder
A Few Selected Recipes from the Blue Ribbon Cook Book	1907	Winnipeg MB		Blue Ribbon Manufacturing Co.
Western Farmers' Handbook	1909	Winnipeg MB		The Farmers' Weekly Telegram
The New Cook Book	1910	Souris MB	Young Ladies' Guild, Fifth Avenue Methodist Church	
St. Luke's Organ Fund Recipe Book	1910	Winnipeg MB	St. Luke's Church	Stovel Company
Unknown	1910	Harney MB		
Knox Church Cook Book	1911	Brandon MB	The Willing Workers of Knox Presbyterian Church	The Record Printing Co.
The Souris Almanac and Cook Book 1911	1911	Souris MB		Sherrin & Co. Chemists and Druggists
Cook Book	1912	Winnipeg MB	The Young Ladies' Club of Westminster Presbyterian Church	
The Reliable Cook Book	1912	Foxwarren MB	The Ladies Aid of the Methodist Church	
Dauphin Ladies' Cook Book	1913	Dauphin MB	Ladies of Dauphin	Dauphin Herald Print
Riverview Presbyterian Church Cook Book	1913	Winnipeg MB	Ladies Aid of Riverview Church	
The Minnedosa Cook Book	1914	Minnedosa MB	Ladies of Minnedosa and vicinity	Women's Hospital Aid, Minnedosa
The Real Home-Keeper	1914	Winnipeg MB		

Selkirk Cook Book	1914	Selkirk MB	Women's Auxililary of Christ Church Anglican	
Rawleigh's 1915 Almanac, Cook Book and Medical Guide	1916	Winnipeg MB		W.T. Rawleigh Co. Ltd.
Norwood Methodist Souvenir Cook Book	1916	Winnipeg MB	Ladies' Aid of Norwood Methodist Church	
Unknown	1917	Reston MB		
Manitoba Farmers' Library monthly publications	1917	Winnipeg MB	Elizabeth Crawford, Charles Henry Lee, R.M. Atkinson, James A. Neilson, V.W. Jackson, Ethel M. Eadie, I. Villenueve, Helen MacDougall, Reuben Wesley Brown, H.B. Sommerfeld	Manitoba Department of Agriculture and immigration
War Recipes	1917	Winnipeg MB	Juvenile "Prisoners of War" Club	Sir Edward Grey Chapter, IODE
Knox Church Cook Book	1917	Winnipeg MB	Knox Presbyterian Church	Christian Press
The 'Home Queen' World's Fair Souvenir Cook Book	1918			Royal Crown Soups
Rawleigh's Almanac Cook Book and Guide to Health 1919	1919	Winnipeg MB		W.T. Rawleigh Co. Ltd.
Meat and Its Substitutes	1920	Winnipeg MB		Manitoba Agricultural College
A World of Useful Information in a Nutshell	1920	Winnipeg MB		Stovel Company
Better Baking	1921	Winnipeg MB		J.R. Watkins Co.
The Country Cook or the Manitoba Agricultural College Cook Book	1922	Winnipeg MB	Mary Catherine Hiltz, Mary Caroline Moxon	Manitoba Agricultural College
The New Hospital Cook Book	1922	Brandon MB	Brandon Graduate Nurses Association	

The Country Homemaker	1922	Virden MB	Margaret Mary Speechly	The Grain Growers' Guide Ltd.
NPLA Cook Book	1923	Winnipeg MB	The Home-Cooking Circle of the Norwood Presbyterian Ladies' Aid	
Cook Book	1924	Neepawa MB	Girls' Auxiliary of the Women's Hospital Aid Society	
Harmsworth Community Cook Book	1924	Virden MB		Empire-Advance Print
Tested Recipes	1924	Winnipeg MB	Ladies of Greenwood Methodist Church	Adult Bible Class
Winnipeg High School Domestic Science Note Book	1924	Winnipeg MB		Russel, Lang & Co. Ltd.
Ranchvale Ladies Aid Cook Book	1925	Rossburn MB		The Review Job Print
Wise Wives Keep Husbands Happy	1925	Winnipeg MB	St. Mark's Anglican Church, Regent's Park United Church	
A Cook Book of Tested Recipes	1926	Winnipeg MB	American Women's Club	
Cook Book	1927	Winnipeg MB	Ladies' Aid Society of Home Street United Church	
The League Cook Book	1927	Winnipeg MB	League of Winnipeg	
A Cook Book of Favorite Recipes	1928	Winnipeg MB	Women's Association of Crescent United Church	
Cook Book	1929	Winnipeg MB	Ladies' Aid of the First Lutheran Church	
A Cook Book of Tested Recipes	1929	Winnipeg MB	Group Number Three of Gordon United Church Ladies' Aid	Reynolds Printing
PEO Cook Book	1929	Selkirk MB	Chapter 'A' of PEO Sisterhood	

Recipes	1929	Winnipeg MB	United Farm Women of Manitoba	
The Young Women's Auxiliary Cook Book	1929	Roland MB	Young Women's Auxiliary of Roland United Church	R.E. Buffy, Roland
All Tested Recipes	1930	Winnipeg MB		Canadian Cook Book Company of Canada
The Canadian Bride's Reference Book	1930	Winnipeg MB		Merton Corporation Ltd.
The Dugald Women's Institute Cook Book	1930	Dugald MB	Dugald Women's Institute	
Favorite Recipes	1930	Winnipeg MB	St. Luke's Parish Guild	Wilson Stationery Co. Ltd.
140 Good Recipes	1930	Winnipeg MB	Women of Augustine United Church	
Winnipeg Laundry Cook Book	1930	Winnipeg MB	Anna S. Welch	Public Press Ltd.
Good Things to Eat	1930	Winnipeg MB	Ladies of St. Ignatius Roman Catholic Church	
The Community Cook Book	1930	Oakview MB	Moline Women's Institute	Saults & Pollard Ltd.
Betty's Scrapbook of Little Recipes for Little Cooks	1931	Winnipeg MB	The Nor'West Farmer	Nor'West Farmer Publishing House
Cook Book and Household Budget	1931	Winnipeg MB	Rhela Leslie	Ladies' Aid Society of Fort Rouge United Church
Cook Book and Household Budget	1931	Winnipeg MB		John Black United Church Ladies' Aid Society
Specially Selected Recipes	1931	Winnipeg MB	Gertrude Dutton	The Western Home
Recipes Old and New, Tried and True	1931	Winnipeg MB	Ladies of the Business Women's Group of King Memorial United Church	Reynolds Printing
Eclipse Tempting Recipes	1931	Winnipeg MB	Dickson Riley	Western Pure Foods Ltd.
A Guide to Good Cooking	1932	Winnipeg MB		

The Easy Way Cake Book	1932	Brandon MB	Anna Lee Scott	Sun Publishing Co.
Souvenir Book and Shoppers' Guide (annual)	1932	Winnipeg MB		Winnipeg Hadassah Council
All Tested Recipes	1934	Winnipeg MB	Commercial Girls' Club	
Choice Recipes	1934	Winnipeg MB	Women's Association of St. Stephens-Broadway United Church	
Household Hints - Cooking Recipes	1934	Winnipeg MB	Lions Club of Winnipeg	
The Waverley Cook Book	1934	Winnipeg MB	May McMillan	Sons of Scotland Benevolent Association
Free Press Cook Book	1935	Winnipeg MB	Madeline Day	Winnipeg Free Press
The Universal Cook Book	1935	Winnipeg MB	Olive Hobson Kyle	Universal Life Assurance
Red & White Health, Diet and General Recipe Book	1935	Pointe du Bois MB		Pointe du Bois Supply Co.
Choice Tested Recipes	1935	Virden MB	Women of Virden Hospital Aid	
Diet Facts and Health Cookery	1935	Winnipeg MB		Health Supply Centre
Favourite Vegetable Recipes	1935	Brandon MB		A.E. McKenzie Co. Ltd.
Home Curing and Preparing of Meats	1935	Winnipeg MB		Standard Chemical Co. Ltd.
Pickling Recipes	1935	Winnipeg MB		Western Vinegars Ltd.
A Cook Book of Tested Recipes	1936	Winnipeg MB	American Women's Club	
Around the Clock with the Free Press Kitchen	1936	Winnipeg MB	Madeline Day	Winnipeg Free Press
Party Entertaining and New Menus for the Winter Season	1936	Winnipeg MB	Jessie Marie DeBoth	Winnipeg Tribune
Everyday Recipe Book	1936	Roblin MB	Willing Workers Circle No. 2 of the Ladies Aid Society of Roblin United Church	

Cook Book	1937	Wawanesa MB	Chesley Methodist Church Ladies' Aid	
Cook Book	1937	Winnipeg MB	Madeline Day	Winnipeg Free Press
Prezervovannia ovochiv i iaryn	1937	Winnipeg MB	Mary Catherine Hiltz	Ukrainian Book Store
Rebekah Cook Book	1937	Winnipeg MB	Rebekah Lodges of Greater Winnipeg	
Theory and Practice in Household Science	1937	Winnipeg MB		Winnipeg Public Schools
Unknown	1937	Winnipeg MB		National Home Monthly
Community Cook Book	1938	Crandall MB	Crandall United Church Mission Band	
A Diary of Celebrated Christmas Recipes	1938	Winnipeg MB		Five Roses Flour
The Manitoba Health Cook Book	1938	Winnipeg MB		United Farm Women
The Winnipeg Home Cook Book	1938	Winnipeg MB	Katharine (Kay) Middleton	Winnipeg Tribune
Favorite Recipes of the Woman's Missionary Society Tuelon United Church	1939	Teulon MB	Woman's Missionary Society Teulon United Church	
Low Cost Recipes	1939	Winnipeg MB	Mary Catherine Hiltz	
Mrs. Becker's Favorite Recipes	1939	Winnipeg MB		Great-West Life Assurance Company
Honey and Sugarless Recipes	1939	Winnipeg MB		Universal Life Assurance
Victory Cook Book	1939	Greenway MB	Greenway Ladies' Aid	
Orange Lodge Cook Book	1940	Winnipeg MB	Ladies' Orange Benevolent Association	
Preserving Recipes for Hardy Home Grown Fruits	1940	Dropmore MB		Manitoba Hardy Plant Nursery

The Commercial and Home-Canning Possibilities of Mullets	1940	Winnipeg MB	University of Manitoba, Manitoba Department of Mines and Natural Resources	
Favorite Recipes of the Parents and Friends of the Members of the Lake Max Branch of the Canadian Junior Red Cross	1940	Boissevain MB	Lake Max Branch of the Canadian Junior Red Cross	
Harrow United Church Cook Book	1940	Winnipeg MB	Harrow United Church	
Cook Book	1940	Winnipeg MB	Women's Auxiliary of the Fort Garry Horse	
The Newport Book of Recipes	1941	Winnipeg MB	Dorothy Faulconer	Newport Cereal Co. Ltd.
Harmsworth Community Cook Book	1941	Elkhorn MB		Elkhorn Mercury Print
Vegetable Cook Book	1941	Winnipeg MB	Katharine (Kay) Middleton	McFayden Seed Co.
Canned Meat Recipes	1945	Winnipeg MB	Dorothy Faulconer	Canada Packers Ltd.
Nordwesten' Kochbuch	1945	Winnipeg MB		Druck und Verlag
Ukrainian-English Cook Book	1945	Winnipeg MB		Ukrainian Book Store and Press
Domashnie miasovyrobnytstvo ta konservuvannia ovochiv i iaryn	1945	Winnipeg MB		Ukrainian Book Store
Fancy Fare	1946	Portage la Prairie MB	Evening Branch of Woman's Auxiliary of St. Mark's Anglican Church	
From Me to You	1946	Winnipeg MB	Corinne Jordan	Paulin Chambers Co. Ltd.
Star Recipes	1946	Elm Creek MB	Elm Creek Chapter of Order of the Eastern Star	
Cook Book	1947	Selkirk MB	Knox Church Junior Aid	
Between Ourselves	1947	Winnipeg MB	Corinne Jordan	Paulin Chambers Co. Ltd.

Favorite Recipes for Home Cooking	1947	Crystal City MB		Colfax Rebekah Lodge
Sunshine Snacks	1948	Winnipeg MB	Sunshine Rebekah Lodge No. 43	
The Evening Circle Cook Book	1948	Winnipeg MB	Evening Circle of St. Vital United Church	
Ravenscourt Recipes	1948	Winnipeg MB	Ravenscourt School Guild	
Cook Book	1949	Winnipeg MB	Westminster United Church Women's Association Circle 3	
Morden Cook Book	1949	Morden MB	Women's Association of Morden United Church	
The St. James' Women's Auxiliary Cook Book	1949	Flin Flon MB	Uptown Branch of the Anglican Women's Association	
Tested Recipes for Home Cooking	1949	Waskada MB	Young Women's Association of Waskada United Church	Deloraine Times Publishing Company Ltd.
Thirtieth Anniversary Cook Book	1949	Winnipeg MB	Women's Missionary Federation	

Acknowledgements

We are thankful to the many people who contributed to this book—most particularly, those who consented to be interviewed for the Manitoba Food History Project and to share their recipes. This book would not exist otherwise.

Funding and assistance for this research was provided by the Social Sciences and Humanities Research Council of Canada, the University of Winnipeg (UW) Research Office (particularly Jino Distasio and Heather Mowat), UW Vice-President of Finance and Administration Michael Emslie, UW Dean of Arts Glenn Moulaison, UW Dean of Graduate Studies Mavis Reimer, UW Safety Office (especially Kevin Smith), UW Marketing and Communications (Kevin Rosen, Eric Roddy, Jennifer Cox, Naniece Ibrahim), UW Financial Services, and UW Human Resources.

This project would have been impossible without the support of Diversity Foods' Ian Vickers, Kirsten Godbout, Kelly Andreas, and Darwin Gaspar. From day one, they were on board with our bizarre ideas, and they were always upbeat and helpful when we were stymied by the idiosyncrasies of our shared food truck.

Thank you to Alexander Freund and Nolan Reilly for inspiring the idea of the Manitoba Food History Truck. And thanks to those who issued invitations to visit and provided a safe landing place for the truck: Winnipeg Public Libraries, Mennonite Heritage Village in Steinbach, St. Norbert Farmers' Market in Winnipeg, the Altona Sunflower Festival, and Canada's National Ukrainian Festival in Dauphin. We're still disappointed that COVID-19 prevented us from attending the Threshermen's Reunion in Austin and from going further afield.

Our thanks to the many students hired as research assistants throughout this project: Amber Ali, Jackson Anderson, Ashley Cross, Alyssa Czemerynzki, Emma Dubeski, Madison

Herget-Schmidt, Michaela Hiebert, Aidan Kingston, Madrin Macgillivray, Quinn MacNeil, Caitlin Mostoway-Parker, Daniel Nychuk, and Rochelle Richards. University of Winnipeg students in the history courses 2120, 3007, 3504, 4530, and 7517 assisted with archival processing; some also had their work published on our project's website, http://manitobafoodhistory.ca.

uw Indigenous Summer Scholars Caitlin Mostoway-Parker and Alyssa Czemerynzki transcribed the recipes for this book. The biographies, based on the oral history interviews, were written by Alyssa Czemerynzki and Janis Thiessen. The first year of the project was coordinated by Sarah Story, who conducted many interviews and also drove the Food History Truck. Scott Price was our graduate research fellow and truck driver during year two. Thank you for your contributions!

We also thank the many curators, archivists, and others who assisted with our research: Stephanie Friesen and James Gorton, Archives of Manitoba; Louise Lawrie, Churchill Library and Archives; Sarah Ramsden, City of Winnipeg Archives; Maria Abiusi, the Food Studio; Gordon Goldsborough, Manitoba Historical Society; Stuart Hay and Megumi Ishibashi, Manitoba Legislative Library; Roland Sawatzky and Nancy Anderson, the Manitoba Museum; Conrad Stoesz, Mennonite Heritage Archives; Andrea Dyck Klassen, Mennonite Heritage Village; Shelley Sweeney, Heather Bidzinski, and Brian Hubner, University of Manitoba Archives & Special Collections; Su Kim Chung and Stacey Fott, University of Nevada Las Vegas Special Collections & Archives; Brett Lougheed and Tanya Wiegand, University of Winnipeg Archives. Thanks as well to Christian Cassidy for his informative blogs on Winnipeg history, and Dave Sauer for sharing news of his own research on Manitoba fruit. We are grateful as well for feedback from those who participated in our roundtable at the Oral History Association annual conference in Montreal in October 2018, from the anonymous readers of earlier drafts of this manuscript, from uw colleague Karen Froman, and from our amazing editor Jill McConkey.

Finally, our thanks to those past and present at University of Manitoba Press who have supported the development of this book over the years, particularly David Carr, Jill McConkey, David Larsen, and Glenn Bergen. Their enthusiasm for this project was matched by their attention to detail, and we are grateful for both.

Notes

INTRODUCTION

1   The restaurant's registration in the Companies Office and its advertisements in newspapers in the 1970s list its name as Ichi Ban (two words), but the current restaurant website uses Ichiban (one word). For consistency, we will refer to the restaurant as Ichi Ban.

2   Parlour Coffee was Winnipeg's first "third-wave" coffee shop, opening on Main Street in 2010. Thom Bargen opened in 2013; in 2022 it had three locations throughout the city and a roastery located in the Barnhammer craft brewery in Winnipeg's West End. The three "waves" of coffee are defined by *Imbibe* magazine: "The first wave represented the spread of coffee around the planet, culminating with the convenient but poor-quality freeze-dried coffee of the post-World War II era. The second wave, exemplified by Starbucks, saw the mass marketing of higher-quality arabica coffees and espresso beverages. The third wave is a response to the homogenization of the second" via "cutting-edge cafés." Richard Reynolds, "Coffee's Third Wave," *Imbibe* (May/June 2006), http://imbibemagazine.com/Coffee-s-Third-Wave (accessed 6 May 2023).

3   Janis Thiessen, quoted in Lorraine Stevenson, "Food History Truck Ready to Roll," *Manitoba Co-operator*, 29 May 2018, https://www.manitobacooperator.ca/country-crossroads/food-history-truck-ready-to-roll/ (accessed 6 May 2023).

4   *Preserves* is also available on all major podcast apps, including Apple, Spotify, and Google.

5   Thiessen, *Snacks*.

6   Anderson, Brady, and Levkoe et al., *Conversations in Food Studies*, 9, 54, 206, 302, 308, 311; Parkhurst Ferguson, *What We Talk About*, 27, 102, 113–15, 118, 121, 137; Brzozowski, Lu, and Social and Economic Dimensions of an Aging Population (SEDAP), "Home Cooking"; Neuhaus, *Manly Meals*, 30, 75.

7   Abbey Perreault, "The Food Truck That Invites You to Cook," *Atlas Obscura*, 19 September 2018, https://www.atlasobscura.com/articles/unusual-food-trucks (accessed 6 May 2023). As Janis told her, "We've had a few 12-year-old boys approach the truck and be completely devastated that we're not selling hot dogs, and to them I apologize."

8   Philadelphia Public History Truck, https://phillyhistorytruck.wordpress.com/about/; StoryCorps, https://storycorps.org/mobile-tour/ (accessed 6 May 2023). Other truck-based oral history projects have emerged since the time we wrote our SSHRC grant application: the DC Humanities Truck (http://humanitiestruck.com, accessed 6 May 2023) and the Chesapeake Heartland Project's African American History Truck (https://chesapeakeheartland.squarespace.com/african-american-humanities-truck, accessed 6 May 2023). None of these other mobile recording studios incorporate cooking as part of the interview process; the Manitoba Food History Truck is thus unique.

9   Kimberley Moore, quoted in "Palatable Past: Travelling Truck Collects Old Prairie Recipes," *National Post*, https://nationalpost.com/pmn/life-pmn/food-life-pmn/palatable-past-travelling-truck-collects-old-prairie-recipes, 1 July 2018 (accessed 6 May 2023).

10 We discuss these challenges in more detail in Thiessen, Davies, and Moore, "Rhymes with 'Truck.'"

11 Friesen, *Canadian Prairies*, 195. For more recent work on the Métis and Indigenous histories of what is now Manitoba, see Teillet, *North-West Is Our Mother*; Daschuk, *Clearing the Plains*; and Peters et al., *Rooster Town*.

12 Friesen, *Canadian Prairies*, 202; Statistics Canada, "Table 98-10-0002-01 Population and Dwelling Counts: Canada and Census Subdivisions (Municipalities)," https://www150.statcan.gc.ca/t1/tbl1/en/tv.action?pid=9810000201 (accessed 6 May 2023).

13 Friesen, *Canadian Prairies*, 210.

14 For the history of Winnipeg's immigrant neighbourhoods, see Loewen and Friesen, *Immigrants in Prairie Cities*, chs. 2, 4, 7; Gourluck, *Mosaic Village*; Paskievich et al., *North End Revisited*; Hiebert, "Class, Ethnicity and Residential Structure."

15 Manitoba Trade and Investment, "Manitoba's Growing Agri-Food Industry," http://www.gov.mb.ca/trade/globaltrade/agrifood/industry/index.html (accessed 3 October 2018); Manitoba Agriculture and Resource Development, "Manitoba Analytics: Food Manufacturing Sales," 17 June 2020, https://www.gov.mb.ca/agriculture/markets-and-statistics/food-and-value-added-agriculture-statistics/pubs/manitoba-food-manufacturing-sales.pdf (accessed 19 July 2021); "Food and Beverage Sector Profile at a Glance," 21 April 2021, https://www.gov.mb.ca/agriculture/markets-and-statistics/food-and-value-added-agriculture-statistics/pubs/food-and-bev-manufacturing-sector-profile.pdf (accessed 19 July 2021).

   By comparison, food and beverage processing is also the largest manufacturing industry in Canada as a whole, accounting for 6.7 percent of GDP and one in eight jobs. Agriculture and Agri-Food Canada, *An Overview of the Canadian Agriculture and Agri-Food System*, https://publications.gc.ca/site/eng/9.505772/publication.html (accessed 11 July 2023), 11–12, 22; "Food and Beverage Sector Profile at a Glance"; Manitoba Agriculture and Resource Development, "Manitoba Analytics: Food Manufacturing Sales."

16 Levine and Striffler, "From Field to Table," 12.

17 Allen and Albala, *Business of Food*; Grumett, Bretherton, and Holmes, "Fast Food"; Helstosky, *Pizza*; Heron, *Booze*; Kraig, *Hot Dog*; Kiple, *Movable Feast*; Levenstein, *Paradox of Plenty*; Nestle, *Food Politics*; Ostry, *Nutrition Policy in Canada*; Parasecoli, *Bite Me*; Parkin, *Food Is Love*; Penfold, *Donut*; Power, "De-centering the Text"; Reiter, *Making Fast Food*; Schlosser, *Fast Food Nation*; Smith, *Hamburger*; Smith, *Popped Culture*; Smith, *Oxford Companion to American Food*; Spitznagel, *Junk Food Companion*; Turner, "Buying, Not Cooking."

18 Pollan, *Food Rules*; Pollan, *Defense of Food*; Pollan, *Omnivore's Dilemma*; Schlosser, *Fast Food Nation*.

19 Thiessen, *Snacks*; Thiessen, "From Faith to Food."

20 Sharpless, *Cooking in Other Women's Kitchens*; Penfold, *Donut*; Southern Foodways Alliance, https://www.southernfoodways.org (accessed 6 May 2023); Culinaria Research Centre, https://utsc.utoronto.ca/culinaria/food-studies-university-toronto (accessed 6 May 2023); see also Culinaria Research Centre and Multicultural History Society of Ontario, "Mapping Scarborough Chinatown," https://culinaria.digital.utsc.utoronto.ca (accessed 6 May 2023).

21 Russell, "Archives, Academy, and Access," 58.

22 British Library, "Collection Guides: Oral Histories of Food Production and Consumption," https://www.bl.uk/collection-guides/oral-histories-of-food-production-and-consumption (accessed 6 May 2023).

23 Russell, "Archives, Academy, and Access," 54.

24 Portelli, *Battle of Valle Giulia*; Portelli, *Death of Luigi Trastulli*; Confino, "Collective Memory and Cultural History"; Frisch, *Shared Authority*; LeGoff, *History and Memory*; LeGoff and Nora, *Constructing the Past*; Connerton, *How Societies Remember*.

25 K'Meyer and Hart, *I Saw It Coming*, 4, 11.

26 "In order to capture these stories without invading someone's personal space, Thiessen and her team created a "public kitchen" in which diverse, safe, and often satiating interviews can be conducted and recorded." Perreault, "Food Truck That Invites You." For recent discussions of oral history safety, see Jessee, "Managing Danger"; Strong, "Shifting Focus."

27 Jackson Anderson, Brendan Dvorak, Zachary Hamilton, and Madison Herget-Schmidt, "The Manitoba Food History Project," *Canada's History*, 28 March 2018, https://www.canadashistory.ca/explore/arts,-culture-society/the-manitoba-food-history-project, (accessed 8 May 2023).

28 "Manitoba Food History Project Trucking Along Remotely," University of Winnipeg Communications, 28 May 2020, https://news-centre.uwinnipeg.ca/all-posts/manitoba-food-history-project-trucking-along-remotely (accessed 9 May 2023).

29 Harvest Moon Oral History, http://www.harvestmoonoh.com (accessed 9 May 2023).

30 *Preserves: A Manitoba Food History Podcast,* https://www.manitobafoodhistory.ca/preserves-pod (accessed 9 May 2023); "What Is Northern Food?" https://www.manitobafoodhistory.ca/northern-food (accessed 9 May 2023).

CHAPTER ONE

1 Winnipeg Architecture Foundation, "Lakeview Square," https://www.winnipegarchitecture.ca/lakeview-square/ (accessed 19 December 2018).

2 This slogan has been used in advertising the Ichi Ban restaurant throughout its history. "Restaurant guide to A Taste of Manitoba," *Winnipeg Free Press,* 9 July 1994, 5; Ichi Ban restaurant website, https://www.ichibanwinnipeg.com/ (accessed 22 November 2018).

3 Photo of Nat Hart, Wally Guberman, and Sam Linhart, *Winnipeg Free Press*, 25 July 1972, 21; George Walkey, "Threads," *Winnipeg Free Press*, 8 July 1972, 5; "Caesar's Palace Quality High," *Winnipeg Free Press*, 11 August 1970, 4G; Gordon Goldsborough, "Memorable Manitobans: Oscar Bert Grubert (1929–2014)," *Manitoba Historical Society*, 17 August 2020, http://www.mhs.mb.ca/docs/people/grubert_o.shtml (accessed 6 May 2023); Steven Hart, interviewed by Janis Thiessen, 6 February 2019, 00:13:28–00:14:55. Currently, the sole director of Ichi Ban Ltd. is Yetta Levit, widow of Jack Levit. Ichi Ban Ltd., file summary (as of 12 February 2019), Companies Office, Government of Manitoba.

4 Advertisement, *Winnipeg Free Press,* 27 April 1973, 24; "Appointment: Mr. Mike Fuji," *Winnipeg Free Press* advertisement, 17 May 1975, 16; Gene Telpner, "Chef Entertains and Cooks," *Winnipeg Tribune,* 9 October 1976, 32. Teppan means iron plate; yaki means grilling. In Japanese, iron plate grilling thus is depicted as two separate characters; in English, this is rendered as teppan yaki, teppanyaki, or teppan-yaki. To conform most closely to the original Japanese, we will use the term teppan yaki.

5 Steven Hart interview, 00:06:22–00:07:00.

6 Ibid., 00:07:03–00:07:36.

7 Hannah Robinson, "Collection Highlight: Nat Hart Professional Papers," blog post, *UNLV Special Collections and Archives,* 18 August 2014, https://www.library.unlv.edu/whats_new_in_special_collections/20 (accessed 14 December 2018).

8 Hart opened the Nat Hart Gourmet Cooking School in Las Vegas in the 1980s, and became head of the food and beverage department at the Desert Inn Hotel and Casino, where he opened the restaurants Ho Wan and La Vie en Rose. He died in Las Vegas in 1995. Muriel Stevens, "Bidding a Fond Farewell to Caesars' Palace Court," *Las Vegas Sun,* 28 April 2000, https://lasvegassun.com/news/2000/apr/28/columnist-muriel-steve (accessed 14 December 2018); University of Nevada at Las Vegas Special Collections and Archives, Nat Hart Professional Papers (MS 00419), "Biographical/Historical Note," https://special.library.unlv.edu/ark%3A/62930/f1b307 (accessed 6 May 2023)

9 Sarah Feldberg, "As Caesars Palace Turns 50, It Remains the Strip-changing Icon It Has Always Been," *Las Vegas Weekly,* 21 July 2016, https://lasvegasweekly.com/news/2016/jul/21/caesars-palace-50-years/ (accessed 28 July 2020).

10 Katarzyna J. Cwiertka, "From Ethnic to Hip: Circuits of Japanese Cuisine in Europe," *Food & Foodways* 13, 4 (2005): 249, https://doi.org/10.1080/07409710590931294 (accessed 9 May 2023).

11 Ichi Ban advertisement, *Winnipeg Free Press,* 26 January 1976, 16.

12 Peng, Chen, and Hung, "Effects of Teppanyaki Restaurant," S1.

13 Chen, Peng, and Hung, "Chef Image's Influence," 154.

14 Ibid., 156.

15 Nat Hart, "Procedures for Ichi Ban and La Grande Canal of Venice," typescript, 27 September 1974, 10, Box 9, Folder 14, Nat Hart Collection, MS-00419, Special Collections & Archives, University Libraries, University of Nevada, Las Vegas.

16 Gail Cabana-Coldwell, "Visual Indulgence," *Ciao!* 2, 1 (1998): 19.

17 Continental Public Relations Limited, Winnipeg, MB, "Public Relations Recommendations for Ichi Ban Limited," typescript, 28 September 1972, 11, Box 9, Folder 14, Nat Hart Collection, MS-00419, Special Collections & Archives, University Libraries, University of Nevada, Las Vegas.

18 Authors have remained faithful to the interviewees' or sources' use of imperial, metric, or a combination of both types of measurements provided in the original recipes.

19 Steven Hart interview, 00:20:42–00:22:21.

20 Steven and Wendy Hart, interviewed by Barbara Tabach, 23 October 2014, transcript, 34–35.

21 Steven Hart interview; So Kim Chung, "Pyramids of Pink Shrimp: A Brief History of Las Vegas Dining, 1940s–1970s," *Nevada in the West* 3, 1 (Spring 2012): 10, https://digitalscholarship.unlv.edu/lib_articles/432 (accessed 9 May 2023).

22 Steven Hart interview, 00:19:56–00:20:13 and 00:22:21–00:22:29.

23 Cwiertka, "From Ethnic to Hip," 249.

24 "Cynthia Wine Says . . .," *Winnipeg Free Press,* 26 May 1973, 72.

25 Pannell Kerr Forster & Associates, "Proposed Ichi Ban Japanese Steak House, Minneapolis, Minnesota, Financial Projections," typescript, n.d., 24, Box 9, Folder 14, Nat Hart Collection, MS-00419, Special Collections & Archives, University Libraries, University of Nevada, Las Vegas.

26 Cwiertka, "From Ethnic to Hip," 248.

27 Ibid.

28 Untitled chart comparing Ichi Ban menu with that of twelve other restaurants, 21 May 1972, Box 9, Folder 8, Nat Hart Collection, MS-00419, Special Collections & Archives, University Libraries, University of Nevada, Las Vegas. The complete dinner menu was later shortened by making tempura an optional à la carte item. Untitled memo, 14 November 1972, Box 9, Folder 8, Nat Hart Collection, MS-00419, Special Collections & Archives, University Libraries, University of Nevada, Las Vegas; Steven Hart interview, 00:01:20–00:02:36.

29 Steven Hart interview, 00:16:47–00:17:05.

30 Cho, *Eating Chinese,* 7.

31 "Cynthia Wine Says . . .," *Winnipeg Free Press*, 15 July 1972, 14.

32 Gene Telpner, "Fare More Than Just Fair in Winnipeg's Restaurants," *Winnipeg Tribune,* 28 October 1978, 35, citing Anne Hardy's *Where to Eat in Canada.*

33 "Review of Ichi Ban," *Ciao!* (13 December 2003): 37.

34 Marion Warhaft, "Ichi Ban Depends on Both Showmanship and Food for Success," *Winnipeg Free Press,* 1 November 1991, D37.

35 "Flamingo Maître d' Nat Hart," newspaper clipping, n.d., Box 9, Folder 5, Nat Hart Collection, MS-00419, Special Collections & Archives, University Libraries, University of Nevada, Las Vegas.

36 Steven Hart interview, 00:45:53–00:48:08.

37 Ibid., 00:52:32–00:53:46.

38 Nat Hart, "Procedures for Ichi Ban and La Grande Canal of Venice," typescript, 27 September 1974, 2, 5, Box 9, Folder 14, Nat Hart Collection, MS-00419, Special Collections & Archives, University Libraries, University of Nevada, Las Vegas.

39 Steven Hart interview, 00:29:56–00:30:17.

40 Winnipeg Architecture Foundation, "Lakeview Square Parkade."

41 Gene Telpner, *Winnipeg Tribune,* 13 March 1973, 25.

42 Winnipeg Architecture Foundation, "Lakeview Square Parkade," https://www.winnipegarchitecture.ca/343-york-avenue/ (accessed 19 December 2018).

43 Steven Hart interview, 00:09:16–00:09:21.

44 Ibid., 00:08:29–00:08:36.

45 Advertisement for La Grande Canal of Venice, *Winnipeg Free Press,* 20 June 1974, 18.

46 Gene Telpner, "On the Town," *Winnipeg Tribune,* 18 April 1975, 27; advertisement for Café Mediterranea, *Winnipeg Free Press,* 28 April 1976, 70; Cynthia Wine, *Winnipeg Free Press,* 10 July 1976, 11.

47 Steven Hart interview, 00:11:32–00:11:46.

48 Cynthia Wine, *Winnipeg Free Press,* 10 July 1976, 11.

49 See Hui, *Chop Suey Nation.*

50 Cwiertka, "From Ethnic to Hip," 247.

51 "Winnipeg Chop Sticks, Do-It-Yourself Kind," *Winnipeg Free Press,* 23 November 1972, 23.

52 "The Fastest Knives in Town!" Ichi Ban advertisement, *Ciao!* (8 February 1997): 35.

53 Darlene Lazenby, "Ichi Ban: Excellent Food, Unusual Experience," *Winnipeg Tribune,* 8 November 1979, 18.

54 Cynthia Wine, *Winnipeg Free Press,* 7 August 1976, 11.

55 "Name Committee to Study Report on Restaurants," *Winnipeg Evening Tribune,* 22 October 1936, 4.

56 "Legal," *Winnipeg Daily Tribune,* 14 August 1903, 5; "A Contractor's Suit," *Manitoba Free Press,* 15 August 1903, 9.

57 "Expensive Waffles," *Manitoba Free Press,* 10 October 1903, 20.

58 Ward, "Japanese in Canada," 3.

59 See Hinther and Mochoruk, *Civilian Internment in Canada.*

60 Hinther and Mochoruk, "Introduction," in *Civilian Internment in Canada,* 7.

61 "Government Apologizes to Japanese Canadians in 1988," *CBC Archives,* 22 September 2018, https://www.cbc.ca/archives/government-apologizes-to-japanese-canadians-in-1988-1.4680546 (accessed 10 May 2023); Miki, "Internment of Japanese Canadians," 384, 389–98.

62 Hinther and Mochoruk, "Introduction," 3–4.

63 Fujiwara, *Ethnic Elites and Canadian Identity,* 24, Table 4; Oikawa, *Cartographies of Violence,* 2, Map 2, 173.

64 Henry Kusano, interviewed by Keiko Miki, 27 October 1987, 00:35:06–00:36:40; Kanaye Connie Matsuo, interviewed by Lillian E. Mukai, 3 September 1987, 00:03:22–00:03:52, 00:10:38–00:13:00, 00:15:33–00:18:57; Sunahara, *Politics of Racism.*

65 Tokunaga Nakai, interviewed by Isabel Hirota, 15 September 1987, 00:11:52–00:25:00; Harold A. Hirose, interviewed by Lillian E. Mukai, 20 October 1987, 00:04:03–00:05:02.

66 "Japan Holds Spotlight at Y Club Ethnic Night," *Winnipeg Free Press,* 11 February 1952, 3.

67 "We, The Women: Aiding 'Problem Girl' Aim of MHFG Auxiliary," *Winnipeg Tribune,* 6 April 1961, 14.

68 Bill Trebilcoe, "Coffee Break," *Winnipeg Free Press,* 28 August 1967, 1.

69 Purple Lantern Restaurant advertisement, *Winnipeg Free Press,* 17 August 1963, 24.

70 Ichi Ban itself would expand to five locations (Winnipeg, Minneapolis, Reno, Palm Springs, and Gimli) before shrinking back to only the original Winnipeg location. The Minneapolis location was the second-last Ichi Ban to close; it had opened in 1980 and folded in 2016. Rick Nelson, "Ichiban in Downtown Minneapolis Closing at End of Month," *Minneapolis Star Tribune,* 18 July 2016, http://www.startribune.com/ichiban-closing-at-the-end-of-the-month/387267061/ (accessed 22 November 2018); Marion Warhaft, "Japanese Cuisine in Home of Vikings," *Winnipeg Free Press,* 17 August 2000, D4.

71 Gene Telpner, "New Capitol Reopens with Benefit Night," *Winnipeg Tribune,* 5 June 1979, 17.

72 The first sushi offered in a North American restaurant was in 1904 in Los Angeles's Little Tokyo. Lee, "Nobu's Influence," 9–10.

73 Marion Warhaft, "Japanese, Korean Fare Yours for the Cooking," *Winnipeg Free Press,* 5 October 1979, 16.

74 "New Yorkers Develop Taste for Sea Urchin and Octopus," *Winnipeg Free Press,* 16 August 1978, 28.

75 Marjorie Gillies, "What's Cooking: Japan's Sushi Pretty to Look at, Good to Eat," *Winnipeg Tribune,* 25 April 1980, 55.

76 "Sushi Pioneer Edohei to Close Saturday," *Winnipeg Free Press,* 23 February 2012, https://www.winnipegfreepress.com/arts-and-life/food/Sushi-forerunner-Edohei-to-close-Saturday-140175353.html (accessed 10 May 2023); Marion Warhaft, "The Art of Sushi," *Winnipeg Free Press,* 4 March 2011, https://www.winnipegfreepress.com/opinion/columnists/the-art-of-sushi-117393228.html (accessed 10 May 2023); Bartley Kives, "A City Sushi Pioneer Closing His Restaurant," *Winnipeg Free Press,* 24 February 2012, https://www.winnipegfreepress.com/local/a-city-sushi-pioneer-closing-his-restaurant-140272893.html (accessed 10 May 2023).

77 Edward Lam, interviewed by Daniel Pastuck, 4 February 2015, 00:02:32–00:03:27; "Edohei Restaurant Closes Doors as 'Father of Sushi' Plans Retirement," *CTV News Winnipeg,* 27 February 2012, https://winnipeg.ctvnews.ca/edohei-restaurant-closes-doors-as-father-of-sushi-plans-retirement-1.773555 (accessed 10 May 2023); "Masa Sugita—Yujiro," *PEGuru,* 1 June 2010, https://peguru.ca/winnipeg-chefs/masa-sugita-yujiro/ (accessed 1 December 2022); Mike Green, "Brand New Winnipeg Restaurants for 2017," *Tourism Winnipeg,* 13 January 2017, https://www.tourismwinnipeg.com/eat-and-drink/peg-city-grub/read,post/577/brand-new-winnipeg-restaurants-for-2017 (accessed 10 May 2023).

78 Advertisement, *Winnipeg Free Press,* 6 October 1994, 8; advertisement, *Winnipeg Free Press,* 29 June 1996, B5.

79 Marion Warhaft, "Yamato's Sushi Is Sublime," *Winnipeg Free Press,* 22 December 2000, D4. The popularity of sushi exploded across Canada in the 1990s, a result of increased diversity of products in food businesses, greater interest in food-related health, increased overseas travel, and the creation of Japanese factories in North America. Tachibana, "'Processing' Sushi/Cooked Japan," 58–59.

80 Steven Hart interview, 00:26:13–00:26:35.

81 Continental Public Relations Limited, "Public Relations Recommendations for Ichi Ban."

82 An Act to Prevent the Employment of Female Labor in Certain Capacities, Statutes of Saskatchewan 1912, c.17.

83 An Act to Prevent the Employment of Female Labor in Certain Capacities, Statutes of Manitoba 1913, c.19.

84 Lindsay Stewart, "Sushi in the City," *Ciao!* (8 December 2001): 33; Kives, "City Sushi Pioneer Closing"; "Master and Apprentice," *Ciao!* (27 May 2000): 24.

85 Marion Warhaft, "Appealing Little Restaurant Offers Tempting Menu, Quiet Ambiance," *Winnipeg Free Press,* 29 April 1988, 34.

86 Jared Story, "Sushi Chef Rolls Back into Business at Japanese Pavilion," *Winnipeg Free Press,* 6 August 2013, https://www.winnipegfreepress.com/our-communities/times/Sushi-chef-rolls-back-into-business-at-Japanese-pavilion-218530771.html (accessed 10 May 2023); "Winnipeg's Original Sushi Restaurant Closing," *CBC Manitoba,* 22 February 2012, https://www.cbc.ca/news/canada/manitoba/winnipeg-s-original-sushi-restaurant-closing-1.1228768 (accessed 10 May 2023).

87 Andrea Ratuski, "The 'Father of Sushi' Rules Kitchen at the Japanese Pavilion," *CBC Manitoba,* 1 August 2014, https://www.cbc.ca/news/canada/manitoba/the-father-of-sushi-rules-kitchen-at-the-japanese-pavilion-1.2723800 (accessed 11 May 2023); "Sushi Class by Chef Sadao Ono—SOLD OUT," Japanese Cultural Association of Manitoba, 21 March 2020, https://www.jcamwpg.ca/events/sushi-class-by-chef-sadao-ono/ (accessed 11 May 2023); "Ramen Sundays," Japanese Cultural Association of Manitoba, 31 October 2021, https://www.jcamwpg.ca/events/ramen-sundays-october-31st-2021-noon-to-1-pm/ (accessed 11 May 2023); "Makunochi Bento Box," Japanese Cultural Association of Manitoba, 13 November 2021, https://www.jcamwpg.ca/events/november-13th-2021-makunouchi-bento-box/ (accessed 11 May 2023).

88 Canada, Department of Labour, *Labour Gazette* (Ottawa: Queen's Printer, 1923), 1382.

89 Lee, "Laws of Gold Mountain," 312–14.

90 Backhouse, *Colour-Coded*; Backhouse, "Nineteenth-Century Canadian Prostitution," 393–94; Valverde, *Age of Light,* 77–103; University of Toronto Libraries, "Legislating the 'White Slave Panic,'

1885–1914," in *Canada's Oldest Profession: Sex Work and Bawdy House Legislation,* https://exhibits.library.utoronto.ca/exhibits/show/bawdy/white-slave-trade (accessed 5 August 2020).

91   "Will Test Law as Regards Orientals," *Manitoba Free Press,* 13 August 1912, 1; "No White Help for Chinamen," *Manitoba Free Press,* 26 February 1914, 14.

92   "Western Canada Labor Conference Report of Proceedings," *Western Labor News,* 4 April 1919, 4.

93   Lee, "Laws of Gold Mountain," 316. There were 150 Chinese-owned laundries, three restaurants, eight groceries, and three greenhouses in Winnipeg by 1920. Yee, *Chinatown,* 70.

94   The discussion changed over time from restricting Chinese Canadian employment of *white* women to *all* women.

95   Petition, 8 December 1921, Committee on Health, Employment of Women or Girls in Chinese Restaurants 1921, 191(1), City of Winnipeg Archives.

96   This is a reference to An Act to Prevent the Employment of Female Labor in Certain Capacities, Statutes of Manitoba 1913, c.19, discussed above.

97   Letter from Jules Preudhomme, City Solicitor, Winnipeg, MB, to C.J. Brown, Clerk of Committee on Health, Winnipeg, MB, 15 November 1921, Committee on Legislation and Reception, Re: employment of women & girls in Chinese restaurants, 1921–1926, A2145 Box 16, File 42, City of Winnipeg Archives; memo from Jules Preudhomme, City Solicitor to Mayor Edward Parnell, Winnipeg, MB, 2 December 1921, Committee on Legislation and Reception, Re: employment of women & girls in Chinese restaurants, 1921–1926, A2145 Box 16, File 42, City of Winnipeg Archives.

98   Statutes of Manitoba 1923, c.101.

99   "Amend Charter of St. Boniface," *Winnipeg Evening Tribune,* 29 December 1923, 12.

100   "Opposes Chinese Hiring White Girls," *Winnipeg Evening Tribune,* 6 February 1919, 2; "Discuss Use of Canteen Funds," *Winnipeg Evening Tribune,* 2 November 1921, 17; letter from Jules Preudhomme, City Solicitor, Winnipeg, MB, to J.S. Hough, of Hough, Campbell &

Ferguson, 24 December 1921, Committee on Legislation and Reception, Re: employment of women & girls in Chinese restaurants, 1921–1926, A2145 Box 16, File 42, City of Winnipeg Archives.

101   Letter from R.H. Barber, Restmore Manufacturing Company [and vice-president of the Asiatic Exclusion League], Calgary, AB, to Public Safety Committee, Winnipeg, MB, 28 November 1921, Committee on Legislation and Reception, Re: employment of women & girls in Chinese restaurants, 1921–1926, A2145 Box 16, File 42, City of Winnipeg Archives; Winnipeg City Council minutes, 3 January 1922, City of Winnipeg Archives; letter from R.H. Barber, Restmore Manufacturing Company [and vice–president of the Asiatic Exclusion League], Calgary, AB, to Winnipeg City Council, 17 December 1921, Committee on Legislation and Reception, Re: employment of women & girls in Chinese restaurants, 1921–1926, A2145 Box 16, File 42, City of Winnipeg Archives.

102   C.F. Macaulay, Asiatic Exclusion League pamphlet, Vancouver, BC, n.d., Committee on Legislation and Reception, Re: employment of women & girls in Chinese restaurants, 1921–1926, A2145 Box 16, File 42, City of Winnipeg Archives. The Asiatic Exclusion League successfully lobbied for federal passage in 1923 of the discriminatory Chinese Exclusion Act, which abolished the head tax but also prohibited virtually all immigration from China and required Chinese Canadians to register with the government.

103   Letter from Consul General of China, to Mayor Edward Parnell, Winnipeg, MB, 29 November 1921, Committee on Legislation and Reception, Re: employment of women & girls in Chinese restaurants, 1921–1926, A2145 Box 16, File 42, City of Winnipeg Archives.

104   Memo from Jules Preudhomme, City Solicitor, to Mayor Edward Parnell, Winnipeg, MB, 2 December 1921, Committee on Legislation and Reception, Re: employment of women & girls in Chinese restaurants, 1921–1926, A2145 Box 16, File 42, City of Winnipeg Archives; letter from Jules Preudhomme, City Solicitor, Winnipeg, MB, to J.S. Hough, of Hough, Campbell & Ferguson, 24 December 1921, Committee on Legislation and Reception, Re: employment of women & girls

in Chinese restaurants, 1921–1926, A2145 Box 16, File 42, City of Winnipeg Archives.

105 Letter from to J.S. Hough, of Hough, Campbell & Ferguson, to Jules Preudhomme, City Solicitor, Winnipeg, MB, 23 December 1921, Committee on Legislation and Reception, Re: employment of women & girls in Chinese restaurants, 1921–1926, A2145 Box 16, File 42, City of Winnipeg Archives.

106 Letter from J.S. Hough, of Hough, Campbell & Ferguson, to J. Preudhomme, City Solicitor, Winnipeg, MB, 15 February 1924, Committee on Legislation and Reception, Re: employment of women & girls in Chinese restaurants, 1921–1926, A2145 Box 16, File 42, City of Winnipeg Archives.

107 "Female Labor Barred from Chinese Cafes," *Manitoba Free Press,* 7 March 1924, 6.

108 Advertisement for Rex Café, 423 Portage Avenue, *Winnipeg Evening Tribune,* 27 February 1925, 22; advertisement for Olympia Café, The Pas, *Hudson's Bay Herald,* 10 April 1913, 8; advertisement for Café Aagaard's Café, Brandon, *Brandon Weekly Sun,* 23 November 1916, 7; advertisement for employment at Royal Café, Portage la Prairie, *Manitoba Free Press,* 17 June 1920, 17; advertisement for Jim Grant's Restaurant, Winnipeg, *Winnipeg Evening Tribune,* 20 July 1925, 7; advertisement for restaurant at the Bell Hotel, Winnipeg, *Winnipeg Evening Tribune,* 7 April 1926, 17; advertisement for Castran's Café, 596 Main Street, *Manitoba Free Press,* 16 March 1929, 5; advertisement for Cocoanut Grove Cabaret, Winnipeg, *Winnipeg Evening Tribune,* 5 May 1937, 19; advertisement for Wesley Lunch, 492 Portage Avenue, *Winnipeg Evening Tribune,* 14 May 1937, 28.

109 Advertisement for Aagard's Café, Brandon, *Brandon Daily Sun,* 10 November 1917, 2.

110 A.L. Driver, letter to the editor, *Manitoba Free Press,* 11 February 1915, 11.

111 Hartmann, "Starbucks and the Third Wave." The term was invented by coffee roaster Trish Rothgeb. Michael Paul Light, "Trish Rothgeb Coined 'Third Wave'—and Is Now Looking Toward Coffee's Future," *Los Angeles Times,* 4 October 2019, https://www.latimes.com/food/story/2019-10-04/third-wave-coffee-trish-rothgeb (accessed 11 May 2023).

112 Aviv, "B/Eating the Past," 71.

113 "Cynthia Wine Says . . .," *Winnipeg Free Press,* 26 May 1973, 72.

114 Ibid.

115 Aviv, "B/Eating the Past," 73.

116 Edward Lam interview, 00:27:57–00:28:40.

117 Ibid., 00:37:29–00:38:47.

118 Manalansan IV, "Beyond Authenticity," 290.

119 Edward Lam interview, 00:09:43–00:11:00.

120 "Cynthia Wine Says . . .," *Winnipeg Free Press,* 26 May 1973, 72.

CHAPTER TWO

1 As the spelling of "drive-in" varies, we use "drive-in" in the general sense. Where spelling varies, it is in accordance with the registered business name, and, following, is capitalized along with the restaurant name.

2 To confuse the matter further, you are able to purchase a "Market Fat Boy," at the Sals Market Store location on King Edward Street. *Sals Market,* "Deals and Specials," https://www.salsmarket.ca/deals-specials (accessed 13 May, 2023).

3 As seen on a reproduction of the restaurant's 1945 menu displayed at the Lombard location in 2020.

4 *Salisbury House,* "Breakfast Lunch and Dinner Menu," https://www.salisburyhouse.ca/menu (accessed May 13, 2023).

5 This is not a complete list. Additional locations can be found on the Salisbury House website's "History" page, https://www.salisburyhouse.ca/history (accessed 13 May 2023).

6 This term is borrowed from *Eating Culture,* in which Seitz and Scapp describe restaurants meant to serve "mass eaters" as distinct from restaurants meant to serve "the privileged diner who can afford not only to eat ("to fill the hole") but to eat very well, with wine to match" (Seitz and Scapp, *Eating Culture,* 9).

7   In 1991, around half of the locations operated twenty-four hours a day. "Salisbury House Started with $130," *Winnipeg Free Press,* 10 July 1991.

8   Like some other memorable Winnipeg enterprises, Winnipeggers did not seem to care all that much about it until it was almost gone. For examples, consider the Winnipeg Jets ("Indelible, Incurable Love Affair: Jets Fans, Players Share Bitter-sweet Memories," *Winnipeg Free Press,* 13 April 1996, D3), the downtown Eaton's Store (Lisa Rochon, "The Height of Stupidity,'" *Globe and Mail,* 15 August 2001), and the Odeon Drive-In Movie Theatre ("Winnipeg's Last Drive in Theatre Fades to Black," *CBC Manitoba,* 10 April 2008).

9   See "Salisbury House Started with $130"; and David Roberts, "Rock Royalty Buys Winnipeg 'Crown Jewel,'" *Globe and Mail,* 24 February 2001, A3.

10   Erwin sold the franchise to Quebec-based Steinberg Company in 1979. It was owned by Interactions Restaurants, Inc. at the time of its sale to this group. Salisbury House was owned by a Quebec-based corporation, which had acquired ownership in the 1970s (Roberts, "Rock Royalty").

11   Katz divested his interest in the company in 2002 and would later make headlines amid conflict-of-interest allegations after the Winnipeg Goldeyes loaned Maple Leaf Distillers (a Sals investor) an undisclosed sum prior to moving into the Esplanade Riel location (Dan Lett, "Should Katz Have Voted," *Winnipeg Free Press,* 1 October 2005, A1, A11).

12   Geoff Kirbyson and Alexandra Paul, "Rocker, Pals Put Winnipeg Institution in Local Hands," *Winnipeg Free Press,* 24 February 2001, A1–A2.

13   Roberts, "Rock Royalty."

14   An *Internet Archive* capture showing a period in 2001, where the Salisbury House Website was temporarily offline before being re-launched. *Internet Archive,* "Wayback Machine," https://web.archive.org/web/20010406230021/http://www.salisburyhouse.ca/ (accessed 13 May 2023).

15   This tour is documented in the film *Fahrenheit 7-11,* which explores Winnipeg's feelings for Cummings, and vice versa.

16   *Fahrenheit 7-11,* Walter Forsberg, dir.; Ultramega, "Panis Angelicus," 17 December 2021, https://www.instagram.com/ultramega204/?hl=en (accessed 13 May 2023); Smoky Tiger "Corporal Compliance" (2021), https://thesmokytiger1.bandcamp.com/album/corporal-compliance (accessed 13 May 2023).

17   "Confusion Corner" is the colloquial name of the Osborne Junction, a convoluted intersection at Pembina Highway, Osborne Street, Donald Street and Corydon Avenue. See: *Wikipedia,* "Confusion Corner," https://en.wikipedia.org/wiki/Confusion_Corner (accessed 13 May 2023).

18   Geoff Kirbyson, "Sals Ready to Say Bonjour," *Winnipeg Free Press,* 30 June 2005, B6. This was not universally celebrated in Winnipeg, as "some St. Boniface residents [hoped] for an exclusive eatery that celebrated Franco-Manitoban cuisine and culture." See Mary Agnes Welch, "St. Boniface Critics Nip at Plan to Put Sals on Bridge," *Winnipeg Free Press,* 17 February 2005, https://www.winnipegfreepress.com/historic/2005/02/17/st-boniface-critics-nip-at-plan-to-put-sals-on-bridge (accessed 13 May 2023); and Bartley Kives, "It's a Game of Crepes," *Winnipeg Free Press,* 28 November 2007, A3.

19   Kirbyson, "Sals Ready to Say Bonjour."

20   When the Esplanade Riel was constructed, equipping this midway stop with the plumbing necessities required for accommodating a restaurant was a source of contention among city residents. It was highly criticized, and the phrase "million-dollar toilet" became synonymous with the restaurant space on the bridge. See Tom Brodbeck, "Taxpayers' Cost Nips in to Esplanade Restaurant Viability," *Winnipeg Sun,* 15 January 2013, https://winnipegsun.com/2013/01/15/taxpayers-cut-nips-in-to-esplanade-restaurant-viability (accessed 13 May 2023); *CBC News,* "Toilet Gets Mayor in Hot Water with Taxpayers," 19 May 2003.

21   Carol Sanders, "Frigid Temps Force Sals to Take Winter Break," *Winnipeg Free Press,* 31 December 2008.

22   Kirbyson and Paul, "Rocker, Pals Put Winnipeg Institution."

23   Dickie Dee is a company founded in Winnipeg that sold its ice cream on the street via tricycles with small freezer compartments; the tricycle's bells alerted

children to a vendor's presence in their neighbourhood in summer. *CBC News*, "Sals Company Names New President, Forms New Financial Plan," 30 March 2006, https://www.cbc.ca/news/canada/manitoba/sals-company-names-new-president-forms-new-financial-plan-1.576116 (accessed 13 May 2023). Shareholders also agreed at this meeting to inject 500,000 dollars into the company to address immediate debts.

24   This is produced locally by Fort Garry Brewing Company.

25   Presumably similar to a kaiser roll, the Salisbury House menu describes the Beef Dip sandwich as "roast beef piled high on Sals own FRESH baked Winni bun." *Salisbury House,* "Breakfast Lunch and Dinner Menu: Sandwiches," https://www.salisburyhouse.ca/menu (accessed 13 May 2023).

26   Facebook, "Salisbury House," 10 September 2021, https://www.facebook.com/page/528065677354727/search/?q=car%20hop (accessed 13 May 2023). The Sals Market web page still notes car hop service, although a phone call placed by Kim on 18 July 2023 confirmed it had been discontinued the winter of 2022–23. See: https://www.salisburyhouse.ca/home (accessed 18 July 2023).

27   Barish actually sold the majority shares of Sals to a group that included local restaurateur Noel Bernier, the Metis Economic Development Fund (MEDF), and lawyer David Filmon. After recovering from a health scare, Barish reacquired his shares two years later. Martin Cash, "He's Got a Little Red Roof Over His Head, Again," *Winnipeg Free Press*, 30 July 2019, https://www.winnipegfreepress.com/arts-and-life/food/2019/07/30/hes-got-a-little-red-roof-over-his-head-again (accessed 13 May 2023).

28   Donohue, *Erwin Story,* 27. This is Ralph Erwin's official biography, written in 1982 by Patrick Donohue and compiled by Phyllis Erwin Ketcheson. It is based on the author's interviews with Ralph and Helen Erwin.

29   Ibid., 29. In 1920 the Martin Erwin Players were contracted by the larger Canadian Chautauquas group.

30   Ibid., 70.

31   Ibid., 76.

32   Ibid.

33   Ibid., 91.

34   Ibid., 76. It is possible that Erwin steered clear of using "hamburger," opting for something "more British" due to widespread anti-German sentiment during this period. See Aspen Moore, "A Short History of Hamburgers," *all the whyzer* blog post, 12 May 2021, https://allthewhyser.com/2021/05/12/a-short-history-of-hamburgers/ (accessed 13 May 2023); and Michaela Hallifax, "Anti-Japanese and Germanphobic Sentiments: Perpetuating Fear and Loathing of the Enemy in Commando Comics," 15, 3 April 2017, https://cla.blog.torontomu.ca/anti-japanese-and-germanphobic-sentiments-perpetuating-fear-and-loathing-of-the-enemy-in-commando-comics-issue-no-15/ (accessed 13 May 2023).

35   *The Erwin Story* states there were "12 restaurants on the street" (Donohue, *Erwin Story*, 92). While the *Henderson's Directories* often do not include every person or business, the 1931 directory lists 272 Fort as vacant, two fish and chips shops, three cafés, and one establishment simply noted "Chinese" (*Henderson's Directorie*s, 1931, 380–81).

36   Donohue, *Erwin Story,* 92.

37   On his travels north from the U.S., Erwin decided these would be a feature of the restaurant. On his way north, he'd met a representative from the Albert Pick Equipment Company. One thing led to another, and with assistance from friend Win Forbes, Ewin would eventually import Silex coffee machines into Winnipeg beginning in 1931 (Donohue, *Erwin Story*, 81, 92–95). The first ad for Silex coffee makers, taken out by City of Winnipeg Hydro Electric Systems, appears in the *Winnipeg Free Press*, 15 December 1931.

38   Donohue, *Erwin Story,* 100. Erwin used Heinz beans in the chili, and his biography makes the claim that, given the popularity of the chili, Heinz requested to use the recipe on the label on their tins.

39   Donohue, *Erwin Story*, 108–9.

40   The earliest Salisbury House advertisement appeared in the *Winnipeg Free Press* in 1932. However, staying open late evidently came with hazards, as through the 1930s the *Winnipeg Free Press* also reported Salisbury House had been robbed at least a half-dozen times.

41 The restaurant was owned by Fred Haddad and was also a grocery store (*The Manitoban*, 9 October 1933, 3). Similarly, if you visit Skinner's drive-in in Lockport, Manitoba, an old menu board (date unknown) lists "Nips" among the menu items.

42 *Winnipeg Free Press*, 17 December 1934.

43 Salisbury House, "Our History Your Sals," https://www.salisburyhouse.ca/history (accessed 15 December 2021). The first Winnipeg newspaper ad for the Flin Flon location appears in a 1940 "Vacation in Manitoba's Northland" spread, *Winnipeg Tribune*, 23 May 1940, 26.

44 Jakle and Sculle, *Roadside Restaurant*, 31–33.

45 Ibid., 39.

46 Gutman, *American Diner*, 14.

47 Elias, *Lunch*, 26.

48 Turner, "Buying not Cooking," 26. Elias indicates that lunch had been a normal part of urban life since at least the 1850s (Elias, *Lunch*, 98).

49 Turner, "Buying not Cooking," 16.

50 Elias, *Lunch*, 29.

51 Turner, "Buying not Cooking," 16.

52 T.H. Buckley, lunch wagon manufacturer, developed the famous "Tile Wagon." Largely for promotional purposes, its interior was lined with opal tile; it boasted nickel-plated, glass-top stools, stained-glass windows, ivory and gold lamps, and brass spittoons (Gutman, *American Diner*, 27).

53 Gutman, *American Diner*, 48. Tierney's company, P.J. Tierney Sons, would become a publicly traded company, which included a "lunch wagon training college" and operated until the stock market crash forced them out of business. With sad irony, Tierney died of acute indigestion.

54 Gutman, *American Diner*, 58.

55 Bluestone, "'Pushcart Evil,'" 71. Early advocates of the night lunch wagon included the Women's Christian Temperance Union of New York, who had purchased several in an effort to lure the hungry out of saloons prior to prohibition. See Gutman, *American Diner*, 62.

56 Bluestone, "'Pushcart Evil,'" 89.

57 Ibid., 70.

58 City of Winnipeg Archives, City of Winnipeg By-Laws, File 314, 1885.

59 Ibid.

60 Ibid., File 3087, 1904, and File 3112, 1904.

61 Ibid., File 12990, 1928.

62 Ibid., File 14677, 1934.

63 See, for example, Ellen Drew in "Reaching for the Sun," *Winnipeg Free Press*, 1 November 1940, 12; and a 1940s exposé about the 1926 hit "A Cup of Coffee, a Sandwich, and You," *Winnipeg Free Press*, 21 September 1940, 33.

64 *Winnipeg Daily Tribune*, 19 March 1903, 11.

65 *Winnipeg Daily Tribune*, 2 April 1903, 11. This was an interesting argument, considering that the night lunch wagon would have operated through the night and not through peak traffic times. The proximity of the Main Street and Higgins Avenue location to the Canadian Pacific Railway Station, where there were presumably trains arriving and some related traffic at all hours, might have influenced this.

66 Although saloons provided a reliable place for lunch, this option would have disappeared with Manitoba's flirtation with prohibition between 1916 and 1923.

67 Statistics Canada. Table 98-10-0357-01 Ethnic or cultural origin by gender and age: Canada, provinces and territories and census divisions. DOI: https://doi.org/10.25318/9810035701-eng. For more on the Greek Canadian experience, see Chimbos, *Canadian Odyssey*, and Vlassis, *Greeks in Canada*.

68 "*Ciao!* reviews: C. Kelekis," *Winnipeg Free Press*, 23 September 2000, 238.

69 Christian Cassidy, "680 Victor Street—Commercial Building (R.I.P.)," *Winnipeg Downtown Places* blog post, 24 July 2021, https://winnipegdowntownplaces.blogspot.com/2021/07/680-victor-street-commercial-building.html?m=1 (accessed 15 May 2023).

70 Geoff Kirbyson and Bill Redekop, "Kelekis Eatery Cashes in Chips," *Winnipeg Free Press*, 1 December 2012. The 1940 *Henderson's Directory* for Winnipeg demotes Kelekis to "pedlar" from "confectioner (1932)."

See Peel's Prairie Provinces, *Henderson's Directory Winnipeg*, 1940, 864, http://peel.library.ualberta.ca/bibliography/921.4.21/636.html?qid=peelbib%7CKelekis%7C%28peelnum%3A000921.4.21%29%7Cscore (accessed 15 May 2023).

71   *Winnipeg Free Press*, "'It's Been a Wonderful 70 Years,'" 30 January 2013, 13. The first was at 935 Main Street, and the second less than a kilometre away at 929 Main Street. See *Henderson's Directory Winnipeg*, 1945, 165 and 663.

72   The eclectic mix of bannock and Italian foods is owing to Faraci's mixed Italian and Métis ancestry. See the Faraci Foods website, "About Us," http://www.faraci-foods.com/about-us/ (accessed 15 May 2023).

73   Anthony Faraci, interviewed by Emily Gartner and Trent Brownlee, 16 May 2019, 00:17:00–00:17:26.

74   *Henderson's Directory Winnipeg*, 1939, 329.

75   Ibid., 771.

76   Turner, "Buying not Cooking," 32.

77   *Henderson's Directory Winnipeg*, 1943, 806.

78   *Henderson's Directory Winnipeg*, 1947.

79   Personal correspondence with Anthony Faraci. Many thanks to the Faraci family for helping to piece together Sam's story.

80   Benson, "Hawking and Peddling," 79.

81   Turner, "Buying not Cooking," 32–34, and Gutman, *American Diner*, 37. Turner argues that in the eastern U.S., although home cooking was more economically frugal, most people supplemented home booking with ready-made food, as it was "cheaper in time, effort, skills, or equipment."

82   Although no last name is included, a 1963 article published in the *Winnipeg Tribune* pays tribute to Nick the Popcorn Man, who took the opposite path, from a restaurant to a popcorn wagon. At eighty years old, he was still selling popcorn from a wagon on the corner of Main Street and Pacific Avenue. *Winnipeg Tribune*, 19 September 1965, 6.

83   "Name Committee to Study Report on Restaurants," *Winnipeg Evening Tribune*, 22 October 1936, 4.

84   *El Toro*, 2018, 00:02:13–00:02:20.

85   Heimann, *Car Hops*, 12.

86   Manitoba Archives, Government Records Departmental File, Companies Office, Business Names Registration Files, GR12625. This tally is an approximation, as it was done manually.

87   Jakle and Sculle, *Fast Food*, 40–41.

88   Heimann, *Car Hops*, 11.

89   Ibid., 14.

90   Ibid., 28.

91   Ibid., 56. Heimann dates the concept of curb service much earlier, however, to a Memphis drugstore that hired runners to carry soda out to patrons (13).

92   Ibid., 32–33.

93   Ibid., 84–85.

94   Ibid., 118.

95   Ibid., 121.

96   Jakle and Sculle, *Fast Food*, 54–55.

97   Donohue, *Erwin Story*, 122–23.

98   This was two years prior to the first Canadian A&W Drive In, which opened in Winnipeg in 1956.

99   *Winnipeg Tribune*, 4 June 1955, 23.

100   *Winnipeg Free Press*, 13 June 1956, 29.

101   *Winnipeg Tribune*, 28 March 1961, 226.

102   Legris, "Drive-in Copes with Cold Winters," *Canadian Hotel Review and Restaurant*, 15 May 1960, 33, 36.

103   Ibid., 33.

104   Ritchie was also involved in another drive-in separate from this franchise, the MotorClub Drive Inn, at 680 St. James Street.

105   *Winnipeg Free Press*, 26 August 1967, 18. The head office of River Rouge Tours was located adjacent to the drive-In.

106   Statistics Canada, "Historical Statistics, Immigration to Canada, by Country of Last Permanent Residence." These data were organized by country of origin, so

would not include others of Greek ethnicity, like Mr. Kelekis, who immigrated from surrounding countries.

107 John Calogeris, interviewed by Janis Thiessen, 20 August 2019, 00:27:20–00:28:00.

108 John Ginakes and Demitris Scouras, interviewed by Zachary Hamilton, 15 December 2017, 00:11:50–00:12:12.

109 Ibid., 00:12:12–00:14:30. The *Henderson's Directory* lists George and John Furtis as occupants during this time.

110 Cory Funk, "'They Stole the Recipe, Which Is Good': How the Fat Boy Burger Became a Winnipeg Icon," *CBC Manitoba*, 3 November 2019, https://www.cbc.ca/news/canada/manitoba/fat-boy-burger-winnipeg-icon-1.5344645 (accessed 16 May 2023).

111 Joe Paraskevas, "A Big Empty Spot in City's Heart," *Winnipeg Free Press*, 23 August 2007, 15.

112 Funk, "'They Stole the Recipe.'" There is still a restaurant in Thunder Bay called the Westort Coney Island, currently owned by Victoria Saites. Theodore Saites, her husband, established the restaurant around 1950. He and the Scouras family immigrated to Canada from Krokilio, Greece. Thank you to Panagiota Saites for clarifying this detail (email correspondence, 2 February 2023).

113 1935 *Henderson's Directory*. The 1952 *Henderson's Directory* lists Herb Cook as the proprietor (*Henderson's Directory Winnipeg*, 1952, 826). Shortly after, Gus left Winnipeg to work on the DEW Line (Funk, "'They Stole the Recipe'").

114 David Sanderson, "Like Father, Like Son," *Winnipeg Free Press*, 23 November 2014, 8.

115 Paraskevas, "Big Empty Spot."

116 See Alexandra Paul, "New Owner Promises Red Top Will Stay the Same," *Winnipeg Free Press*, 22 December 2018, 37; "Winnipeg's Iconic Red Top Drive-In Will Stay the Same, New Owner Says," *CBC News*, 23 December 2018, https://www.cbc.ca/news/canada/manitoba/red-top-winnipeg-new-owner-1.4957750 (accessed 15 May 2023).

117 Paul, "New Owner Promises Red Top" and *CBC News*, "*Winnipeg's iconic* Red Top."

118 John Calogeris interview, 00:02:56–03:50.

119 "Spiros (Nick) Calogeris," *Winnipeg Free Press*, 26 December 1989, 51.

120 Maureen Scurfield, "Famous Burger Joint Draws Worldly Crowd," *Winnipeg Free Press*, 4 August 2010, 13.

121 Manitoba Archives, Government Records Departmental File, Companies Office, Business Names Registration Files, GR12625.

122 After leaving Junior's on Main Street, Gus Scouras would take the name "Junior's" with him, and establish the Junior's restaurant chain in Winnipeg. There are hints of a naming dispute in this matter, but there are not enough public records to write about this in any detail. This gap in records also leaves some question as to what the name of 170 Main Street was between 1971 and 1981, when it became VJ's.

123 Funk, "'They Stole the Recipe.'"

124 John Calogeris interview, 00:21:30–00:22:00.

125 John Ginakes and Demitris Scouras interview, 00:48:00–00:50:00.

126 The Coney Island Lunch at 564½ Main Street, which first appeared in the *Henderson's Directory* in 1934, is easily confused in the directory with the Original Coney Island located at 421 Portage (owned by Clifford Needham), which appears in the directory the following year. See: *Henderson's Directory Winnipeg*, 1934, 1022; and *Henderson's* 1935, 1029. However, the two locations are listed together as "Original Coney Island Lunch" spots in a 1934 advertisement in *The Manitoban*, so ownership in the first and second year is not entirely clear.

127 Erick Trickey, "The Origin of the Coney Island Hot Dog is a Uniquely American Story: They Also Have Very Little to Do with the New York City Amusement Park," *Smithsonian Magazine*, "History," 30 June 2016, https://www.smithsonianmag.com/history/origins-coney-island-hot-dog-uniquely-american-story-180959659/ (accessed 19 May 2023).

128 Arielle Godbout, "History of Red Top and Family Intertwined for 50 Years," *Winnipeg Free Press*, 12 August 2010, https://www.winnipegfreepress.com/our-commu-

nities/herald/History-of-Red-Top-and-family-inter-twined-for-50-years-100378284.html (accessed 15 May 2023).

129 *You Gotta Eat Here!*, Food Network Canada, https://www.foodnetwork.ca/shows/you-gotta-eat-here/recipe/red-top-burger/12529/ (accessed 30 April 2021).

130 "Obituary: Peter Speros Scouras," *Winnipeg Free Press*, 4 March 2017, https://passages.winnipegfreepress.com/passage-details/id-243675/SCOURAS_PETER (accessed 15 May 2023).

131 "Winnipeg's Iconic Red Top Drive-In."

132 Trickey, "The Origin of the Coney Island Hot Dog."

133 Ibid.

134 Stern and Stern, *500 Things to Eat.*

135 Grimm and Yung, *Coney Detroit*, 1–2.

136 Adam Waito, "Good Old-Fashioned Eats: Thunder Bay's Best Diners and Greasy Spoons," *Northern Ontario Travel*, 7 March 2019, https://www.northernontario.travel/thunder-bay/thunder-bay-s-best-diners-greasy-spoons-and-comfort-food (accessed 19 May 2023). Thank you to Bartley Kives for pointing us toward this source.

137 Although Saites was not related to the Saites who established the Westfort Coney Island, and the Westfort Coney Island was not the same "Coney Island" restaurant where the Scourases learned to make Greek chili, all these men had a connection in that they immigrated from Krokilio, Greece. Thank you to Panagiota Saites for clarifying these details.

138 *Henderson's Directory Winnipeg*, 1937. Andrew Petrakos is listed in that year's directory as "Andy Pestroskas." The spelling of his name varies with the source and the decade, as is common with ethnicized names in sources such as the *Henderson's Directory* and Census data.

139 *Winnipeg Tribune*, 1 March 1935.

140 Thank you to Christian Cassidy, author of the *West End Dumplings* blog, for steering us in this direction.

141 John Calogeris interview, 00:03:02–00:04:40. Junior (John Petrakos) partnered with Steve Hrousalas in purchasing Rae and Jerry's Steak House on Portage Avenue. See "Steak House Changes Hands After 18 Years," *Winnipeg Free Press,* 21 March 1975, 3.

142 "Junior's: A Local Success Story," *Winnipeg Tribune*, 9 February 1979, 17 and 22. In this article, Petrakos is spelled "Petrakis."

143 Salisbury House website, https://www.salisburyhouse.ca/locations#:~:text=From%20classic%20breakfasts%20to%20hearty,everyone%20at%20your%20favourite%20Sals! (accessed 7 October 2023).

144 Until the COVID-19 pandemic began to put strain on the restaurant industry beginning March 2019, the Pembina Highway and Fermor Avenue locations were open all night. At the time of writing, there are no longer any Salisbury Houses open twenty-four hours.

145 *CTV News Winnipeg*, "'Those Are Memories You Retain for a Long Time'; Main Street and Matheson Salisbury House up for Sale," 5 February 2023, https://winnipeg.ctvnews.ca/those-are-memories-you-retain-for-a-long-long-time-main-and-matheson-salisbury-house-up-for-sale-1.6261013 (accessed 19 May 2023).

146 Funk, "'They Stole the Recipe.'"

147 John Calogeris interview, 00:42:17–00:42:41.

148 "Winnipeg Landmark Thunderbird Pours Cold Water on 'Grande' Plans for Starbucks Next Door," *CBC Manitoba*, 2 December 2022, https://www.cbc.ca/news/canada/manitoba/winnipeg-thunderbird-star-bucks-1.6670055 (accessed 19 May 2023).

149 George Freeman, "The Trouble with Winnipeg," *The Manitoban*, 4 November 1941, 4.

150 For an expertly crafted exploration of this "ambivalence," see Kives and Scott, *Stuck in the Middle.*

151 *First We Feast*, "The Burger Scholar: Canadian Burgers," 21 February 2022. In this YouTube episode, "Burger Scholar" (George Motz) assigns credit for the Fat Boy to the Scouras brothers. https://youtu.be/e6zUff1UgRo (accessed 19 May 2023).

152 "Winnipeg Fat Boy," 28 November 2021, https://www.instagram.com/thewrendanforth/?hl=en (accessed 19 May 2023).

CHAPTER THREE

1   Fujiwara, *Ethnic Elites and Canadian Identity*, 23.
    A testament to the significance of the Ukrainian
    population in Manitoba is the Holodomor memorial
    in front of Winnipeg's city hall, erected in 1984 on the
    fiftieth anniversary of the famine/genocide in Ukraine.
    "Holodomor Monument Commemorating the 50th
    Anniversary," Ukrainian Canadian Congress Mani-
    toba, 24 July 2020, https://uccmanitoba.ca/2020/07/
    holodomor-monument-commemorating-the-50th-an-
    niversary/ (accessed 19 May 2023).

2   Zembrzycki, "'We Didn't Have a Lot,'" 134.

3   Also known as the informal, invisible, secondary,
    irregular, or criminal food economy. Reimer, "Informal
    Economy," 24.

4   Education professor Srabani Maitra references Statistics
    Canada data demonstrating that the work of Canadian
    women has become increasingly informalized and do-
    mesticized since the 1990s. Maitra, "Are We Not Being
    Entrepreneurial?," 330.

5   Knezevic, "Illicit Food," 413.

6   Patsy Kozek, "Elma," *Steinbach Carillon*, 20 August
    2009, 9A.

7   Marion Pederson, "Marchand," *Steinbach Carillon*, 8
    January 2004, 12A.

8   Jean Wensel obituary, *Winnipeg Free Press*, 11 October
    2007, 32.

9   Classified advertisement, *Selkirk Journal*, 2 November
    1998, 43.

10 Classified advertisement, *Winnipeg Free Press*, 7 July
    1966, 33.

11 Classified advertisement, *Brandon Sun*, 14 December
    1967, 16.

12 Classified advertisement, *Winnipeg Free Press*, 19 Sep-
    tember 1969, 32.

13 Classified advertisement, *Winnipeg Free Press*, 2 January
    1967, 25.

14 Patricia McIntyre and Maureen Martin Osland, inter-
    viewed by Kimberley Moore, 3 July 2019, 00:05:56–
    00:06:44.

15 Helen McEwan, interviewed by Janis Thiessen, Kent
    Davies, and Kimberley Moore, 14 June 2019, 00:31:47–
    00:32:02. .

16 Manitoba Agriculture, "Direct Marketing Your Food
    Product," https://www.gov.mb.ca/agriculture/food-and-
    ag-processing/pubs/direct-marketing-your-food-prod-
    uct.pdf (accessed 23 May 2023).

17 Government of Manitoba, "Public Health Act, Food
    and Food Handling Establishments Regulation," Sec-
    tion 1, https://web2.gov.mb.ca/laws/regs/current/_pdf-
    regs.php?reg=339/88%20R (accessed 23 May 2023).

18 Manitoba Health, Seniors and Active Living, "Farmers'
    Market Guidelines," June 2019, https://www.gov.mb.ca/
    health/publichealth/environmentalhealth/protection/
    docs/farmers_market.pdf (accessed 14 September
    2021).

19 Holly Moore, "Complex Rules for Home-based Food
    Spark Need for Commercial Kitchens," *CBC News*, 18
    July 2015, https://www.cbc.ca/news/canada/manitoba/
    complex-rules-for-home-based-food-spark-need-for-
    commercial-kitchens-1.3153095 (accessed 23 May
    2023).

20 Government of Manitoba, "Public Health Act, Food
    and Food Handling," Section 3(4)a.

21 Ibid., Sections 19.3, 20, and 21.

22 Rachel Bergen, "Manitoba Chefs Giving up on Tradi-
    tional Trappist-style Cheese, Blame Costly Provincial
    Roadblocks," *CBC News Manitoba*, 22 November
    2019, https://www.cbc.ca/news/canada/manitoba/
    trappist-cheese-monk-prairie-tradition-1.5367918
    (accessed 23 May 2023); Government of Manitoba,
    "Public Health Act, Food and Food Handling," Section
    17.

23 City of Winnipeg Archives, City of Winnipeg By-
    Laws, Box 1 files 7 and 11, 1874.

24 Ibid., Box 1 file 51, 1875.

25 Ibid., Box 1 file 48, 1875; Box 1 file 73, 1877; Box 1 file
    91, 1878.

26 Ibid., Box 1 file 722, 1894.

27 Ibid., Box 1 file 8085, 1913.

28 As Jennifer McDonald explains, "Cottage foods are products for human consumption produced in a private home for commercial sale." McDonald, "Relationship Between Cottage Food Laws," 21.

29 Government of Saskatchewan, "Government Removes Barriers on Homebased Food Business," 29 June 2016, https://www.saskatchewan.ca/government/news-and-media/2016/june/29/homebased-food-businesses (accessed 23 May 2023); Government of Saskatchewan, "Food Safety," Section 4, https://www.saskatchewan.ca/residents/environment-public-health-and-safety/food-safety#home-food-processing (accessed 23 May 2023); Government of Saskatchewan, "Key Proposed Changes to The Food Safety Regulations–September 2022," 3, 1, https://publications.saskatchewan.ca/#/products/113120 (accessed 23 May 2023).

30 McDonald, "Relationship Between Cottage Food Laws," 21.

31 Betty Shumka, interviewed by Janis Thiessen, 3 August 2019, 00:01:40–00:01:53.

32 Ibid., 00:24:25–00:25:30.

33 Ibid., 00:21:10–00:21:40.

34 Ibid., 00:03:11–00:03:40.

35 Ibid., 00:23:48–00:42:11.

36 Ibid., 00:26:20–0:27:08.

37 McDonald, "Relationship Between Cottage Food Laws," 26. Sara Teitelbaum and Thomas Beckley, by contrast, find in their study of rural Canadian self-provisioning that there is "no clear relationship between income and participation in the informal economy." Teitelbaum and Beckley, "Harvested, Hunted and Home Grown," 118.

38 McDonald, "Relationship Between Cottage Food Laws," 27.

39 United Nations Food and Agriculture Organization (UNFAO), *The Informal Food Sector: Municipal Support Policies for Operators* (Rome, 2003), 1.

40 Ibid., 3; Maitra, "Are We Not Being Entrepreneurial?" 335.

41 For example, 18 percent of people in Rangamati, Bangladesh, are employed in the informal food sector;

32 percent in Guayaquil, Ecuador; 48 percent in Lagos, Nigeria. UNFAO, *Informal Food Sector,* 22.

42 Ommer and Turner, "Informal Rural Economies," 156; Thompson, *Whigs and Hunters*; Peluso, "*Whigs and Hunters,*" 313.

43 Reimer, "Informal Economy in Non-Metropolitan Canada," 24.

44 Knezevic, "Illicit Food," 414.

45 Kulinski, "'It Comes with Practice,'" 13.

46 Anthropologist Charlotte van de Vorst notes that more profitable farms, rural depopulation, and increased regulation of food meant that fewer Manitoba farm women produced food for sale in their homes after the Second World War. Van de Vorst, *Making Ends Meet*, 85–86.

47 Maria Bohuslawsky, "Fear Strangles Corner Stores," *Winnipeg Free Press*, 23 January 1988, 49.

48 Ibid.

49 Elizabeth Fraser, "Bannock Lady Won't Be Deterred," *Winnipeg Free Press*, 26 August 2013, A4.

50 "Salutes for Human Rights," *Winnipeg Free Press*, 28 November 2014, B5.

51 Larry Kusch, "Bannock Lady Extends Reach in Point Douglas," *Winnipeg Free Press*, 31 December 2015, A7; Riley Martin, "Manitoba Election 2016: Point Douglas Riding," *Global News*, 18 April 2016, https://globalnews.ca/news/2592509/manitoba-election-2016-point-douglas-riding/ (accessed 23 May 2023).

52 Carol Sanders, "Spring Roll Fundraiser a Wrap," *Winnipeg Free Press*, 2 April 2014, B1.

53 "Gilbert Plains Receives Grant for Community Hall Kitchen," *Grandview Exponent*, 1 November 2016, 11; "Teulon-Rockwood Centennial Centre Receiving $10K," *Stonewall Argus,* 3 November 2016, 8.

54 "Hadashville Rec Centre Gets Kitchen Upgrade," *Beausejour Clipper,* 15 December 2016, 5.

55 Manitoba Health, "Notice to Home-Based Food Businesses," https://www.gov.mb.ca/health/publichealth/environmentalhealth/protection/home.html (accessed 23 May 2023). According to the Internet

Archive's Wayback Machine, this announcement was first posted in July 2016, (https://web.archive.org/web/20160724021753/https://www.gov.mb.ca/health/publichealth/environmentalhealth/protection/home.html) (accessed 23 May 2023).

56 Holly Caruk, "Home-based Food Sales Stirring up Trouble with Manitoba's Health Inspectors," *CBC News*, 18 December 2017, https://www.cbc.ca/news/canada/manitoba/home-based-food-sale-inspectors-manitoba-1.4449379 (accessed 23 May 2023).

57 "Deerboine Homemade Goods Sale Unlikely to Be Held Again," *Brandon Sun*, 12 August 2016, A2.

58 Austin Grabish, "Illegal Home Kitchens Taking a Bite Out of Restaurant Business, Says Winnipeg Café Owner," *CBC News Manitoba*, 6 April 2021, https://www.cbc.ca/news/canada/manitoba/home-kitchens-restaurant-business-concerns-1.5968976 (accessed 23 May 2023).

59 Eva Wasney, "Feeling the Heat," *Winnipeg Free Press*, 30 June 2021, https://www.winnipegfreepress.com/arts-and-life/food/feeling-the-heat-574743332.html (accessed 23 May 2023).

60 Ibid.; "Home Cooks Could Be in Hot Water," *Winnipeg Free Press*, 3 July 2021, G2.

61 Grabish, "Illegal Home Kitchens."

62 Corey Mintz, "Perogy Pinch: The Prairies' Fine, and Dying, Art," *Globe and Mail*, 1 December 2017, A1.

63 "St. Joseph's Parish Perogy Miracle," St. Joseph's Ukrainian Catholic Church, https://www.stjosephukrwinnipeg.ca/st-joseph/ (accessed 23 May 2023).

64 "'We Make the Best Perogies in Manitoba': Holy Eucharist Promises Winnipeg's Largest Perogy Bash," *CBC News*, 14 April 2018, https://www.cbc.ca/news/canada/manitoba/perogy-fundraiser-winnipeg-bash-1.4619389 (accessed 23 May 2023).

65 Mintz, "Perogy Pinch"; Allan Besson, "Quest for the Best Perogy," *Winnipeg Free Press*, 28 November 2010, https://www.winnipegfreepress.com/local/quest-for-the-best-perogy-110930074.html (accessed 23 May 2023).

66 Western Ukrainians say "pyrohy" (as Joyce Sirski-Howell does here), eastern Ukrainians say "varenyky," and Poles say "pierogi." "Perogy" is perhaps the most common term used in Manitoba.

67 Joyce Sirski-Howell, interviewed by Janis Thiessen, 3 August 2019, 00:35:02–00:39:40.

68 A bridge between the mass-produced perogy and the hand-pinched perogy was provided by the 1976 invention of Hunky Bill's Perogy Maker: see Madison Herget-Schmidt, "A Perogy Story," Manitoba Food History Project, 2 August 2022, https://www.manitobafoodhistory.ca/story-maps/2022/08/02/perogy (accessed 23 May 2023).

69 Classified advertisement, *Winnipeg Free Press*, 29 August 1970, 34.

70 Lois Braun, "Memorable Manitobans: Marion Bodnar Staff (1926–2004)," *Manitoba Historical Society*, 18 February 2021, http://www.mhs.mb.ca/docs/people/staff_mb.shtml (accessed 23 May 2023); "Alycia's," *Ciao!* (2010), http://www.ciaowinnipeg.com/alycias/ (accessed 23 May 2023).

71 Sharon Staff and Roger Leclerc, interviewed by Russ Gourluck, 22 July 2009, 00:00:30-00:01:18.

72 Ibid., 00:02:38–00:03:15.

73 Ibid., 00:04:33–00:05:19.

74 Roger Leclerc describes the dramatic increase in costs of potatoes and flour (two essential ingredients for a Ukrainian restaurant) in the 2009 Sharon Staff and Roger Leclerc interview with Russ Gourluck; these cost increases may have been the cause of the restaurant's 2011 closure.

75 "Former Iconic Ukrainian Restaurant in North End Finds New Home in Gimli," *CBC News*, 17 June 2016, https://www.cbc.ca/news/canada/manitoba/alycias-ukrainian-perogies-opens-in-gimli-1.3640607 (accessed 23 May 2023); David Sanderson, "The Second Coming of Alycia's," *Winnipeg Free Press*, 3 December 2017, https://www.winnipegfreepress.com/local/the-second-coming-of-alycias-461588533.html (accessed 23 May 2023); Shane Gibson, "Alycia's Restaurant Is Coming Back to Winnipeg," *CBC News*, 4 February 2018, https://www.cbc.ca/news/canada/manitoba/alycias-winnipeg-ukrainian-royal-albert-1.4518937 (accessed 23 May 2023).

76 Sevala's Ukrainian Deli, "About Us," https://www.seva-las.com/-about-us (accessed 23 May 2023); Truderung, *Transcona's Story*, 145; David Sanderson, "Better than Baba's?" *Winnipeg Free Press*, 3 January 2021, https://www.winnipegfreepress.com/local/better-than-ba-bas-573520212.html (accessed 23 May 2023); Murray McNeill, "Processors Feed Appetite for Traditional Ukrainian Food Perogy Paradise," *Winnipeg Free Press*, 23 June 2012, J5.

77 Bill Redekop, "Perogies Just Like Baba Used to Make," *Winnipeg Free Press*, 30 March 2015, https://www.winnipegfreepress.com/local/perogies-just-like-baba-used-to-make-297967281.html (accessed 23 May 2023).

78 Lyndenn Behm, "Rural Entrepreneur Makes Lots of Dough by Maintaining Quality," *Brandon Sun*, 13 October 1996, 1.

79 Murray McNeill, "Processors Feed Appetite for Traditional Ukrainian Food Perogy Paradise," *Winnipeg Free Press*, 23 June 2012, https://www.winnipegfreepress.com/special/ourcityourworld/ukraine/processors-feed-appetite-for-traditional-ukrainian-food-perogy-paradise-160104815.html (accessed 23 May 2023).

80 "Naleway Foods," *Canadian Business Journal* (13 February 2021), https://www.cbj.ca/naleway_foods/ (accessed 23 May 2023); David Sanderson, "Perogy Punk," *Winnipeg Free Press*, 16 April 2016, https://www.winnipegfreepress.com/arts-and-life/food/perogy-punk-375893031.html (accessed 23 May 2023); Doug Lunney, "Perogy Planet: The Next Generation," *Winnipeg Sun*, 8 January 2016, https://winnipegsun.com/2016/01/08/perogy-planet-the-next-generation (accessed 23 May 2023); Jared Story, "A Tasty Family Tradition," *Winnipeg Free Press*, 4 January 2016, https://www.winnipegfreepress.com/our-communities/lance/A-tasty-family-tradition-364142261.html (accessed 23 May 2023).

81 Ben Knight, "Perogies on the Prairies: Manitoba's European Community Keeping Traditions Alive," *Yahoo News Canada*, 21 September 2015, https://ca.news.yahoo.com/perogies-on-the-prairies--manitoba-s-european-community-keeping-traditions-alive-013001910.html (accessed 23 May 2023).

82 Julie van Rosendaal, "Bringing Back the Perogy Bee," *Globe and Mail*, 23 November 2016, L4.

83 Brian Laghi, "Perogy Empire Grew with Soviet Technology," *Globe and Mail*, 6 June 1997, A2.

84 Joyce Sirski-Howell interview, 00:45:24–00:45:41.

85 Ibid., 00:40:25–00:40:46.

86 Ibid., 00:28:16–00:28:34.

87 A rare exception is the interviews with perogy ladies conducted by Sarah Story, in her private possession, which she featured in her presentation as Janis's student at the Canadian Food History Symposium on 4 April 2013 at the University of Winnipeg.

CHAPTER FOUR

1 Gonzales, "Kitchenlessness," 72.

2 Joanelle Wichers and Geralyn Wichers, interviewed by Sarah Story, 2 July 2018, 01:39:55–01:40:06.

3 Ibid., 00:05:28–00:08:58.

4 Chornoboy, *Faspa*, 44.

5 Ibid., 44–45. Traditional Mennonite hog butchering has been an annual event at the Mennonite Heritage Village in Steinbach, https://mennoniteheritagevillage.com (accessed 23 May 2023).

6 Tipton-Martin, *Jubilee*, 223.

7 Ibid., 218. See also Miller, *Black Smoke*, 11–13.

8 *Barbecue Pitmasters* is a reality TV show that began airing on TLC in 2009; "Bubba" is a nickname for a white man from the southern United States.

9 Michael W. Twitty, "Barbecue Is an American Tradition—of Enslaved Africans and Native Americans," *The Guardian*, 4 July 2015, https://www.theguardian.com/commentisfree/2015/jul/04/barbecue-american-tradition-enslaved-africans-native-americans (accessed 23 May 2023). See also Twitty, *Cooking Gene*, 310–17.

10 Miller, *Black Smoke*, 33.

11 "A Barbecue," *Manitoba Daily Free Press*, 31 July 1890, 8.

12 Advertisement, *Winnipeg Tribune*, 23 August 1890, 8; advertisement, *Winnipeg Tribune*, 27 August 1890, 4.

13 Though the area that was Elm Park is now part of Winnipeg, it was not so in 1890. Five departing trains and three returning trains shuttled barbecue attendees to the event that day. Ibid.

14 "Two Big Picnics," *Manitoba Daily Free Press,* 29 August 1890, 8.

15 "Over 2,400 People Present," *Winnipeg Tribune,* 29 August 1890, 3.

16 Advertisement for interprovincial picnic, *Brandon Daily Sun,* 27 August 1930, 16.

17 "Inter-Provincial Picnic Promises to Be Big Event, Labor Day, September 1st," *Roblin Review,* 28 August 1930, 1.

18 "Monarch of Mushers Setting Fast Pace in Big Dog Derby," *Winnipeg Free Press,* 5 March 1930, 10.

19 "About $1,000 'Treaty' Paid Chipeweyans at Churchill," *Winnipeg Free Press,* 16 July 1932, 30.

20 "Homecoming Plans Complete," *The Manitoban,* 30 September 1930, 1.

21 Laura Lou Brookman, "The Leap Year Bride," *Winnipeg Tribune,* 1 October 1932, 40.

22 Classified advertisement, *Winnipeg Free Press,* 13 May 1931, 20.

23 Ibid.; classified advertisement, *Winnipeg Free Press,* 31 July 1931, 18; *Henderson's Directory Winnipeg,* 1932, 449. *Henderson's* lists the latter as Roycroft rather than Raycroft.

24 Classified advertisement, *Winnipeg Free Press,* 2 September 1933, 31; *Henderson's Directory Winnipeg,* 1932, 736, 816, 889.

25 "Woman Charged After Stabbing of Her Husband," *Winnipeg Free Press,* 19 March 1954, 1.

26 Classified advertisement, *Winnipeg Free Press,* 10 January 1935, 16; advertisement, *Winnipeg Tribune,* 1 May 1935, 6; classified advertisement, *Winnipeg Free Press,* 24 May 1935, 17. Eaton's was demolished in 2002 and an arena was opened at that location in 2004.

27 *Henderson's Directory Winnipeg,* 1947, 354, 697.

28 Advertisement, *Winnipeg Free Press,* 20 June 1934, 22; *Henderson's Directory Winnipeg,* 1933, 370, 572, 1276.

29 *Henderson's Directory Winnipeg,* 1933, 316, 589.

30 *Henderson's Directory Winnipeg,* 1947, 203.

31 John M. 'Jack' Bumsted, "Memorable Manitobans: Silvio Jack DiCosimo," *Manitoba Historical Society,* 5 March 2008, http://www.mhs.mb.ca/docs/people/dicosimo_sj.shtml (accessed 24 May 2023).

32 Classified advertisement, *Winnipeg Tribune,* 6 October 1942, 15; "Holdup Nets $75; Thief Sneaks $60," *Winnipeg Free Press,* 20 October 1942, 20.

33 Classified advertisement, *Winnipeg Free Press,* 7 September 1948, 20; classified advertisement, *Winnipeg Free Press,* 15 May 1947, 27; classified advertisement, *Winnipeg Free Press,* 9 September 1948, 25.

34 Christian Cassidy, "Manitoba Black History: Percy Haynes," *West End Dumplings* blog, 8 February 2012, https://westenddumplings.blogspot.com/2012/02/manitoba-black-history-percy-haynes.html (accessed 24 May 2023); Christian Cassidy, "Recipe for Success: Restaurateur, Musician and Athlete Excelled at Virtually Everything," *Winnipeg Free Press,* 8 February 2015, https://www.winnipegfreepress.com/local/recipe-for-success-291186151.html (accessed 24 May 2023).

35 Sheila Craig, "Where Southerners Seek Chicken," *Winnipeg Tribune,* 4 December 1954, 25. Two decades later, the seating had expanded to accommodate sixty-five. Cynthia Wine, "Cynthia Wine Says . . .," *Winnipeg Free Press,* 9 December 1972, 17.

36 Advertisement, *Winnipeg Free Press,* 7 November 1952, 4.

37 His first name was often misspelled as "Percy" in local newspapers.

38 Though he is a significant figure in Black history in this province, there are no archived oral history interviews with Haynes. He is one of the musicians featured, however, in the documentary *Prairie Soul: Black Rhythms from the Heartland* (Adrian Peek, 1991); trailer on YouTube at https://www.youtube.com/watch?v=MqPD3-1sn5Y.

39 See Walker, "Critical Histories of Blackness."

40 Christian Cassidy, "An Unceremonious End for One of Winnipeg's Historic Black Cultural Hubs," *West*

End Dumplings blog, 24 July 2020, https://westend-dumplings.blogspot.com/2020/07/an-unceremonious-end-for-one-of.html (accessed 24 May 2023).

41   Vernon, "Introduction," in *Black Prairie Archives*, 13; Sapoznik, "Where the Historiography Falls Short."

42   Winks, *Blacks in Canada*, 303. Karina Vernon notes that they also arrived from Kansas, Texas, and Missouri. Vernon, "Introduction," in *Black Prairie Archives*, 19–20.

43   Hartman, "Churches of Early Winnipeg"; Manitoba Historical Society, "MHS Resources: Historic Sites of Manitoba," 28 April 2019, http://www.mhs.mb.ca/docs/sites/index.shtml (accessed 24 May 2023).

44   "Dining Car Dispute," *Manitoba Free Press*, 30 May 1918, 10. Saje Mathieu examines the history of Black railway workers and their exclusion from White labour unions in *North of the Color Line*.

45   Saje Mathieu, quoted in Bryce Hoye, "A Century Ago, Winnipeg Railways Became 'Birthplace' of Fight for Black Canadian Workers' Rights," *CBC News Manitoba*, 29 February 2020, https://www.cbc.ca/news/canada/manitoba/sleeping-car-porters-winnipeg-1.5477349 (accessed 24 May 2023). For the comparable situation in Montreal's Little Burgundy neighbourhood, see High, "Little Burgundy."

46   For example, a 1914 newspaper article describes that a local politician, at a meeting of "colored voters," "spoke of a college companion in Halifax who was a colored man, and told the audience that they should be satisfied so long as the government did not legislate against them." "Big Surprise for Roblin Candidates," *Manitoba Free Press*, 4 July 1914, 11.

47   Adomako-Ansah and Joachim, *Black on the Prairies*, 11.

48   Melissa Fundira, "What These 10 Graphics Say About Black People on the Prairies," *CBC Saskatchewan*, 25 April 2021, https://www.cbc.ca/news/canada/saskatchewan/black-on-the-prairies-by-the-numbers-1.5990990 (accessed 24 May 2023).

49   Markus Chambers was elected to Winnipeg City Council in 2018; Uzoma Asagwara, Audrey Gordon, and Jamie Moses were elected as MLAs in 2019. George Waldron Prout, whose mother identified as having Black ancestry though he apparently did not, was elected as an MLA in 1915. Gordon Goldsbor-

ough, "Memorable Manitobans: George Waldron Prout (1878–c1980)," *Manitoba Historical Society*, 8 November 2021, http://www.mhs.mb.ca/docs/people/prout_gw.shtml (accessed 24 May 2023).

50   Advertisement, *Winnipeg Free Press*, 13 September 1963, 21; "Educational Video Will Highlight Black Music," *Brandon Sunday*, 5 January 1992, 12.

51   Advertisement, *Winnipeg Tribune*, 29 September 1962, 15; "Cynthia Wine Says . . .," *Winnipeg Free Press*, 9 December 1972, 17; Cheryl Arnold, "Successful City Restaurant Began with Young Girl's Dream," *Winnipeg Free Press*, 29 February 1988, 13.

52   "'Soul' Launches Logan Hopeful," *Winnipeg Free Press*, 19 September 1977, 12.

53   Stevens Wild, "Landmark Restaurant Closes Doors," *Winnipeg Free Press*, 28 September 1996, A6.

54   Obituary for Olive Mae Berryman, *Winnipeg Free Press*, 28 May 1999, C10.

55   Parr, *Domestic Goods*, 64, 77–79.

56   The local newspaper reported that Bob McLean from Pilot Mound served as pit master, assisted by Ron Tolton (Oak Lake), Allan Rose (Souris), Ernie Ellis and Bill Mooney (both from Wawanesa), and Duke Campbell (Carberry). "Big Crowd Expected at Livestock Field Day," *Russell Banner*, 23 June 1960, 1.

57   "Barbecuing Chicken," *Lac du Bonnet Springfield Leader*, 23 June 1959, 4.

58   Johnson Hardware Company Ltd., advertisement, *Brandon Daily Sun*, 15 June 1959, 5.

59   Matthews, "One Nation over Coals," 7, 26.

60   Lax and Mertig, "Perceived Masculinity of Meat," 424.

61   Hudson's Bay Company, *Round the Clock Hostess* (Winnipeg: Hudson's Bay Company, 1948), 12, from *What Canada Ate*, Archival & Special Collections, University of Guelph Library, Guelph, ON, https://whatcanadaate.lib.uoguelph.ca/items/show/63 (accessed 24 May 2023).

62   Contois, *Diners, Dudes & Diets*, 2.

63   Leer, "New Nordic Men," 317–18.

64   Contois, *Diners, Dudes & Diets*, 49.

65 Danysk, "'A Bachelor's Paradise,'" 159–60.

66 Ibid., 168.

67 Royden Loewen, interviewed by Janis Thiessen, 12 March 2019, 00:01:48–00:02:27, 00:13:00–00:15:13.

68 Ibid., 00:15:32–00:16:12.

69 Ibid., 00:16:13–00:16:48.

70 Ibid., 00:17:08–00:17:30.

71 Ibid., 00:17:50–00:19:38.

72 Ibid., 00:26:37–00:27:00.

73 Contois, *Diners, Dudes & Diets*, 130.

74 Kevin Smith, interviewed by Janis Thiessen and Sarah Story, 29 June 2018, 00:37:30–00:38:43, 01:14:28–01:14:37.

75 Ibid., 00:38:50–00:39:57.

76 Royden Loewen, interviewed by Arshdeep Kaur and Colin Rier, 14 May 2019, 01:03:54–01:04:47.

77 Ibid., 01:06:00–01:08:13.

78 Ibid., 01:09:23.

79 Ibid., 00:15:57–00:18:54.

80 Kevin Smith interview, 00:23:51–00:24:28.

81 Ibid., 00:29:53–00:30:16.

82 Ibid., 00:24:31–00:24:37.

83 Ibid., 00:17:43–00:18:04.

84 "Safety Office," University of Winnipeg, https://www.uwinnipeg.ca/safety/ (accessed 24 May 2023).

85 Kevin Smith interview, 01:15:31–01:15:44.

86 Ibid., 01:16:21–01:16:58.

87 "Pinoy/Pinay" is an informal term that Filipinx in diaspora use to describe themselves. Filipinx is the gender-inclusive term for people from the Philippines.

88 Bonifacio, *Pinay on the Prairies*, 115–16.

89 Krispin and Peegy Ontong, interviewed by Sarah Story and Janis Thiessen, 6 July 2018, 01:27:47–01:28:57.

90 Malek, "*Silangan* Rising," 51–52. Filipinx Americans underwent a similar process of diasporic redefinition. See Mabalon, "As American as Jackrabbit Adobo."

91 Krispin and Peegy Ontong interview, 03:08:01–03:09:48.

92 The total Filipinx population in Winnipeg, however, is smaller than in Toronto or Vancouver: in 2016, 9.49 percent of Winnipeggers were Filipinx. Malek, "Filipinos in Canada," 3, citing 2016 Canadian Census data.

93 Malek, "*Silangan* Rising," 36; Chen, *From Sunbelt to Snowbelt*, 13–14.

94 Malek, *Filipinos in Canada*, 2.

95 Ibid., 18–19.

96 Krispin and Peegy Ontong interview, 00:14:28–00:15:51.

97 Bonifacio, *Pinay on the Prairies*, 246.

98 Regine Cabato, "Anthony Bourdain: Sisig Will 'Win the Hearts and Minds of the World,'" *CNN Philippines*, 9 June 2017, https://www.cnnphilippines.com/news/2017/06/05/anthony-bourdain-sisig.html (accessed 24 May 2023).

99 Folklorama itself began in 1970. Steve Whysall, "Folklorama a Sure Cure for Summer Blues," *Winnipeg Free Press*, 8 August 1978, 6; Folklorama advertisement, *Winnipeg Free Press*, 26 July 1997, 23.

100 Bartley Kives, "Familiarity Breeds Appetite," *Winnipeg Free Press*, 9 January 2013, D1.

101 Malek, "Filipinos in Canada," 19.

102 Casa Bueno advertisement, *Winnipeg Free Press*, 13 August 1989, 6.

103 Mike Maunder, "Take a Walk on the Wild Side," *Winnipeg Free Press*, 26 April 1999, A8.

104 Marion Warhaft, "Loaded with Taste, Easy on the Wallet," *Winnipeg Free Press*, 15 January 2010, D3.

105 Marion Warhaft, "Attention, Hungry Shoppers: You've Lucked Out," *Winnipeg Free Press*, 30 April 2010, D3.

106 Marion Warhaft, "Takeout Treats," *Winnipeg Free Press,* 28 August 2014, 5.

107 Kris Ontong, "Seafood City Opens in Winnipeg," *Filipino Journal* 33, no. 23 (5–20 December 2019), https://filipinojournal.com/seafood-city-opens-in-winnipeg/ (accessed 24 May 2023).

108 Jill Wilson, "From the Street to the Strip," *Winnipeg Free Press,* 30 March 2017, 5; Melissa Martin, "New Eats on Our Streets," *Winnipeg Free Press,* 2 July 2012, B1.

109 Peegy Ontong in Krispin and Peegy Ontong interview, 01:48:05–10:48:09.

110 Krispin and Peegy Ontong interview, 00:01:14.

111 Ibid., 00:23:37–00:24:53.

112 Ibid., 00:28:47–00:29:10.

113 Ibid., 00:26:06–00:26:34.

114 Ibid., 01:24:39–01:27:46.

115 Aidan Geary, "A Narrow Window for Reunification," *CBC News,* 27 January 2019, https://newsinteractives.cbc.ca/longform/family-reunification (accessed 24 May 2023).

116 Krispin and Peegy Ontong interview, 02:02:53–02:03:24.

117 Ibid., 02:30:49–02:31:01.

118 Ilana Simon, "Bring Your Appetite," *Winnipeg Free Press,* 1 August 2001, D1.

119 Krispin and Peegy Ontong interview, 03:14:28–03:14:40.

CHAPTER FIVE

1 In 2016, 67.9 percent of the population in the Churchill community area were Indigenous. Winnipeg Regional Health Authority, "Churchill Community Area Profile, 2020," https://wrha.mb.ca/files/cha-2019-profile-churchill.pdf (accessed 24 May 2023).

2 See "Federal Government gives OmniTRAX 30 Days to Restore Rail Line to Churchill, Man.," *CBC News Manitoba,* 13 October 2017, https://www.cbc.ca/news/canada/manitoba/ottawa-sends-notice-to-omnitrax-1.4354131 (accessed 24 May 2023); "Crews Working Daily to Repair Broken Rail Line to Churchill in Northern Manitoba," *CTV News,* 12 September 2018, https://www.ctvnews.ca/canada/crews-working-daily-to-repair-broken-rail-line-to-churchill-in-northern-manitoba-1.4090912 (accessed 24 May 2023); Mason DePatie, "$40 Million Churchill Railway Upgrade Applauded by Northern Communities," *CTV News,* 7 August 2021, https://winnipeg.ctvnews.ca/40-million-churchill-railway-upgrade-applauded-by-northern-communities-1.5538260 (accessed 24 May 2023).

3 Tuck, "Suspending Damage," 412.

4 Brittany Luby, "Kill the 'Indian' and Save the 'Wild': Vocabularies with Political Consequences in Indigenous Studies," *NICHE: Network in Canadian History & Environment* blog post, 10 December 2018, https://niche-canada.org/2018/12/10/kill-the-indian-and-save-the-wild-vocabularies-with-political-consequences-in-indigenous-studies/ (accessed 24 May 2023). Emphasis in the original.

5 For discussion of the extensive evidence that Indigenous peoples have inhabited the Americas for 60,000 to 100,000 years, see Steeves, *Indigenous Paleolithic.*

6 Quoted in Corey Mintz, "The History of Food in Canada Is the History of Colonialism," *The Walrus* (27 March 2020), https://thewalrus.ca/the-history-of-food-in-canada-is-the-history-of-colonialism/ (accessed 24 May 2023).

7 Cochrane et al., *Kéhté Ochek Sípí Minowasowak,* 22.

8 Brandson, "Cache for Leaner Times," 12–13; Lorson, "Igloo Restaurant."

9 The Itsanitaq Museum was formerly named the Eskimo Museum.

10 See Kent Davies, "What is Northern Food?," https://www.manitobafoodhistory.ca/northern-food (accessed 24 May 2023).

11 Wheeler, "Reflections on the Social Relations," 194. See also the introduction to Julie Cruikshank, *Life Lived Like a Story.*

12 Wheeler, "Reflections on the Social Relations," 201.

13   University of Winnipeg, Research Ethics, *Guidance Document 9*, 8 June 2022, https://www.uwinnipeg.ca/research/docs/ethics/guidance-document-9---guidance-for-research-with-indigenous-communities-and-participants.pdf (14 October 2022).

14   Arctic Bay tape 2, 1966, Helen Burgess oral interview recordings, HB1994/24, T39-17, Archives of Manitoba; Camil D. Coupal oral history interview, 22 July 1983, Flin Flon Oral History Project fonds, PR1984-72, C631, Archives of Manitoba; Harry Guymer oral history interview, 14 July 1983, Flin Flon Oral History Project fonds, PR1984-72, C630, Archives of Manitoba; William Thomas oral history interview, 30 July 1987, Ma-Mow-We-Tak Friendship Centre oral history project records, 1987-213, C1220-C1221, Archives of Manitoba; Charles McPherson oral history interview, 15 May 1993, Métis Women of Manitoba Inc. oral history project records, 1997-44, C2431 and C2432, Archives of Manitoba; Jean LeClerc oral history interview, 15 May 1993, Métis Women of Manitoba Inc. oral history project records, 1997-44, C2433, Archives of Manitoba; Sam Chun oral history interview, 16 September 1988, Manitoba Chinese Historical Society fonds, PR1988-213, C1150, Archives of Manitoba; D.H. Learmonth oral history interview, 23 May 1958, J.W. Anderson fonds, 1976/73, T6/1, Archives of Manitoba; Ashton Alston oral history interview, 13 August 1958, J.W. Anderson fonds, 1976/73, T6/9, Archives of Manitoba; Muriel Cook oral history interview, 8 September 1983, Oral history interviews with long-service employees of the Hudson's Bay Company Fur Trade and Northern Stores Departments, HB1984/15, T11-66, Archives of Manitoba; R.H. Cook oral history interview, 7 September 1983, Oral history interviews with long-service employees of the Hudson's Bay Company Fur Trade and Northern Stores Departments, HB1984/15, T11-63, Archives of Manitoba; J.C. Currie, W. Cave, and W. Willis oral history interviews, 11 September 1978, Oral history interviews with long-service employees of the Hudson's Bay Company Fur Trade and Northern Stores Departments, HB1984/15, T11-1, Archives of Manitoba; Mary Swaffield oral history interview, Oral history interviews with long-service employees of the Hudson's Bay Company Fur Trade and Northern Stores Departments, HB1984/15, T11-24, Archives of Manitoba.

15   Hudson's Bay Company Centenary Celebrations, outtakes reel, 9 of 10, 1919, HB2011/001, F119-27, Archives of Manitoba.

16   Allan and Mary Code oral history collection, interviews 480–97, Manitoba Museum. Interviews 481, 484, 488, and 492 are in Chipewyan and have no English transcripts or summaries.

17   Glenn Wingie, interviewed by Janis Thiessen, 10 June 2019.

18   Ibid.

19   North Star Bus Lines, *Story of Churchill*, 1.

20   Ibid., 5; Brandson, *Churchill Hudson Bay*, 101.

21   Churchill Library and Archives, Churchill, MB, 003.4.20, Imperial Oilways brochure (March 1965), Nick Nickels, "Churchill Grain Rush," 8. The first grain shipment through Churchill was carried by the *S.S. Ungava Queen* in 1919. Brandson, *Churchill Hudson Bay*, 3, 113.

22   Joe Stover, interviewed by Kent Davies, 16 June 2019, 00:11:55–00:14:40.

23   "Port of Churchill Moves under 100% Local and Indigenous Ownership," *RealAgriculture*, 11 March 2021, https://www.realagriculture.com/2021/03/port-of-churchill-moves-under-100-local-and-indigenous-ownership/ (accessed 24 May 2023).

24   Greer, "Settler Colonialism and Beyond."

25   E.M. Fraser, "Canoes Trail Whales in the Hudson Bay," *Winnipeg Free Press*, 11 August 1962, 19.

26   Churchill Library and Archives, "Canoes Trail Whales"; Churchill Library and Archives, Churchill, MB, Churchill Ladies Club scrapbooks, 002.14.27, "Mammoth" scrapbook, "Hunt Whales on Inland Sea," *Wainwright Star-Chronicle*, 20 October 1965, 7.

27   Forbes Powell, interviewed by Janis Thiessen, 17 August 2018, 00:01:10–00:01:17.

28   Ibid., 00:03:05–00:03:14.

29   Ibid., 00:04:43–00:05:13.

30   Ibid., 00:06:17–00:06:31.

31   Ibid., 00:06:54–00:08:04.

32 Ibid., 00:03:34–00:04:25.

33 John Arnalukjuaq, quoted in Keith and Stewart, "Churchill Oral History Project," 9.

34 "Catching the White Whale in Waters of Hudson Bay Exciting," *Stonewall Argus,* 1 February 1950, 6; "Whales Caught by Canoe in Hudson Bay Processed by New Industry at Churchill," *Winnipeg Free Press,* 24 November 1949, 14; E.M. Fraser, "Canoes Trail Whales in the Hudson Bay," *Winnipeg Free Press,* 11 August 1962, 19; "First Whale Oil Shipment Passes through Dauphin," *Dauphin Herald and Press,* 12 October 1950, 4; "White Whale Meat Makes New Treat for Businessmen," *Dauphin Herald and Press,* 27 July 1950, 1; "Harpoons Yield to Nets in North Whaling," *Winnipeg Tribune,* 3 November 1949, 2; W.J. Swain, "I Saw: The Port of Churchill," *Grandview Exponent,* 1 September 1949, 3; Forbes Powell interview, 00:05:07–00:05:25.

35 Women's Auxiliary of the Chapel of the Good Shepherd and the Ladies of St. Paul's Anglican Mission, *Northern Kitchen,* 10.

36 Churchill Library and Archives, Churchill, MB, Churchill Ladies Club scrapbooks, 002.14.27, "Mammoth" scrapbook, "Churchill's Whale Plant Is Resuming Operations," undated newspaper clipping, 43; Robert Lowery, "No Pact on Prices as Whaling Season Nears," *Winnipeg Free Press,* 7 May 1969, 16.

37 John McManus, "Mink Rancher Slaughters Stock," *Winnipeg Free Press,* 26 January 1970, 1; Peter Neufeld, "Valley Vistas," *Brandon Sun,* 3 December 1971, 9; "Whale Hunting to Be Allowed," *Winnipeg Tribune,* 27 March 1965, 7; "Beluga Whales Split Ministers," *Winnipeg Free Press,* 7 March 1973, 6.

38 Brandson, *Churchill Hudson Bay,* 211.

39 Ibid., 3–11.

40 Helen Webber, interviewed by Kimberley Moore, Kent Davies, Janis Thiessen, 14 June 2019.

41 Ibid., 01:04:32–01:04:38.

42 Patricia McIntyre and Maureen Martin Osland, interviewed by Kimberley Moore, 3 July 2019, 00:02:55–00:03:47.

43 Ibid., 00:29:58–00:30:18.

44 Helen Webber interview, 00:56:38–00:57:33.

45 Patricia McIntyre and Maureen Martin Osland interview, 00:20:10–00:20:23.

46 Ben Larson in *Muskeg Special,* Gregory Zbitnew, dir., transcript. The film is made from footage recorded in 1979. Our thanks to Morgan Brightnose for drawing *Muskeg Special* to our attention.

47 Bob Lowery, "Tunnel Gardening Greening the North," *Winnipeg Free Press,* 3 July 1975, 18.

48 See Milloy, *National Crime*; TRC, *Knock on the Door*; Stevenson, *Intimate Integration.*

49 Brandson, *Churchill Hudson Bay,* 203–4.

50 Patricia McIntyre and Maureen Martin Osland interview, 00:07:51–00:08:26.

51 Helen Webber interview, 01:05:57–01:06:36.

52 Helen McEwan, interviewed by Janis Thiessen, Kent Davies, and Kimberley Moore, 14 June 2019, 01:04:21–01:05:49.

53 Brandson, *Churchill Hudson Bay,* 204–5.

54 Helen McEwan interview, 01:08:34–01:09:14.

55 Bob Lowery, "'Tent Gardens' Providing Fresh Vegetable Crops in North," *Winnipeg Free Press,* 5 October 1974, 10.

56 Ibid.

57 Lowery, "Tunnel Gardening"; Bob Lowery, "Portree Proves 'Magic' of Northern Peat Moss," *Winnipeg Free Press,* 11 December 1975, 70.

58 Bob Lowery, "Trapper Finds a Green Thumb in Tunnel-garden," *Winnipeg Free Press,* 18 July 1977, 11.

59 Bob Lowery, "Trapper's 'Weird Wigwam' Feeds Northern Towns," *Winnipeg Free Press,* 20 September 1978, 15; "Plastic Tunnel Garden Protects Tomatoes," *Medicine Hat News,* 18 October 1978, 23.

60 George Ponask in *Muskeg Special,* Gregory Zbitnew, dir., transcript.

61 Bob Lowery, "Katimavik Youths Help Northerner Beat Cold," *Winnipeg Free Press,* 18 April 1980, 4.

62 Murray Harvey, "You Can't Eat Discussion, Harvey Talks Opportunity," *The Pas Opasquia Times,* 1 February 2017, 7.

63 Bob Lowery, "Action Sought on Rail Service," *Winnipeg Free Press,* 11 August 1977, 76.

64 Bob Lowery, "Concern in the North," *Winnipeg Free Press,* 10 December 1977, 94.

65 Carley Basler, interviewed by Kimberley Moore, Janis Thiessen, and Kent Davies, 13 June 2019, 00:04:31–00:10:31.

66 Ibid., 00:13:40–00:14:30.

67 Ibid., 00:11:08–00:12:50.

68 Ibid., 00:20:35–00:21:40; Cameron MacIntosh, "Hydroponic Produce Is Blooming in Churchill, Man.," *CBC News,* 20 March 2018, https://www.cbc.ca/news/canada/manitoba/churchill-hydroponic-produce-1.4568847 (accessed 24 May 2023).

69 Carley Basler interview, 00:37:50–00:40:39.

70 Stephanie Puleo, interim executive director of the Churchill Northern Studies Centre, quoted in Cameron MacLean, "Churchill Hydroponic Garden Project Serves Up Fresh Greens in Northern Town," *CBC News,* 4 January 2018, https://www.cbc.ca/news/canada/manitoba/churchill-vegetables-shipping-container-cnsc-1.4473799 (accessed 24 May 2023).

71 Stephanie Gordon, "Year-round Hydroponic Project Hits 40,000-unit Milestone," *Greenhouse Canada,* 16 March 2021, https://www.greenhousecanada.com/year-round-hydroponic-project-hits-40000-unit-milestone/ (accessed 24 May 2023).

72 Helen Webber interview, 01:23:16–01:23:30.

73 Wally Daudrich and Jason Ransom, interviewed by Kent Davies, Kimberley Moore, and Janis Thiessen, 17 June 2019, 00:03:25–00:04:12.

74 Lazy Bear Lodge, "Café," https://www.lazybearlodge.com/lazy-bear-lodge/cafe (accessed 24 May 2023).

75 Brandson, "A Cache for Leaner Times," 15; Helen Webber interview, 00:50:36–00:50:49; Nunavut Development Corporation, "Kivalliq Arctic Foods," https://ndcorp.nu.ca/we-invest/subsidiaries/kivalliq-arctic-foods/ (accessed 24 May 2023).

76 Carley Basler interview, 01:17:22–01:18:51.

77 Joe Stover interview, 00:34:30–00:38:50.

78 Helen Webber interview, 00:34:20–00:34:28.

79 Ibid., 00:31:02–00:33:17.

80 Ibid., 00:41:15–00:42:20.

81 Helen McEwan interview, 00:12:28–00:13:08.

82 Brandson, "Country Food," 12.

83 Patricia McIntyre and Maureen Martin Osland interview, 00:37:55–00:38:49.

84 Banfield, "Caribou Crisis"; Alexandra Paul, "Addressing the Fatal Ordeal of the Dene," *Winnipeg Free Press,* 13 August 2016, https://www.winnipegfreepress.com/featured/2016/08/13/relocation-and-reconciliation (accessed 24 May 2023); Kelly Malone, "Manitoba's Sayisi Dene: Forced Relocation, Racism, Survival," *CBC News Manitoba,* 19 August 2016, https://www.cbc.ca/news/canada/manitoba/manitoba-sayisi-dene-relocation-1.3722564 (accessed 24 May 2023).

85 Bussidor and Bilgen-Reinart, *Night Spirits,* 56–57.

86 Ibid., 146; Paul, "Addressing the Fatal Ordeal." See also *Nuhoniyeh—Our Story,* Allen Code and Mary Code, dirs.

87 Brandson, *From Tundra to Forest,* 8.

88 Eva Anderson, quoted in Bussidor and Bilgen-Reinart, *Night Spirits,* 61.

89 Newton, Fast, and Henley, "Sustainable Development," 284.

90 Quoted in Paul, "Addressing the Fatal Ordeal."

91 Ibid.

92 Helen Webber interview, 00:10:34–00:10:52.

93 Ibid., 00:35:54–00:37:07.

94 Ibid., 00:46:14–00:46:36.

95 Ibid., 00:18:40–00:20:23.

96 "About the Authors," *Blueberries & Polar Bears,* accessed 17 June 2021, https://blueberriesandpolarbears.com/about/ (accessed 24 May 2023).

97 Helen McEwan interview, 00:23:120–00:23:48.

98   Ibid., 00:25:45–00:26:31 and 00:39:07–00:40:06.

99   The popularity of Thompson's pizza is such that there is now a pizzeria in Winnipeg that offers it: T-Town Style Pizza. It is described as "Chicago style with a New York twist." T-Town Style Pizza, "Our Story," https://ttown-stylepizza.com/our-story/ (accessed 24 May 2023).

100   Tuck and Yang, "Decolonization Is Not a Metaphor," 3.

CHAPTER SIX

1   See, for example, Ellis, *Ministry of Agriculture;* Foster, *Developing West*; Katz and Lehr, *Last Best West*.

2   Historian Norma Hall observes, for example, that "Red River Métis settlers did farm (deliberately), they worked (hard) while farming, and farmed to a greater extent and with greater success (and intelligence) than the history writing about Red River, in the main, openly accepts." Hall, *Casualty of Colonialism*.

3   Mason and Robidoux, "Introduction," in *A Land Not Forgotten*, 3.

4   See, for example, Mysyk, *Manitoba Commercial Market Gardening*; Marchildon, *Agricultural History*; Russell, *How Agriculture Made Canada*; Perry, Jones, and Morton, *Place and Replace*; Carter, *Lost Harvests*; Peotto and Nelson, "Food Production in the Wabigoon Basin."

5   Manitoba Culture, Heritage and Citizenship, *First Farmers*, 1–2.

6   Diana Robson, "A Brief History of Indigenous Agriculture," *Manitoba Museum: Botany*, blog post, 18 February 2020, https://manitobamuseum.ca/a-brief-history-of-indigenous-agriculture/ (accessed 28 May 2023); Flynn and Syms, "Manitoba's First Farmers." European biases against Indigenous knowledge meant that they did not adopt Indigenous practices of nixtamalization of corn or eating it with beans; the result was pellagra when corn was introduced to Europe.

7   Manitoba Culture, Heritage and Citizenship, *First Farmers*, 1–3, 6.

8   Carter, "Erasing and Replacing," 14.

9   Ibid., 16, 18.

10   Kimmerer and Lake, "Maintaining the Mosaic," 37.

11   Ibid., 37–40.

12   Ibid., 38.

13   Carter, *Lost Harvests,* ix.

14   Ibid., 162.

15   Ibid., 231, citing Glenbow-Alberta Institute, John McDougall Papers, "The Future of the Indians," n.d. (1902).

16   Canada, Royal Commission on Aboriginal Peoples, *Report of the Royal Commission on Aboriginal Peoples,* Volume 1, *Looking Forward, Looking Back* (Ottawa: Government of Canada, 1996), 271, hereafter RCAP; Mysyk, *Manitoba Commercial Market Gardening*, 37.

17   Eric Tang, "Agriculture: The Relationship Between Aboriginal and Non-Aboriginal Farmers," *Western Development Museum/Saskatchewan Indian Cultural Centre Partnership Project* (2003), 5–6, http://apihtawikosisan.com/wp-content/uploads/2012/05/FNAgriculture.pdf, cited in Vowel, *Indigenous Writes*, 328.

18   Carter, *Lost Harvests,* 136.

19   RCAP, 371.

20   Ibid., 272; Indian Act, RSC 1985, c 1-5, s 32.

21   Friesen, "Grant Me Wherewith," 147.

22   Carter, *Imperial Plots*, 30.

23   Carter, "Erasing and Replacing," 15.

24   RCAP, 613.

25   Nickels, "Examining the Future," 59.

26   Ibid., 60.

27   Ibid., 65.

28   Ibid., 65–66.

29   Manomin is also spelled "manoomin."

30   Government of Manitoba, Indigenous Reconciliation and Northern Relations, *Community Profiles,* November 2020, https://www.gov.mb.ca/inr/publications/community_profiles.html (accessed 28 May 2023); David Square, "Gone Wild," *Winnipeg Free Press,* 11 December 2010, C1; Government of Manitoba, Environment, Climate and Parks, *Regions*, https://gov.mb.ca/sd/about/parks-and-regional-services/regions/index.html;

Government of Manitoba, "Whiteshell Area Wild Rice Harvest Underway," media bulletin, 31 August 2016, https://news.gov.mb.ca/news/index.html?item=39131&posted=2016-08-31 (accessed 28 May 2023).

31 Kathi Avery Kinew explains that an older name for manomin is the Anishinaabe term *manito gitigaan*, "the living gift of the Creator." Kinew, "Manito Gitigaan Governing," x.

32 Ibid., 4.

33 See, for example, Destination Canada, "Want a Once-in-a-Lifetime Northern Lights Experience? Head to Canada," *New York Times*, https://www.nytimes.com/paidpost/destination-canada/want-a-once-in-a-lifetime-northern-lights-experience-head-to-canada.html (accessed 28 May 2023).

34 Kinew, "Manito Gitigaan Governing," 46.

35 Margaret Lehman with Niisaachewan Anishinaabe Nation, "Cooking with Manomin: Comparing Regional Differences in Expression," *NICHE: Network in Canadian History & Environment*, blog post, 26 June 2020, https://niche-canada.org/2020/06/26/cooking-with-manomin-comparing-regional-differences-in-expression/ (accessed 28 May 2023).

36 Ibid.

37 Melissa Hryb, "Did you know? (The Wild Rice Edition)," *Spectator Tribune*, 7 June 2016, https://spectatortribune.com/wild-rice-manitoba/ (accessed 28 May 2023).

38 Moodie, "Manomin," 76.

39 Luby et al., "Beyond Institutional Ethics," 5–6.

40 Margaret Lehman, "Defending Manomin: The Advocacy Work of Winona LaDuke," *NICHE*, blog post, 1 December 2021, https://niche-canada.org/2021/12/01/defending-manomin-the-advocacy-work-of-winona-laduke/ (accessed 28 May 2023).

41 LaDuke, "Wild Rice Moon."

42 Moodie, "Manomin," 71.

43 Ibid., 72.

44 Ibid., 73.

45 Ibid., 72–73; Margaret Lehman, "Building a Common Vocabulary: A Cornerstone of Community-Engaged Research," *NICHE: Network in Canadian History & Environment*, blog post, 5 June 2020, https://niche-canada.org/2020/06/05/building-a-common-vocabulary-a-cornerstone-on-community-engaged-research/ (accessed 28 May 2023).

46 See our discussion of the ethics of conducting oral history interviews with Indigenous people in Chapter 5.

47 See University of Regina, Canadian Plains Research Center, "Indian History Film Project," https://ourspace.uregina.ca/handle/10294/26 (accessed 28 May 2023).

48 Kinew, "Manito Gitigaan Governing," 46.

49 Ibid., 47.

50 Alvin Hagar, interviewed by Ranald Thurgood, 9 August 1982, transcript, 23.

51 Lithman, "Capitalization of a Traditional Pursuit," 13–14.

52 Kinew, "Manito Gitigaan Governing," 44.

53 Lithman, "Capitalization of a Traditional Pursuit," 16–17.

54 Kinew, "Manito Gitigaan Governing," 165–66.

55 Lithman, "Capitalization of a Traditional Pursuit," 14–15.

56 Alvin Hagar interview transcript, 23. See also Vennum, *Wild Rice*, 81–150.

57 Manitoba, *Manitoba Wild Rice Industry*, 20.

58 Luby, *Dammed*, 6, 96–97, 116–17; Mehltretter, Luby, and Bradford, "Hydroelectric Power and Anishinaabe Diets."

59 Kamal, "Recipe for Change," 137, 142–44, 162.

60 Campbell et al., "Contemporary Food Supply," 105.

61 Kamal, "Recipe for Change," 161, 166.

62 Kinew, "Manito Gitigaan Governing," 172.

63 "Foiled by Inches," *Indian News* 22, no. 6 (September 1981): 4.

64 Alvin Hagar interview transcript, 22.

65 "Foiled by Inches," *Indian News.*

66 Canadian Flavors, "Du Bois Wild Rice Ltd." (2022), https://www.canadianflavors.com/canadian-suppliers/du-bois-wild-rice-ltd/ (accessed 28 May 2023); Cinda Chavich, "Not Really Rice, but Truly Canadian," *Globe and Mail,* 10 October 2007, https://www.theglobe-andmail.com/life/not-really-rice-but-truly-canadian/article18146882/ (accessed 28 May 2023).

67 See, for example, Teillet, *North-West Is Our Mother*; Friesen, *Canadian Prairies.*

68 Wild Man Ricing, https://www.wildmanricing.ca (accessed 28 May 2023).

69 Naosap Harvest, https://www.naosapharvest.com (accessed 28 May 2023).

70 Julienne Isaacs, "Naosap Harvest: Growing Wild Rice in Manitoba's North," *Canadian Organic Growers,* blog post, 12 September 2017, https://www.cog.ca/article/naosap-harvest-growing-wild-rice-manitobas-north/ (accessed 28 May 2023); Government of Manitoba Agriculture, Food Safety, "Food Processing and Distribution Facilities with Manitoba Agriculture Issued Permits," https://www.gov.mb.ca/agriculture/food-safety/regulating-food/food-processing-and-distribution-facilities-with-mafrd-issued-permits.html (accessed 28 May 2023).

71 NWC Wild Rice Company, https://nwcwildrice.ca (accessed 28 May 2023); Brittany Warner, "Indigenous-Owned Wild Rice Company Showcases the Importance of Community-Minded Business," *RealAgriculture,* 12 July 2022, https://www.realagriculture.com/2022/07/indigenous-owned-wild-rice-company-showcases-the-importance-of-community-minded-business/ (accessed 28 May 2023).

72 This is the manomin sold in Manitoba by Kookum's Pantry, an online and pop-up store that sells only Indigenous-produced goods. Kookum's Pantry, "Pickerel & Wild Rice," https://www.kookums.ca/product-page/wild-rice-full-pound (accessed 28 May 2023).

73 "Manomin Wild Rice magazine advertisement," MCC Menno Wiebe Native Concerns Collection, MHA.

74 "Manitoba Indian Brotherhood President David Courchene Awarded Honorary Degree," *Indian News* 13, no. 2 (May 1970): 6; Lithman, "Capitalization of a Traditional Pursuit,"18.

75 Susan Hiebert, "Swan Lake Reserve News," *Indian News* 14, no. 11 (1972): 7; Lithman, "Capitalization of a Traditional Pursuit," 18–19.

76 Lithman, "Capitalization of a Traditional Pursuit," 19; "Ritual Has Changed with Time," *Indian News* 22, no. 7 (October 1981): 6. In 1972, the second such cooperative was formed: the Anishinabeg Man-O-Min Co-operative. Its purpose was to harvest and market manomin in Ontario near Kenora and Dryden. It folded in 1975 due to a combination of interference by the Department of Indian Affairs and management issues. "Native News," *Indian News* 15, no. 4 (September 1972): 8; "A Helping Hand for Indians," *Indian News* 16, no. 2 (June 1973): 7; Kinew, "Manito Gitigaan Governing," 170.

77 Manitoba, *Manitoba Wild Rice Industry,* 2.

78 "Ritual Has Changed with Time."

79 "Wild Rice Industry to Be Probed," *Indian News* 22, no. 7 (October 1981): 6; "Ritual Has Changed with Time."

80 "Wild Rice Industry to Be Probed."

81 Ibid.

82 Ibid.

83 Kinew, "Manito Gitigaan Governing," 270; Manitoba, "Whiteshell Area Wild Rice Harvest Underway."

84 Manitoba, *Manitoba Wild Rice Industry,* 1.

85 Ibid., 11–12.

86 Manitoba, Public Inquiry into the Administration of Justice and Aboriginal People, A.C Hamilton, and C.M Sinclair, *Report of the Aboriginal Justice Inquiry of Manitoba* (Winnipeg: Public Inquiry into the Administration of Justice and Aboriginal People, 1991), 190, hereafter AJI; "The Paypom Treaty," *Kiinawin Kawindomowin Story Nations*, https://storynations.utoronto.ca/index.php/the-paypom-treaty/ (accessed 28 May 2023).

87 Brittany Luby, "Kill the 'Indian' and Save the 'Wild': Vocabularies with Political Consequences in Indigenous Studies," *NICHE: Network in Canadian History & Environment*, blog post, 10 December 2018,

https://niche-canada.org/2018/12/10/kill-the-in-dian-and-save-the-wild-vocabularies-with-politi-cal-consequences-in-indigenous-studies/ (accessed 18 July 2023). Ontario had passed its own Wild Rice Harvesting Act in 1970. Government of Ontario, Wild Rice Harvesting Act, RSO 1970, c. 497.

88 AJI, 189; Kinew, "Manito Gitigaan Governing," 183–84, 271.

89 AJI, 190–91.

90 Ibid., 191.

91 Government of Manitoba, C.C.S.M. c. W140, The Wild Rice Act, revised 1 October 2015, https://web2. gov.mb.ca/laws/statutes/ccsm/w140e.php (26 June 2022).

92 LaDuke, "Wild Rice Moon"; "Manomin Wild Rice magazine advertisement," MCC Menno Wiebe Native Concerns Collection, Series 9, Manomin Wild Rice Materials 1980s, Volume 4718: 14, MHA; LaDuke, "Ricekeepers."

93 Frank Bibeau, quoted in LaDuke, "Ricekeepers."

94 LaDuke, "Wild Rice and Ethics."

95 The Manomin Project, @manominproject on Instagram, https://www.instagram.com/manominproject/ (accessed 28 May 2023).

96 The Manomin Project, "About the Project," http://niche-canada.org/manomin/about/ (accessed 28 May 2023).

97 Government of Canada, Panel on Research Ethics, "TCPS2 (2018): Introduction," https://ethics.gc.ca/eng/tcps2-eptc2_2018_introduction.html (accessed 28 May 2023).

98 Luby et al., "Beyond Institutional Ethics," 11.

99 Ibid., 5–6.

CHAPTER SEVEN

1 Corey Mintz, "Where Are Canada's Indigenous Restaurants?" BuzzFeed News, 27 April 2017, https://www.buzzfeed.com/coreymintz/where-are-canadas-indige-nous-restaurants (accessed 28 May 2023).

2 Portions of the following were previously published as Preserves podcast episode 4, "1491," 15 April 2019, https://www.manitobafoodhistory.ca/pre-serves-pod/2019/04/15/ep-4 (accessed 28 May 2023), written and narrated by Janis Thiessen.

3 Mintz, "Where Are Canada's Indigenous Restaurants?"

4 Gora, "Cuisine of its Own." See also Phillipps and Skinner, "Bannock," 61–62.

5 (Martens), Dennis, and Hart, "Feeding Indigenous People in Canada." See also Daschuk, Clearing the Plains.

6 Physical and sexual abuse by those running these "schools" was also rampant. (Martens), Dennis, and Hart, "Feeding Indigenous People in Canada," 655–56. See also Mosby, "Administering Colonial Science"; Truth and Reconciliation Commission of Canada, Canada's Residential Schools.

7 (Martens), Dennis, and Hart, "Feeding Indigenous People in Canada," 655.

8 Long Plain First Nation, "New Winnipeg Hotel Announces Grand Opening," press release, 28 July 2022, https://lpband.ca/2022/07/new-winnipeg-hotel-an-nounces-grand-opening/ (accessed 28 May 2023); Eva Wasney, "A Menu of Memories," Winnipeg Free Press, 5 December 2022, https://www.winnipegfreepress.com/arts-and-life/2022/12/05/a-menu-of-memories (accessed 28 May 2023).

9 Feast Café Bistro, http://www.feastcafebistro.com (accessed 28 May 2023).

10 Kekuli Café, https://www.kekulicafe.com (accessed 28 May 2023).

11 L'Autochtone Taverne Americaine, https://www.lautochtone.com (accessed 28 May 2023).

12 Mr. Bannock, https://www.mrbannock.com (accessed 28 May 2023).

13 Salmon n' Bannock, https://www.salmonandbannock.net (accessed 28 May 2023); Priya Bhat, "Salmon n' Bannock Expands to YVR, the First Indigenous Restaurant to Open in a Canadian Airport," CBC News, 16 December 2022, https://www.cbc.ca/news/canada/british-columbia/salmon-bannock-indigenous-restau-rant-yvr-airport-vancouver-1.6689601 (accessed 28 May 2023).

14 Kū-kŭm Kitchen, http://www.kukum-kitchen.com (accessed 21 February 2023); Julia Whalen, "Seal Meat on the Menu at Toronto Restaurant Sparks Dueling Petitions, Online Debate," *CBC News,* 11 October 2017, https://www.cbc.ca/news/canada/toronto/seal-meat-debate-kukum-1.4347858 (accessed 28 May 2023).

15 Nk'Mip Cellars, https://www.nkmipcellars.com/About-Us (accessed 28 May 2023); Indigenous World Winery, https://www.indigenousworldwinery.com (accessed 28 May 2023).

16 Gora, "From Meat to Metaphor," 95, 97.

17 Geoff Kirbyson, "State of the Nation: Indigenous Business in Manitoba," *Manitoba Inc. Magazine,* https://manitoba-inc.ca/state-of-the-nation-indigenous-business-in-manitoba/ (accessed 28 May 2023).

18 "Socreds Renege, Say Indians," *Victoria Daily Colonist,* 31 December 1975, 16.

19 "Clubs May Dine on Moose," 15 April 1965, *Winnipeg Tribune* clippings file, 5698 Restaurants-1978 18-1845 NP, University of Manitoba Archives.

20 Emphasis in original unpublished report. Yvonne Monkman, Mary Richard, Joy Fedorick, "Bungees," unpublished report, January 1976, Bungees correspondence Communities Economic Development Fund, 1976–1979, Indian & Métis Friendship Centre of Winnipeg fonds, P746-3, Archives of Manitoba; "Native Restaurant Part of New Goal," *Winnipeg Free Press,* 4 October 1973, 23.

21 Interdepartmental memo from Helen Pastuck, research assistant, Northeast Development Initiative, re "Native Restaurant," 20 February 1976, Bungees correspondence, 1975–1980, Indian & Métis Friendship Centre of Winnipeg fonds, P746-2, Archives of Manitoba.

22 Ibid.

23 "Province Funds Feasibility Study of Native Food Restaurants in City," *Winnipeg Free Press,* 25 February 1977, 6.

24 Letter from H.J. Jones, general manager, Communities Economic Development Fund, to Mary Richard, 26 November 1979, Bungees correspondence Communities Economic Development Fund, 1976–1979, Indian

25 Letter from H.J. Jones, Communities Economic Development Fund, to Yvonne Monkman, 7 July 1976, Bungees correspondence Communities Economic Development Fund, 1976–1979, Indian & Métis Friendship Centre of Winnipeg fonds, P746-3, Archives of Manitoba.

26 Letter from H.J. Jones, Communities Economic Development Fund, to Mary Richard, executive director IMCF, 13 July 1977, Bungees correspondence Communities Economic Development Fund, 1976–1979, Indian & Métis Friendship Centre of Winnipeg fonds, P746-3, Archives of Manitoba.

27 After interviewing possible consultants, H.B. & Partners were chosen. The consultants Laventhol & Horwath, invited to submit a proposal, had noted: "There are some interesting problems which come to mind immediately, not the least of which would be overcoming the negative image of native people that some Winnipeger's [sic] hold, and also the lack of trained native personnel who are available for such a venture." Letter from Robert Lederman, Laventhol & Horwath, to Lang Watson, Employment and Immigration Canada, 28 January 1980, Bungees correspondence, 1975–1980, Indian & Métis Friendship Centre of Winnipeg fonds, P746-2, Archives of Manitoba; letter from Mary Richard, president IMFC, to Harvey Bostrom, H.B. & Partners, 20 February 1980; letter from Mary Richard, president IMFC, to Laventhol & Horwath, 14 February 1980, Bungees correspondence contracts etc., 1977–1981, Indian & Métis Friendship Centre of Winnipeg fonds, P746-4, Archives of Manitoba.

28 Yvonne Monkman, Mary Richard, Joy Fedorick, "Bungees," unpublished report, January 1976, Bungees correspondence Communities Economic Development Fund, 1976–1979, Indian & Métis Friendship Centre of Winnipeg fonds, P746-3, Archives of Manitoba.

29 Registration under the Business Names Registration Act, 25 April 1975, Bungees correspondence registration incorporation, 1977 & 1980, Indian & Métis Friendship Centre of Winnipeg fonds, P746-6, Archives of Manitoba. Monkman worked as a teacher aide at the Indian and Métis Friendship Centre, where she was also a board member. She was a board

member of the Selkirk chapter of the Manitoba Métis Federation and Ma Mawi Chi Itata, as well as a member of Manitoba's Task Force on Child Care. Richard was a Métis woman who served as president of the Aboriginal Council of Winnipeg, president of the Indigenous Women's Collective, president of Circle of Life Thunderbird House, and director of the Indian and Métis Friendship Centre (among other responsibilities). Gordon Goldsborough, "Memorable Manitobans: Mary Margaret Richard," *Manitoba Historical Society*, 4 October 2021, http://www.mhs.mb.ca/docs/people/richard_mm.shtml (accessed 28 May 2023); "Province Establishes Day Care Committee," *Hamiota Echo*, 7 November 1989, 17; "Child Care Committee Named," *Russell Banner*, 20 September 1989, 1; Lindsay Vanstone, "Selkirk Chapter of Métis Federation Re-elects Jack Park," *Selkirk Journal*, 30 April 2001, 2; Wally Dennison, "Munroe Fired but Legality of Board Meeting Questioned," *Winnipeg Free Press*, 11 April 1973, 1; Edward Unrau, "Native School Starts," *Winnipeg Free Press*, 24 January 1970, 8.

30   Yvonne Monkman, Mary Richard, Joy Fedorick, "Bungees," unpublished report, January 1976, Bungees correspondence Communities Economic Development Fund, 1976–1979, Indian & Métis Friendship Centre of Winnipeg fonds, P746-3, Archives of Manitoba.

31   Ibid.

32   See Chapter One 1 for further details of those restaurants' décor.

33   Yvonne Monkman, Mary Richard, Joy Fedorick, "Bungees," unpublished report, January 1976, Bungees correspondence Communities Economic Development Fund, 1976–1979, Indian & Métis Friendship Centre of Winnipeg fonds, P746-3, Archives of Manitoba.

34   Letter from Don Marks, IMFC, to Hugh Jones, Communities Economic Development Fund, 14 October 1976, Bungees correspondence Communities Economic Development Fund, 1976–1979, Indian & Métis Friendship Centre of Winnipeg fonds, P746-3, Archives of Manitoba.

35   Letter from Mary Richard and Yvonne Monkman, Bungees Restaurant, to Allan Cochrane, president IMFC, 10 September 1981, Bungees correspondence contracts etc., 1977–1981, Indian & Métis Friend-

ship Centre of Winnipeg fonds, P746-4, Archives of Manitoba; Letter from Ray Barbour and Helen Henry, IMFC, to Ivy Domin, Phyllis Keeper, Darlene Tomasson, Rose Laquette, Milly Stonechild, Bernice McKenzie, Tom Lavallee, Bernice Desnomie, Little Val, and Bubbles, 23 February 1977, Bungees correspondence, 1975–1980, Indian & Métis Friendship Centre of Winnipeg fonds, P746-2, Archives of Manitoba.

36   Diner feedback from four anonymous individuals, Bungees correspondence questionnaires, 1977, Indian & Métis Friendship Centre of Winnipeg fonds, P746-5, Archives of Manitoba.

37   Muck a Muck restaurant served Indigenous food in Vancouver in the 1970s, but it was owned by an art gallery and not by Indigenous people. Letter from Helen Pastuck, research assistant, Manitoba Department of Northern Affairs, to Muck a Muck restaurant, Vancouver, BC, 26 January 1976, Bungees correspondence, 1975–1980, Indian & Métis Friendship Centre of Winnipeg fonds, P746-2, Archives of Manitoba. Bungee restaurant explained that Bungee is a Plains-Ojibwa group also known as Saulteaux or Nakaw-n-niuk. Bass, *Restaurant Menu Guide*, 19.

38   Goldsborough, "Memorable Manitobans: Mary Margaret Richard"; Lawrence Barkwell, "Mary Richard, OM (1940–2010)," Gabriel Dumont Institute of Native Studies and Applied Research, Virtual Museum of Métis History and Culture, https://www.metismuseum.ca/media/document.php/14512.Mary%20Richard.pdf (accessed 28 May 2023); Mary Margaret Richard obituary, *Winnipeg Free Press*, 13 September 2010, https://passages.winnipegfreepress.com/passage-details/id-168864/RICHARD_MARY (accessed 28 May 2023).

39   Val Werier, "Two Women Who Made It," *Winnipeg Free Press*, 9 January 1985, 11.

40   Advertisement for the Teepee Restaurant & Lounge, *Winnipeg Free Press*, 2 February 1984, 35; Marion Warhaft, "Dining Out: Bungees' Native Cooking Delights," *Winnipeg Free Press*, 27 August 1982, 18; Marion Warhaft, "Dining Out: Fish So Good You Forget It's Diet Right," *Winnipeg Free Press*, 27 March 1981, 30.

41   Bass, *Restaurant Menu Guide*, 10.

42   Gordon Sinclair, "Winnipeg Arena Goes High-Tech," *Winnipeg Free Press*, 2 October 1984, 25; Frain Cory,

"Jackson Unrecognized Commodity Full of Talent," *Winnipeg Free Press,* 21 July 1983, 31; Advertisement for the Teepee Restaurant & Lounge, *Winnipeg Free Press,* 2 February 1984, 35.

43   Val Werier, "Two Women Who Made It," *Winnipeg Free Press,* 9 January 1985, 11; the Teepee Restaurant & Lounge, file summary (as of 25 January 2023), Companies Office, Government of Manitoba.

44   CBC Manitoba, "Profile: Steven Watson," 30 March 2016, https://www.cbc.ca/news/canada/manitoba/steven-watson-1.3513442 (accessed 28 May 2023); National Centre for Truth and Reconciliation, "TRC Reports," https://nctr.ca/records/reports/ (accessed 28 May 2023).

45   See, for example, Colpitts, *Pemmican Empire;* and Binnema, *Common & Contested Ground.*

46   Briley, "History of Refrigeration"; Freidberg, "Freshness from Afar."

47   Steven Watson, interviewed by by Janis Thiessen, Kent Davis, and Kimberley Moore, Commonwealth College, Winnipeg, MB, 16 January 2019.

48   Ibid., 00:03:39–00:04:03.

49   Ibid., 00:18:30–00:19:19.

50   Ibid., 00:05:03–00:06:28.

51   Ibid., 00:57:49–00:58:06.

52   Ibid., 01:02:45–01:03:13.

53   See Daschuk, *Clearing the Plains.*

54   Moss and Gardner-O'Toole, *Aboriginal People;* Waisberg and Holzkamm, "'Tendency to Discourage Them.'"

55   "First Nations Were First Farmers in Manitoba," *Manitoba Co-operator,* 4 July 2016, https://www.manitobacooperator.ca/news-opinion/news/first-nations-were-first-farmers-in-manitoba-2/ (accessed 28 May 2023); Flynn and Syms, "Manitoba's First Farmers"; Shannon VanRaes, "Treaty Rights to Farm Were Not Fulfilled," *Manitoba Co-operator,* 3 March 2015, https://www.manitobacooperator.ca/crops/treaty-rights-to-farm-were-not-fulfilled/ (accessed 28 May 2023); Carter, *Lost Harvests,* 209–13, 253.

56   Harris, *Fish, Law, and Colonialism.*

57   Steven Watson interview, 01:04:18–01:04:37.

58   Though the province did switch to a private marketing system for fishers in 2018, the St. Laurent fish-processing plant has not been built. Jade Markus, "'It's a Mess': Manitoba Fishers Missing Close to $1 Million in Payments," *CBC News,* 15 January 2018, https://www.cbc.ca/news/canada/manitoba/it-s-a-mess-manitoba-fishers-missing-close-to-1-million-in-payments-1.4487242 (accessed 28 May 2023).

59   Murray McNeill, "New Plant Would Be a Reel Asset," *Winnipeg Free Press,* 31 May 2016, B5; "St. Laurent Hoping to Revive Plans for Fish Processor," *Manitoba Fishing,* http://manitobafishing.net/st-laurent-hoping-to-revive-plans-for-fish-processor/ (accessed 28 May 2023); "Province of Manitoba Withdrawals from Freshwater Fish Marketing Act," *Fisher River Cree Nation,* https://fisherriver.ca/current-issues/ (accessed 15 April 2019).

60   Kristin Annable, "Fishers Demand Marketing Freedom," *Winnipeg Free Press,* 5 July 2016, https://www.winnipegfreepress.com/local/fisher-demands-marketing-freedom-385621681.html (accessed 28 May 2023).

61   Steven Watson interview, 00:05:04–00:05:17.

62   Ibid., 00:05:51–00:06:42.

63   Ibid., 00:29:59–00:30:41.

64   Ibid., 00:24:33.

65   Ibid., 00:31:56–00:32:26.

66   Ibid., 01:05:30–01:06:15.

67   Ibid., 01:17:17–01:17:51.

68   Emily Chung, "Indigenous Clam Farming Technology Is as Old as Egyptian Pyramids," *CBC News,* 27 February 2019, https://www.cbc.ca/news/science/clam-gardens-dating-1.4761214 (accessed 28 May 2023); Smith et al., "3500 Years of Shellfish Mariculture."

69   Mt. Pleasant, "Paradox of Plows and Productivity."

70   Kimmerer, *Braiding Sweetgrass,* 128–40; Mt. Pleasant, "Food Yields and Nutrient Analyses."

71   Steven Watson interview, 00:06:55–00:07:30.

72 Ibid., 00:11:02–00:12:00. Fred Wiseman (Missisquoi Abenaki) agrees that the fourth sister is tobacco, though he says it could also be sunflowers, sunchokes, or ground cherries. By contrast, Taylor Keen (Omaha and Cherokee) identifies the fourth sister as sunflowers, while Alanna Norris (Red Lake Ojibwe) identifies it as either sunflowers or manomin. Grant Gerlock, "Tribes Revive Indigenous Crops, and the Food Traditions That Go with Them," *NPR The Salt,* 18 November 2016, https://www.npr.org/sections/thesalt/2016/11/18/502025877/tribes-revive-indigenous-crops-and-the-food-traditions-that-go-with-them (accessed 28 May 2023); Seward Community Co-op, "Honoring Indigenous Food Traditions," 28 December 2021, https://seward.coop/honoring-indigenous-food-traditions/ (accessed 28 May 2023); "Tribal Traditions: Updated Cuisine," *Edible Vermont,* 19 November 2020, https://ediblevermont.ediblecommunities.com/food-thought/tribal-traditions-updated-cuisine (accessed 28 May 2023).

73 Kimmerer, *Braiding Sweetgrass,* 212; Watts, "Smudge This," 151, 159–60.

74 Steven Watson interview, 00:37:28–00:00:38:15.

75 Ibid., 00:39:22–00:39:45.

76 The "Sixties Scoop" is a term for government policies that resulted in the removal of Indigenous children from their homes and their placement in foster homes prior to adoption by white families. See Stevenson, *Intimate Integration.*

77 Steven Watson interview, 00:29:57–00:31:24.

78 Million, "Telling Secrets"; Mosby, "Administering Colonial Science."

79 Truth and Reconciliation Commission of Canada, *Knock on the Door.*

80 Steven Watson interview, 00:34:30–00:35:00.

81 Blumenthal, McKean, and Foord, *Historic Heston.*

82 Steven Watson interview, 00:51:44–00:52:28.

83 Ibid., 01:27:08–01:01:27:53.

84 Ibid., 01:28:08–01:01:29:20.

85 Ibid., 00:42:47–00:43:08.

CONCLUSION

1 Driver, *Culinary Landmarks,* xxxiii, 921.

2 Sharpless, "Cookbooks as Resources," 197.

3 Driver, *Culinary Landmarks,* 921.

4 Ibid., 923.

5 Busch, "Learning by Pinches and Dashes," 23.

6 Ibid.

7 Wilmshurst, "How to Eat." Anny Gaul discusses a similar process in Egypt: cookbooks produced by middle-class women helped shape the national and cultural identity of Egypt. Gaul, "From Kitchen Arabic to Recipes."

8 Kenneally, "Cuisine of the Tundra," 290–91.

9 Mary Maushard, "Sugar Pie and Seal Flippers," *Winnipeg Free Press,* 12 June 1982, 93.

10 Ray, *Ethnic Restaurateur,* 194.

11 Corey Mintz, "Where Are Canada's Indigenous Restaurants?" *BuzzFeed News,* 27 April 2017, https://www.buzzfeed.com/coreymintz/where-are-canadas-indigenous-restaurants (accessed 28 May 2023).

12 As Corey Mintz reminds us, "There is no one 'Indigenous cuisine' any more than there is an 'Asian cuisine.' Canada is a big place." Ibid.

13 "Society and state operate on the false equivalence of Indigenous and minority groups, undertake powerful narrative erasures, and show an uneven appreciation and weak grasp of Indigeneity, along with a disinclination to improve that understanding." Grey and Newman, "Beyond Culinary Colonialism," 725.

14 Eric Ritskes, "The Invention of Canada's Relationship to Indigenous Foods: Bannock French Toast with Saskatoon Berry and Birch Syrup Compote," *Anise to Za'atar* blog post, 10 June 2020, https://anisetozaatar.com/2020/06/10/the-invention-of-canadas-relationship-to-indigenous-foods-bannock-french-toast-with-saskatoon-berry-and-birch-syrup-compote/ (accessed 28 May 2023).

15 Doonan, "Wild Cuisine and Canadianness," 14.

16 Grey and Newman, "Beyond Culinary Colonialism," 717.

17 Ibid., 719. Emphasis in original. Our editor, Jill Mc-Conkey, observes that this gentrification of Indigenous cuisine by settlers occurs at the same time as "Indigenous communities face circumscribed access due to shrinking harvest territory, industry-related changes to habitat, and high costs due to limited infrastructure." Personal communication to the authors, 20 January 2022.

18 Hay, *Inventing the Thrifty Gene*, 2, 3. "In other words, Canadian scientists have assisted in the sanitizing of state policies and the whitewashing of settler colonial history. By providing evidence of the long history of human experiments, malnutrition studies, vaccine trials, and gene-hunting studies that led to the rise and reinvention of the thrifty gene, I diagnose settler colonial science as a symptom of Canadians' genocidal way of relating to and thinking about Indigenous peoples." Hay, *Inventing the Thrifty Gene*, 4. See also Krotz, *Diagnosing the Legacy*.

19 Lazy Bear Lodge, "A One-of-a-kind Dining Experience," https://www.lazybearlodge.com/lazy-bear-lodge/cafe (accessed 28 May 2023). See Chapter 5 for further discussion of northern Manitoba food.

20 Grey and Newman, "Beyond Culinary Colonialism," 725.

21 Doreen Klassen, "'You Must Be at Least 85!' Low German Mennonites in Mexico and Belize 'Research' a Kanadier Anthropologist," unpublished paper presented at the Mennonite Studies conference "Departing Canada, Encountering Latin America: Reflections on the Centenary of Mennonite Emigration from Canada to Mexico and Paraguay," University of Winnipeg, 22 October 2022.

22 Pilcher, "Whole Enchilada," 694.

23 Ibid.

24 Iacovetta, Korinek, and Epp, "Introduction," in *Edible Histories*, 22.

25 Russell, "Archives, Academy, and Access," 53; British Library, "Collection Guides: Oral Histories of Food Production and Consumption," https://www.bl.uk/collection-guides/oral-histories-of-food-production-and-consumption (accessed 28 May 2023).

26 Portelli, "Oral History as Genre," 25.

27 Ibid., 38.

28 Raviv, "Food, Art, and the Challenges," 2.

29 Ibid., 4.

30 Doonan, "Wild Cuisine and Canadianness," 24.

Bibliography

ORAL HISTORY INTERVIEWS

Basler, Carley. Interviewed by Kimberley Moore, Janis Thiessen, and Kent Davies, 13 June 2019, Churchill Northern Studies Centre, Churchill, MB. Digital audio recording. Manitoba Food History Project, Oral History Centre Archive, University of Winnipeg, Winnipeg, MB [hereafter UW OHCA].

Calogeris, John. Interviewed by Janis Thiessen, 20 August 2019, Winnipeg, MB. Digital audio recording. Manitoba Food History Project, UW OHCA.

Daudrich, Wally, and Jason Ransom. Interviewed by Kent Davies, Kimberley Moore, and Janis Thiessen, 17 June 2019, Churchill, MB. Digital audio recording. Manitoba Food History Project, UW OHCA.

Faraci, Anthony. Interviewed by Emily Gartner and Trent Brownlee, 16 May 2019, Winnipeg, MB. Digital audio recording. Manitoba Food History Project, UW OHCA.

Ginakes, G. John, and Demitris Scouras. Interviewed by Zachary Hamilton, 15 December 2017, Winnipeg, MB. Digital audio recording. Manitoba Food History Project, UW OHCA.

Hagar, Alvin. Interviewed by Ranald Thurgood, 9 August 1982, Toronto, ON. Transcript. Indian History Film Project, University of Saskatchewan Indigenous Studies Portal, https://iportal.usask.ca/record/29505. Accessed 7 June 2023.

Hart, Steven. Interviewed by Janis Thiessen, 6 February 2019, Las Vegas, NV. Digital audio recording. Manitoba Food History Project, UW OHCA.

Hart, Steven, and Wendy Hart. Interviewed by Barbara Tabach, 23 October 2014. Southern Nevada Jewish Heritage Project, University of Nevada at Las Vegas.

Hirose, Harold A. Interviewed by Lillian E. Mukai, 20 October 1987. Japanese Canadians in Manitoba oral history project, C861, Archives of Manitoba.

Kusano, Henry. Interviewed by Keiko Miki, 27 October 1987. Japanese Canadians in Manitoba oral history project, C863, Archives of Manitoba.

Lam, Edward. Interviewed by Daniel Pastuck, 4 February 2015, Winnipeg, MB. Janis Thiessen, HIST-3007, UW OHCA.

Loewen, Royden. Interviewed by Janis Thiessen, 12 March 2019, Winnipeg, MB. Digital audio recording. Manitoba Food History Project, UW OHCA.

Loewen, Royden. Interviewed by Arshdeep Kaur and Colin Rier, 14 May 2019, Winnipeg, MB. Digital audio recording. Manitoba Food History Project, UW OHCA.

McEwan, Helen. Interviewed by Janis Thiessen, Kent Davies, and Kimberley Moore, 14 June 2019, Churchill, MB. Digital audio recording. Manitoba Food History Project, UW OHCA.

McIntyre, Patricia, and Maureen Martin Osland. Interviewed by Kimberley Moore, 3 July 2019, Gimli, MB. Digital audio recording. Manitoba Food History Project, UW OHCA.

Matsuo, Kanaye Connie. Interviewed by Lillian E. Mukai, 3 September 1987. Japanese Canadians in Manitoba oral history project, C840, Archives of Manitoba.

Nakai, Tokunaga. Interviewed by Isabel Hirota, 15 September 1987. Japanese Canadians in Manitoba oral history project, C847, Archives of Manitoba.

Ontong, Krispin, and Peegy Ontong. Interviewed by Sarah Story and Janis Thiessen, 6 July 2018, Steinbach, MB. Digital audio recording. Manitoba Food History Project, UW OHCA.

Powell, Forbes. Interviewed by Janis Thiessen, 17 August 2018, Winnipeg, MB. Digital audio recording. Manitoba Food History Project, UW OHCA.

Shumka, Betty. Interviewed by Janis Thiessen, 3 August 2019, Dauphin, MB. Digital audio recording, Manitoba Food History Project, UW OHCA.

Sirski-Howell, Joyce. Interviewed by Janis Thiessen, 3 August 2019, Dauphin, MB. Digital audio recording. Manitoba Food History Project, UW OHCA.

Smith, Kevin. Interviewed by Janis Thiessen and Sarah Story, 29 June 2018, Steinbach, MB. Digital audio recording, Manitoba Food History Project, UW OHCA.

Staff, Sharon, and Roger Leclerc. Interviewed by Russ Gourluck, 22 July 2009, Winnipeg, MB. Voices of the North End, PastForward: Winnipeg's Digital Public History, Winnipeg Public Library, http://pastforward.winnipeg.ca/digital/collection/voicesofne/id/1/rec/1. Accessed 7 June 2023.

Stover, Joe. Interviewed by Kent Davies, 16 June 2019, Churchill, MB. Digital audio recording. Manitoba Food History Project, UW OHCA.

Watson, Steven. Interviewed by Janis Thiessen, Kent Davies, and Kimberley Moore, 16 January 2019, Commonwealth College, Winnipeg, MB. Digital audio recording. Manitoba Food History Project, UW OHCA.

Webber, Helen. Interviewed by Kimberley Moore, Kent Davies, and Janis Thiessen, 14 June 2019, Churchill, MB. Digital audio recording. Manitoba Food History Project, UW OHCA.

Wichers, Joanelle, and Geralyn Wichers. Interviewed by Sarah Story, 2 July 2018, Steinbach, MB. Digital audio recording. Manitoba Food History Project, UW OHCA.

Wingie, Glenn. Interviewed by Janis Thiessen, 10 June 2019, Winnipeg, MB. Notes from an unrecorded interview. Manitoba Food History Project, UW OHCA.

GOVERNMENT SOURCES AND ARCHIVES

Churchill Library and Archives, Churchill, MB.

City of Winnipeg Archives, City of Winnipeg By-Laws.

City of Winnipeg Council Minutes, City of Winnipeg Archives.

City of Winnipeg Legislation & Reception Committee, City of Winnipeg Archives.

Government of Canada, Agriculture and Agri-Food Canada.

Government of Canada, Department of Labour, *Labour Gazette.*

Government of Canada, Panel on Research Ethics.

Government of Canada, Royal Commission on Aboriginal Peoples.

Government of Manitoba, Agriculture and Resource Development.

Government of Manitoba, Companies Office.

Government of Manitoba, Environment, Climate and Parks, *Regions.*

Government of Manitoba, Health and Seniors Care.

Government of Manitoba, Health, Seniors and Active Living.

Government of Manitoba, Indian Act, RSC 1985.

Government of Manitoba, Indigenous Reconciliation and Northern Relations, *Community Profiles.*

Government of Manitoba, *The Manitoba Wild Rice Industry: A Commission of Inquiry.*

Government of Manitoba, The Public Health Act, Food and Food Handling Establishments Regulation, CCSM c. P210.

Government of Manitoba, *Report of the Aboriginal Justice Inquiry.*

Government of Manitoba, Trade and Investment.

Government of Manitoba, The Wild Rice Act, CCSM c. W140.

Government of Ontario, Wild Rice Harvesting Act, RSO 1970, c. 497.

Library of Parliament Research Branch.

Manitoba Archives, Government Records Departmental File, Companies Office, Business Names Registration Files.

Manitoba Museum, Winnipeg, MB.

Mennonite Central Committee Menno Wiebe Native Concerns Collection, Mennonite Heritage Centre Archives, Winnipeg, MB.

Nat Hart Collection, MS-00419, Special Collections and Archives, University Libraries, University of Nevada, Las Vegas.

Ontario Ministry of Health.

Peel's Prairie Provinces, *Henderson's Directories Winnipeg.*

Statistics Canada.

Statutes of Manitoba.

Statutes of Saskatchewan.

Mac Runciman fonds, University of Manitoba Archives and Special Collections.

Winnipeg Tribune Personalities Collection, University of Manitoba Archives and Special Collections.

Winnipeg Tribune fonds, University of Manitoba Archives and Special Collections.United Nations Food and Agriculture Organization.

What Canada Ate, Archival and Special Collections, University of Guelph Library, Guelph, ON.

Winnipeg Regional Health Authority, Winnipeg, MB.

MEDIA

Atlas Obscura

Beausejour Clipper

Brandon Daily Sun

Brandon Weekly Sun

BuzzFeed News

Canada's History

Canadian Business Journal

CBC Archives

CBC Manitoba

CBC News

CBC Saskatchewan

Ciao!

CNN Phiippines

CTV News

CTV News Winnipeg

Dauphin Herald and Press

Filipino Journal

Global News

Globe and Mail

Grandview Exponent

Guardian

Hamiota Echo

Henderson's Directory

Hudson's Bay Herald

Imbibe

Indian News

Lac du Bonnet Springfield Leader

Las Vegas Sun

Las Vegas Weekly

Los Angeles Times

Manitoba Co-operator

Manitoba Daily Free Press

Manitoba Free Press

Manitoba Inc. Magazine

The Manitoban

Medicine Hat News

Minneapolis Star Tribune

National Post

New York Times

NICHE: Network in Canadian History & Environment

NPR The Salt

Pas Opasquia Times

RealAgriculture

Roblin Review

Russell Banner

Selkirk Journal

Spectator Tribune

Steinbach Carillon

Stonewall Argus

Toronto Star

Victoria Daily Colonist

The Walrus

Western Labor News

Winnipeg Evening Tribune

Winnipeg Free Press

Winnipeg Sun

Winnipeg Tribune

Yahoo News Canada

WEBSITES

Unless otherwise noted, the following websites were accessed 7 June 2023.

A&W Canada, http://www.aw.ca.

African American History Truck, https://chesapeakeheartland.squarespace.com/african-american-humanities-truck.

Anise to Za'atar, http://anisetozaatar.com.

L'Autochtone Taverne Americaine, https://www.lautochtone.com.

Blueberries & Polar Bears, https://blueberriesandpolarbears.com/.

British Library, http://www.bl.uk.

British Library, "Collection Guides: Oral Histories of Food Production and Consumption," https://www.bl.uk/collection-guides/oral-histories-of-food-production-and-consumption.

Canadian Flavors, https://www.canadianflavors.com.

Canadian Organic Growers, https://www.cog.ca.

Culinaria Research Centre, https://utsc.utoronto.ca/culinaria/food-studies-university-toronto.

Culinaria Research Centre and Multicultural History Society of Ontario, "Mapping Scarborough Chinatown," https://culinaria.digital.utsc.utoronto.ca.

DC Humanities Truck, http://humanitiestruck.com.

Edible Vermont, https://ediblevermont.ediblecommunities.com.

Feast Café Bistro, https://feastcafebistro.com.

Fisher River Cree Nation, http://fisherriver.ca.

Gabriel Dumont Institute of Native Studies and Applied Research, Virtual Museum of Métis History and Culture, https://www.metismuseum.ca.

Greenhouse Canada, https://www.greenhousecanada.com.

Harvest Moon Oral History, http://www.harvestmoonoh.com.

Ichi Ban restaurant, https://www.ichibanwinnipeg.com/.

Indigenous World Winery, https://www.indigenousworldwinery.com.

Internet Archive, Wayback Machine, https://web.archive.org.

Japanese Cultural Association of Manitoba, https://www.jcamwpg.ca/.

Kekuli Café, https://www.kekulicafe.com.

Kiinawin Kawindomowin Story Nations, https://storynations.utoronto.ca/index.php/the-paypom-treaty/.

Kookum's Pantry, https://www.kookums.ca.

Kū-kŭm Kitchen, http://www.kukum-kitchen.com (accessed 21 February 2023).

Lazy Bear Lodge, http://www.lazybearlodge.com.

Long Plain First Nation, https://lpband.ca/.

Manitoba Fishing, http://manitobafishing.net.

Manitoba Food History Project, https://www.manitobafoodhistory.ca/.

Manitoba Historical Society, http://www.mhs.mb.ca/.

Manomin Project, https://www.instagram.com/manominproject/ and https://niche-canada.org/manomin/.

Mennonite Heritage Village, https://mennoniteheritagevillage.com.

Mr. Bannock, https://www.mrbannock.com.

Naosap Harvest, https://www.naosapharvest.com.

National Centre for Truth and Reconciliation, http://nctr.ca.

NiCHE: Network in Canadian History & Environment, https://niche-canada.org.

Nk'Mip Cellars, https://www.nkmipcellars.com/About-Us.

Nunavut Development Corporation, "Kivalliq Arctic Foods," https://ndcorp.nu.ca/we-invest/subsidiaries/kivalliq-arctic-foods/.

NWC Wild Rice Company, https://nwcwildrice.ca.

PEGuru, http://peguru.ca.

Philadelphia Public History Truck, https://phillyhistorytruck.wordpress.com/about/.

Preserves: A Manitoba Food History Podcast, https://www.manitobafoodhistory.ca/preserves-pod.

St. Joseph's Ukrainian Catholic Church, https://www.stjosephukrwinnipeg.ca/st-joseph/.

Salisbury House, https://www.salisburyhouse.ca.

Salmon n' Bannock, https://www.salmonandbannock.net.

Sevala's Ukrainian Deli, http://www.sevalas.com/.

Seward Community Co-op, https://seward.coop.

Southern Foodways Alliance, https://www.southernfoodways.org.

StoryCorps, https://storycorps.org/mobile-tour/.

Tourism Winnipeg, http://www.tourismwinnipeg.com.

T-Town Style Pizza, https://ttownstylepizza.com.

Ukrainian Canadian Congress Manitoba, https://uccmanitoba.ca.

University of Nevada Las Vegas Special Collections and Archives, https://www.library.unlv.edu/whats_new_in_special_collections.

University of Regina, Canadian Plains Research Center, "Indian History Film Project," https://ourspace.uregina.ca/handle/10294/26.

University of Toronto Libraries, *Canada's Oldest Profession: Sex Work and Bawdy House Legislation.* https://exhibits.library.utoronto.ca/exhibits/show/bawdy.

University of Winnipeg Communications, https://news-centre.uwinnipeg.ca.

University of Winnipeg Research Office, https://www.uwinnipeg.ca/research/.

West End Dumplings, http://westenddumplings.blogspot.com.

"What is Northern Food?" https://www.manitobafoodhistory.ca/northern-food.

Wild Man Ricing, https://www.wildmanricing.ca.

Winnipeg Architecture Foundation, https://www.winnipegarchitecture.ca/.

Winnipeg Downtown Places, http://winnipegdowntownplaces.blogspot.com.

FILMS

49th Parallel. Directed by Michael Powell, 1941. Culver City, CA: Columbia Pictures.

El Toro. Directed by Danielle Sturk, 2018. Winnipeg, MB.

Fahrenheit 7-11. Directed by Walter Forsberg, and edited by Matthew Rankin, 2011.

Muskeg Special. Directed by Gregory Zbitnew, 2007. Winnipeg Film Group. Transcript, http://www.dreamlogiccorporation.com/MuskegSpecial_Transcript.html. Accessed 24 May 2023.

Nuhoniyeh—Our Story. Directed by Allen Code and Mary Code, 1993. Super 8 film, 55 min. Watertown: Documentary Educational Resources, Inc. https://youtu.be/wRnxepJx_48. Accessed 24 May 2023.

Prairie Soul: Black Rhythms from the Heartland. Directed by Adrian Peek, 1991.

BOOKS, JOURNAL ARTICLES, UNPUBLISHED PAPERS

Adomako-Ansah, Sarah, and Natasha Joachim. *Black on the Prairies: Teacher Guide.* CBC, 2021, https://s3.documentcloud.org/documents/21185424/cbc–black-on-the-prairies-teacher-guide.pdf. Accessed 7 June 2023.

Allen, Gary, and Ken Albala, eds. *The Business of Food: Encyclopedia of the Food and Drink Industries.* Westport, CT: Greenwood Press, 2007.

Anderson, Colin R., Jennifer Brady, and Charles Z. Levkoe, eds. *Conversations in Food Studies.* Winnipeg: University of Manitoba Press, 2016.

Aviv, Dan Mendelsohn. "B/Eating the Past: A Night Out at the 'Cardo Culinaria.'" *Contemporary Jewry* 22, no. 1 (January 2001): 65–79.

Backhouse, Constance. *Colour-Coded: A Legal History of Racism in Canada, 1900–1950.* Toronto: University of Toronto Press, 1999.

———. "Nineteenth-Century Canadian Prostitution Law Reflection of a Discriminatory Society." *Histoire Sociale/Social History* 18, no. 36 (November 1985): 387–423.

Banfield, Alexander W.F. "The Caribou Crisis." *The Beaver* (Spring 1956): 3–7.

Bass, Jerry, ed. *Restaurant Menu Guide & Cook Book.* Winnipeg, MB: Welmar-Case, 1981.

Benson, John. "Hawking and Peddling in Canada 1867–1914." *Histoire Sociale/Social History* 18, no. 35 (1985): 75–83.

Bertaux, Daniel, and Isabelle Bertaux-Wiame. "Artisanal Bakery in France: How It Lives and Why It Survives." In *The Petite Bourgeoisie: Comparative Analysis of the Uneasy Stratum,* edited by Frank Bechhofer and Brian Elliot, 155–89. London: Macmillan, 1981.

———. "Life Stories in the Bakers' Trade." In *Biography and Society: The Life History Approach in the Social Sciences,* edited by Daniel Bertaux, 169–89. London: Sage, 1981.

Binnema, Theodore. *Common & Contested Ground: A Human and Environmental History of the Northwestern Plains.* Toronto: University of Toronto Press, 2004.

Bluestone, Daniel M. "'The Pushcart Evil': Peddlers, Merchants, and New York City's Streets, 1890–1940." *Journal of Urban History* 18, no. 1 (1991): 68–92.

Blumenthal, Heston, Dave McKean, and Romas Foord. *Historic Heston.* London: Bloomsbury, 2014.

Bonifacio, Glenda Tibe. *Pinay on the Prairies: Filipino Women and Transnational Identities.* Vancouver: University of British Columbia Press, 2013.

Brandson, Lorraine. "A Cache for Leaner Times." *Eskimo* 68 (Fall–Winter 2004–2005): 12–16.

———. *Churchill Hudson Bay: A Guide to Natural and Cultural Heritage.* Rev. ed. Churchill: Churchill Eskimo Museum, 2016.

———. "Country Food: Sustainer of Life." *Eskimo* 66 (Fall–Winter 2003–2004): 7–13.

———. *From Tundra to Forest: A Chipewyan Resource Manual.* Winnipeg: Manitoba Museum of Man and Nature, 1981.

Briley, George C. "A History of Refrigeration." In *100 Years of Refrigeration: A Supplement to ASHRAE Journal.* American Society of Heating, Refrigerating, and Air-Conditioning Engineers (November 2004): S31–S34.

Brzozowski, Matthew, Yuqian Lu, and SEDAP Research Program. "Home Cooking, Food Consumption and Food Production among the Unemployed and Retired Households." SEDAP [Social and Economic Dimensions of an Aging Population] Paper, No. 151. Hamilton: SEDAP Research Program, 2006.

Busch, Jane C. "Learning by Pinches and Dashes: Using Cookbooks as Research Documents." *History News* 52, no. 2 (Spring 1997): 22–25.

Bussidor, Ila, and Üstün Bilgen-Reinart. *Night Spirits: The Story of the Relocation of the Sayisi Dene.* Winnipeg: University of Manitoba Press, 1997.

Campbell, Marian L., Ruth M.F. Diamant, Brian D. Macpherson, and Judy L. Halladay. "The Contemporary Food Supply of Three Northern Manitoba Cree Communities." *Canadian Journal of Public Health/Revue Canadienne de Santé Publique* 88, no. 2 (1997): 105–8.

Carter, Sarah. "Erasing and Replacing: Property and Homestead Rights of First Nations Farmers of Manitoba and the Northwest, 1870s–1910s." In *Place and Replace: Essays on Western Canada,* edited by Adele Perry, Esyllt W. Jones, and Leah Morton, 14–39. Winnipeg: University of Manitoba Press, 2013.

———. *Imperial Plots: Women, Land, and the Spadework of British Colonialism on the Canadian Prairies*. Winnipeg: University of Manitoba Press, 2016.

———. *Lost Harvests: Prairie Indian Reserve Farmers and Government Policy*. 2nd ed. Montreal: McGill-Queen's University Press, 2019.

Chen, Anne, Norman Peng, and Kuang-peng Hung. "Chef Image's Influence on Tourists' Dining Experiences." *Annals of Tourism Research* 56 (2016): 154–57.

Chen, Anita Beltran. *From Sunbelt to Snowbelt: Filipinos in Canada*. Calgary: Canadian Ethnic Studies Journal, 1998.

Chimbos, Peter D. *The Canadian Odyssey: The Greek Experience in Canada*. Toronto: McClelland and Stewart, 1980.

Cho, Lily. *Eating Chinese: Chinese Restaurants and Diaspora*. Toronto: University of Toronto Press, 2018.

Chornoboy, Eleanor Hildebrand. *Faspa: A Snack of Mennonite Stories*. Winnipeg: Interior Publishing, 2003.

Chung, So Kim. "Pyramids of Pink Shrimp: A Brief History of Las Vegas Dining, 1940s–1970s." *Nevada in the West* 3, no. 1 (Spring 2012): 9–14.

Cochrane, Carol, Janna Barkman, Shailesh Shukla, Virginia Grabowski, Gerry Mason, Brielle Beaudin, University of Winnipeg, and Fisher River Cree Nation. Reprint ed. *Kêhté Ochek Sipí Minowasowak: The Forgotten Traditional Foods of Fisher River: Community Food Security Manual*. Winnipeg: University of Winnipeg, 2021.

Colpitts, George. *Pemmican Empire: Food, Trade, and the Last Bison Hunts in the North American Plains,* *1780–1882*. New York: Cambridge University Press, 2015.

Confino, Alon. "Collective Memory and Cultural History: Problems of Method." *American Historical Review* 102, no. 5 (December 1997): 1386–1403.

Connerton, Paul. *How Societies Remember*. New York: Cambridge University Press, 1989.

Contois, Emily J.H. *Diners, Dudes & Diets: How Gender and Power Collide in Food Media and Culture*. Chapel Hill: University of North Carolina Press, 2020.

Cruikshank, Julie. *Life Lived Like a Story: Life Stories of Three Yukon Native Elders*. American Indian Lives. Lincoln: University of Nebraska Press, 1990.

Cwiertka, Katarzyna J. "From Ethnic to Hip: Circuits of Japanese Cuisine in Europe." *Food and Foodways* 13, no. 4 (2005): 241–72.

Danysk, Cecilia. "'A Bachelor's Paradise': Homesteaders, Hired Hands, and the Construction of Masculinity, 1880–1930." In *Making Western Canada: Essays on European Colonization and Settlement,* edited by Catherine Cavanaugh and Jeremy Mouat, 154–85. Toronto: Garamond Press, 1996.

Daschuk, James W. *Clearing the Plains: Disease, Politics of Starvation, and the Loss of Indigenous Life*. Regina: University of Regina Press, 2019.

Donohue, Patrick. *The Erwin Story*. Toronto: Self-published, 1982.

Doonan, Natalie. "Wild Cuisine and Canadianness: Creeping Rootstalks and Subterranean Struggle." *Gastronomica* 18, no. 3 (Fall 2018): 14–27.

Driver, Elizabeth. *Culinary Landmarks: A Bibliography of Canadian Cookbooks, 1825–1949*. Toronto: University of Toronto Press, 2016.

Elias, Megan. *Lunch: A History.* Toronto: Rowman and Littlefield, 2014.

Ellis, Joseph Henry. *The Ministry of Agriculture in Manitoba, 1870–1970.* Winnipeg: Economics and Publications Branch, Manitoba Department of Agriculture, 1971.

Flynn, Catherine, and E. Leigh Syms. "Manitoba's First Farmers." *Manitoba History* 31 (Spring 1996). http://www.mhs.mb.ca/docs/mb_history/31/ firstfarmers.shtml. Accessed 7 June 2023.

Foster, John E. *The Developing West: Essays on Canadian History in Honor of Lewis H. Thomas.* Edmonton: University of Alberta Press, 1983.

Freidberg, Susanne. "Freshness from Afar: The Colonial Roots of Contemporary Fresh Foods." *Food and History* 8, no. 1 (2010): 257–78.

Friesen, Gerald. *The Canadian Prairies: A History.* Toronto: University of Toronto Press, 1987.

Friesen, Jean. "Grant Me Wherewith to Make My Living." In *Aboriginal Resource Use in Canada: Historical and Legal Aspects,* edited by Kerry Abel and Jean Friesen, 141–55. Winnipeg: University of Manitoba Press, 1991.

Frisch, Michael. *A Shared Authority: Essays on the Craft and Meaning of Oral and Public History.* Albany, NY: SUNY Press, 1991.

Fujiwara, Aya. *Ethnic Elites and Canadian Identity: Japanese, Ukrainians, and Scots, 1919–1971.* Winnipeg: University of Manitoba Press, 2012.

Gaul, Anny. "From Kitchen Arabic to Recipes for Good Taste: Nation, Empire, and Race in Egyptian Cookbooks." *Global Food History* (2021): 1–30.

Gonzales, Gema Charmaine. "Kitchenlessness, or the Migrant's Affair with Food." *Gastronomica* 21, no. 2 (Summer 2021): 71–72.

Gora, L. Sasha. "A Cuisine of its Own: Culinary Colonialism in Canada." Public lecture, Institute of Historical Research, University of London, 6 October 2022.

———. "From Meat to Metaphor: Beavers and Conflicting Imaginations of the Edible." In *Canadian Culinary Imaginations,* edited by Shelley Boyd and Dorothy Barensco, 93–113. Montreal and Kingston: McGill-Queen's University Press, 2020.

Gourluck, Russ. *The Mosaic Village: An Illustrated History of Winnipeg's North End.* Winnipeg: Great Plains Publications, 2010.

Greer, Allan. "Settler Colonialism and Beyond." *Journal of the CHA* 30, no. 1 (2019): 61–86.

Grey, Sam, and Lenore Newman. "Beyond Culinary Colonialism: Indigenous Food Sovereignty, Liberal Multiculturalism, and the Control of Gastronomic Capital." *Agriculture and Human Values* 35, no. 3 (2018): 717–30.

Grimm, Joe, and Katherine Yung. *Coney Detroit.* Detroit: Painted Turtle Press, 2012.

Grumett, David, Luke Bretherton, and Stephen R. Holmes. "Fast Food: A Critical Theological Perspective." *Food, Culture and Society* 14, no. 3 (September 2011): 375–92.

Gutman, Richard J.S. *American Diner: Then and Now.* Baltimore: Johns Hopkins University Press, 2000.

Hall, Norma. *Casualty of Colonialism: Red River Métis Farming, 1810–1870.* (2015). https:// resistancemothers.wordpress.com/a-casualty-of-colonialism/. Accessed 7 June 2023.

Harris, Douglas C. *Fish, Law, and Colonialism: The Legal Capture of Salmon in British Columbia.* Toronto: University of Toronto Press, 2001.

Hartman, James B. "The Churches of Early Winnipeg." *Manitoba History* 45 (Spring/Summer 2003). http://www.mhs.mb.ca/docs/mb_history/45/winnipegchurches.shtml. Accessed 7 June 2023.

Hartmann, John. "Starbucks and the Third Wave." In *Coffee—Philosophy for Everyone: Grounds for Debate,* edited by Scott F. Parker and Michael W. Austin, 166–83. Chichester, West Sussex: John Wiley & Sons, 2011.

Hay, Travis. *Inventing the Thrifty Gene: The Science of Settler Colonialism.* Winnipeg: University of Manitoba Press, 2021.

Heimann, Jim. *Car Hops and Curb Service: A History of American Drive-In Restaurants, 1920–1960.* San Francisco: Chronicle Books, 1996.

Helstosky, Carol. *Pizza: A Global History.* London: Reaktion, 2008.

Heron, Craig. *Booze: A Distilled History.* Toronto: Between the Lines, 2003.

Hiebert, Daniel. "Class, Ethnicity and Residential Structure: The Social Geography of Winnipeg, 1901–1921." *Journal of Historical Geography* 17, no. 1 (1991): 56–86.

High, Steven. "Little Burgundy: The Interwoven Histories of Race, Residence, and Work in Twentieth-Century Montreal." *Urban History Review* 46, no. 1 (Fall 2017): 23–44.

Hinther, Rhonda L., and Jim Mochoruk, eds. *Civilian Internment in Canada: Histories and Legacies.* Winnipeg: University of Manitoba Press, 2020.

Hui, Ann. *Chop Suey Nation: The Legion Café and Other Stories from Canada's Chinese Restaurants.* Madeira Park, BC: Douglas and McIntyre, 2019.

Iacovetta, Franca, Valerie J. Korinek, and Marlene Epp. "Introduction." In *Edible Histories, Cultural Politics: Towards a Canadian Food History,* edited by Franca Iacovetta, Valerie J. Korinek, and Marlene Epp, 3–28. Toronto: University of Toronto Press, 2012.

Jakle, John A., and Keith A. Sculle. *The Roadside Restaurant in the Automobile Age.* Baltimore: Johns Hopkins University Press, 1999.

Jessee, Erin. "Managing Danger in Oral Historical Fieldwork." *Oral History Review* 44, no. 2 (2017): 322–47.

Johnson, Michele A., and Funké Aladejebi, eds. *Unsettling the Great White North: Black Canadian History.* Toronto: University of Toronto Press, 2022.

Kamal, Asfia Gulrukh. "A Recipe for Change: Reclamation of Indigenous Food Sovereignty in O-Pipon-Na-Piwin Cree Nation." PhD diss., University of Manitoba, 2018.

Katz, Yossi, and John C. Lehr. *The Last Best West: Essays on the Historical Geography of the Canadian Prairies.* Jerusalem: Magnes Press, The Hebrew University, 1999.

Keith, Darren, and Andrew Stewart. "The Churchill Oral History Project: Interviews with Inuit Elder John Arnalukjuaq." *Research Links: A Forum for Natural, Cultural and Social Studies* 7, no. 3 (Winter 1999): 7–18.

Kenneally, Rhona Richman. "The Cuisine of the Tundra." *Food, Culture and Society* 11, no. 3 (2015): 287–313.

Kimmerer, Robin Wall. *Braiding Sweetgrass: Indigenous Wisdom, Scientific Knowledge, and the*

Teachings of Plants. Minneapolis: Milkweed Editions, 2013.

———, and Frank Kanawha Lake. "Maintaining the Mosaic: The Role of Indigenous Burning in Land Management." *Journal of Forestry* 99, no. 11 (November 2001): 36–41.

Kinew, Kathi Avery. "Manito Gitigaan Governing in the Great Spirit's Garden: Wild Rice in Treaty #3: An Example of Indigenous Government Public Policy Making and Intergovernmental Relations between the Boundary Waters Anishinaabeg and the Crown, 1869–1994." PhD diss., University of Manitoba, 1995.

Kiple, Kenneth F. *A Movable Feast: Ten Millennia of Food Globalization*. Cambridge and New York: Cambridge University Press, 2007.

Kives, Bartley, and Bryan Scott. *Stuck in the Middle: Dissenting Views of Winnipeg*. Winnipeg: Great Plains Publications, 2013.

Klassen, Doreen. "'You Must Be at Least 85!' Low German Mennonites in Mexico and Belize 'Research' a Kanadier Anthropologist." Unpublished paper presented at the Mennonite Studies conference "Departing Canada, Encountering Latin America: Reflections on the Centenary of Mennonite Emigration from Canada to Mexico and Paraguay," University of Winnipeg, 22 October 2022.

K'Meyer, Tracy, and Joy Hart. *I Saw It Coming: Worker Narratives of Plant Closings and Job Loss*. New York: Palgrave Macmillan, 2009.

Knezevic, Irena. "Illicit Food: Canadian Food Safety Regulation and Informal Food Economy." *Critical Policy Studies* 10, no. 4 (2016): 410–25.

Kraig, Bruce. *Hot Dog: A Global History*. London: Reaktion, 2009.

Krotz, Larry. *Diagnosing the Legacy: The Discovery, Research, and Treatment of Type 2 Diabetes in Indigenous Youth*. Winnipeg: University of Manitoba Press, 2018.

Kulinski, Wiktor. "'It Comes with Practice': Pierogi-Making as Preserving and Imagining Polonia." *Canadian Theatre Review* 189 (Winter 2022): 13–16.

LaDuke, Winona. "Ricekeepers." *Orion Magazine* (2007). https://orionmagazine.org/article/ricekeepers/. Accessed 7 June 2023.

———. "Wild Rice and Ethics." *Cultural Survival Quarterly Magazine* 28, no. 3 (September 2004). https://www.culturalsurvival.org/publications/cultural-survival-quarterly/wild-rice-and-ethics. Accessed 7 June 2023.

———. "Wild Rice Moon." *Yes!* (1 July 2000). https://www.yesmagazine.org/issue/food/2000/07/01/wild-rice-moon. Accessed 7 June 2023.

Lax, Jacob B., and Angela G. Mertig. "The Perceived Masculinity of Meat: Development and Testing of a Measure Across Social Class and Gender." *Food, Culture and Society* 23, no. 3 (June 2020): 416–26.

Lee, Paul. "Nobu's influence: New York to Nikkei." Unpublished paper, n.d.

Lee, Victor. "The Laws of Gold Mountain: A Sampling of Early Canadian Laws and Cases that Affected People of Chinese Ancestry." *Manitoba Law Journal* 21, no. 2 (1992): 301–24.

Leer, Jonatan. "New Nordic Men: Cooking, Masculinity and Nordicness in René Redzepi's *Noma* and Clay Meyer's *Almanac*." *Food, Culture and Society* 22, no. 3 (2019): 316–33.

LeGoff, Jacques. *History and Memory*. New York: Columbia University Press, 1996.

LeGoff, Jacques, and Pierre Nora, eds. *Constructing the Past: Essays in Historical Methodology.* New York: Cambridge University Press, 1984.

Legris, George. "Drive-in Copes with Cold Winters." *Canadian Hotel Review and Restaurant* (15 May 1960): 33, 36.

Levenstein, Harvey A. *Paradox of Plenty: A Social History of Eating in Modern America.* Berkeley: University of California Press, 2003.

Levine, Susan, and Steve Striffler. "From Field to Table in Labor History." *Labor: Studies in Working-Class History of the Americas* 12, no. 1–2 (2015): 3–12.

Lithman, Yngve Georg. "The Capitalization of a Traditional Pursuit: The Case of Wild Rice in Manitoba." *Two Papers on Canadian Indians.* University of Manitoba, Center for Settlement Studies, Series 5: Occasional Papers, No. 5–6. Winnipeg: Center for Settlement Studies, University of Manitoba, 1973.

Loewen, Royden, and Gerald Friesen. *Immigrants in Prairie Cities: Ethnic Diversity in Twentieth-Century Canada.* Toronto: University of Toronto Press, 2018.

Lorson, Georges. "Igloo Restaurant: Recipes for Eskimo Dishes." *Eskimo* 65 (September 1963): 16–17.

Luby, Brittany. *Dammed: The Politics of Loss and Survival in Anishinaabe Territory.* Winnipeg: University of Manitoba Press, 2020.

Luby, Brittany, Samantha Mehltretter, Robert Flewelling, Margaret Lehman, Gabrielle Goldhar, Elli Pattrick, Jane Mariotti, Andrea Bradford, and Niisaachewan Anishinaabe Nation. "Beyond Institutional Ethics: Anishinaabe Worldviews and the Development of a Culturally Sensitive Field Protocol for Aquatic Plant Research." *Water* 13, no.

5 (2021): 709. https://doi.org/10.3390/w13050709. Accessed 7 June 2023.

Mabalon, Dawn Bohulano. "As American as Jackrabbit Adobo: Cooking, Eating, and Becoming Filipina/o American before World War II." In *Eating Asian America: A Food Studies Reader,* edited by Robert Ji-Song Ku, Martin F. Manalansan IV, and Anita Mannur, 147–76. New York and London: New York University Press, 2013.

Mac Con Iomaire, Mairtin. "Hidden Voices from the Culinary Past: Oral History as a Tool for Culinary Historians." Dublin Institute of Technology, School of Culinary Arts and Food Technology, conference papers, 2010. http://arrow.dit.ie/cgi/viewcontent.cgi?article=1008&context=tfschcafcon. Accessed 7 June 2023.

McDonald, Jennifer. "The Relationship between Cottage Food Laws and Business Outcomes: A Quantitative Study of Cottage Food Producers in the United States." *Food Policy* 84 (2019): 21–34.

Maitra, Srabani. "Are We Not Being Entrepreneurial? Exploring the Home/Work Negotiation of South Asian Immigrant Women Entrepreneurs in Canada." In *Home-Based Work and Home-Based Workers, 1800–2021,* edited by Malin Nilsson, Indrani Mazumdar, and Silke Neunsinger, 329–46. Leiden: Brill, 2022.

Malek, Jon G. *Filipinos in Canada.* The Canadian Historical Association Immigration and Ethnicity in Canada Series, no. 38. Ottawa: The Canadian Historical Association, 2021.

———. "*Silangan* Rising: Crafting the Filipino Self and the Other in the Diaspora." *Philippine Studies: Historical and Ethnographic Viewpoints* 67, no. 1 (March 2019): 31–58.

Manalansan IV, Martin F. "Beyond Authenticity: Rerouting the Filipino Culinary Diaspora." In *Eating Asian America: A Food Studies Reader,* edited by Robert Ji-Song Ku, Martin F. Manalansan IV, and Anita Mannur, 288–300. New York and London: New York University Press, 2013.

Manitoba Culture, Heritage and Citizenship. *First Farmers in the Red River Valley.* Winnipeg: Historic Resources, 1994.

Marchildon, Gregory P., ed. *Agricultural History: History of the Prairie West Series.* Vol. 3. Regina: Canadian Plains Research Center, University of Regina, 2011.

(Martens), Tabitha Robin, Mary Kate Dennis, and Michael Anthony Hart. "Feeding Indigenous People in Canada." *International Social Work* 65, no. 4 (2022): 652–62.

Mason, Courtney W., and Michael A. Robidoux. "Introduction: Food Security in Rural Indigenous Communities." In *A Land Not Forgotten: Indigenous Food Security and Land-Based Practices in Northern Ontario,* edited by Michael A. Robidoux and Courtney W. Mason, 1–15. Winnipeg: University of Manitoba Press, 2017.

Mathieu, Saje. *North of the Color Line: Migration and Black Resistance in Canada, 1870–1955.* Chapel Hill: University of North Carolina Press, 2010.

Matthews, Kristin L. "One Nation over Coals: Cold War Nationalism and the Barbecue." *American Studies* 50, no. 3/4 (Fall/Winter 2009): 5–34.

Mehltretter, Samantha, Brittany Luby, and Andrea Bradford. "Hydroelectric Power and Anishinaabe Diets: What Oral Testimony Suggests About Managing Food (In)Security on Reserve." *Arcadia: Explorations in Environmental History* 33 (Summer 2020). https://www.environmentandsociety.org/arcadia/hydroelectric-power-and-anishinaabe-diets-what-oral-testimony-suggests-about-managing-food. Accessed 7 June 2023.

Miki, Art. "The Internment of Japanese Canadians: A Human Rights Violation." In *Civilian Internment in Canada,* edited by Rhonda L. Hinther and Jim Mochoruk, 384–405. Winnipeg: University of Manitoba Press, 2020.

Miller, Adrian. *Black Smoke: African Americans and the United States of Barbecue.* Chapel Hill: University of North Carolina Press, 2021.

Million, Dian. "Telling Secrets: Sex, Power and Narratives in Indian Residential School Histories." *Canadian Woman Studies* 20, no. 2 (Summer 2000): 92–107.

Milloy, John S. *A National Crime: The Canadian Government and the Residential School System, 1879 to 1986.* Winnipeg: University of Manitoba Press, 1999.

Moodie, D. Wayne. "Manomin: Historical-Geographical Perspectives on the Ojibwa Production of Wild Rice." In *Aboriginal Resource Use in Canada: Historical and Legal Aspects,* edited by Kerry Abel and Jean Friesen, 71–79. Winnipeg: University of Manitoba Press, 1991.

Mosby, Ian. "Administering Colonial Science: Nutrition Research and Human Biomedical Experimentation in Aboriginal Communities and Residential Schools, 1942–1952." *Histoire sociale/Social History* 46, no. 91 (May 2013): 145–72.

Moss, Wendy, and Elaine Gardner-O'Toole. *Aboriginal People: History of Discriminatory Laws.* Ottawa: Library of Parliament Research Branch, 1991.

Mt. Pleasant, Jane. "Food Yields and Nutrient Analyses of the Three Sisters: A Haudenosaunee Cropping System." *Ethnobiology Letters* 7, no. 1 (2016): 87–98.

———. "The Paradox of Plows and Productivity: An Agronomic Comparison of Cereal Grain Production under Iroquois Hoe Culture and European Plow Culture in the Seventeenth and Eighteenth Centuries." *Agricultural History* 85, no. 4 (Fall 2011): 460–92.

Mysyk, Avis. *Manitoba Commercial Market Gardening, 1945–1997.* Regina: Canadian Plains Research Center, University of Regina, 2000.

Nestle, Marion. *Food Politics: How the Food Industry Influences Nutrition and Health.* Berkeley: University Presses of California, 2007.

Neuhaus, Jessamyn. *Manly Meals and Mom's Home Cooking: Cookbooks and Gender in Modern America.* Baltimore: Johns Hopkins University Press, 2003.

Newton, Steven Timothy, Helen Fast, and Thomas Henley. "Sustainable Development for Canada's Arctic and Subarctic Communities: A Backcasting Approach to Churchill, Manitoba." *Arctic* 55, no. 3 (2002): 281–90.

Nickels, Bret. "Examining the Future of First Nations Agriculture by Exploring the Implications of the Manitoba Indian Agricultural Program." In *Place and Replace: Essays on Western Canada,* edited by Adele Perry, Esyllt W. Jones, and Leah Morton, 59–75. Winnipeg: University of Manitoba Press, 2013.

North Star Bus Lines. *The Story of Churchill, Manitoba.* Churchill: North Star Bus Lines Ltd., 1971.

Oikawa, Mona. *Cartographies of Violence: Japanese Canadian Women, Memory, and the Subjects of the Internment.* Toronto: University of Toronto Press, 2012.

Ommer, Rosemary E., and Nancy J. Turner. "Informal Rural Economies in History." *Labour/Le Travail* 53 (Spring 2004): 127–57.

Ostry, Aleck Samuel. *Nutrition Policy in Canada, 1870–1938.* Vancouver: University of British Columbia Press, 2006.

Parasecoli, Fabio. *Bite Me: Food in Popular Culture.* Oxford and New York: Berg Publishers, 2008.

Parkhurst Ferguson, Priscilla. *What We Talk About When We Talk About Food.* Los Angeles: University of California Press, 2014.

Parkin, Katherine J. *Food Is Love: Food Advertising and Gender Roles in Modern America.* Philadelphia: University of Pennsylvania Press, 2006.

Parr, Joy. *Domestic Goods: The Material, the Moral, and the Economic in the Postwar Years.* Toronto: University of Toronto Press, 1999.

Paskievich, John, Alison Gillmor, George Melnyk, and J.S. Osborne. *The North End Revisited: Photographs.* Winnipeg: University of Manitoba Press, 2017.

Peluso, Nancy Lee. "*Whigs and Hunters: The Origins of the Black Act,* by E.P. Thompson." *The Journal of Peasant Studies* 44, no. 1 (2017): 309–21.

Penfold, Steve. *The Donut: A Canadian History.* Toronto: University of Toronto Press, 2008.

Peng, N., A.H. Chen, and K.P. Hung. "The Effects of Teppanyaki Restaurant Stimuli on Diners' Emotions and Loyalty." *International Journal of Hospitality Management* 60 (January 2017): 1–12.

Peotto, Tom, and Connie Nelson. "Food Production in the Wabigoon Basin: The First Nine Thousand Years." *Canadian Historical Review* 103, no. 4 (December 2022): 563–89.

Perks, Rob. "The Roots of Oral History: Exploring Contrasting Attitudes to Elite, Corporate and Business History in Britain and the U.S." *Oral History Review* 37, no. 2 (2010): 215–24.

Perry, Adele, Esyllt W. Jones, and Leah Morton, eds. *Place and Replace: Essays on Western Canada.* Winnipeg: University of Manitoba Press, 2013.

Peters, Evelyn, Matthew Stock, and Adrian Werner, with Lawrie Barkwell. *Rooster Town: The History of an Urban Métis Community, 1901–1961.* Winnipeg: University of Manitoba Press, 2018.

Phillipps, Breanna, and Kelly Skinner. "Bannock: Using a Contested Bread to Understand Indigenous and Settler Relations and Ways Forward within Canada." In *Recipes and Reciprocity: Building Relationships in Research,* edited by Hannah Tait Neufeld and Elizabeth Finnis, 55–78. Winnipeg: University of Manitoba Press, 2022.

Pilcher, Jeffrey M. "The Whole Enchilada: A Full Plate of Food History." *The Journal of American History* 103, no. 3 (December 2016): 694–96.

Pollan, Michael. *Food Rules: An Eater's Manual.* New York: Penguin Books, 2009.

———. *In Defense of Food: An Eater's Manifesto.* New York: Penguin Books, 2008.

———. *The Omnivore's Dilemma: A Natural History of Four Meals.* New York: Penguin, 2006.

Portelli, Alessandro. *The Battle of Valle Giulia: Oral History and the Art of Dialogue.* Madison: University of Wisconsin Press, 1997.

———. *The Death of Luigi Trastulli and Other Stories: Form and Meaning in Oral History.* New York: State University of New York Press, 1990.

———. "Oral History As Genre." In *Narrative and Genre: Contexts and Types of Communication,* edited by Mary Chamberlain and Paul Thompson, 23–45. Reprint ed. New Brunswick, USA, and London, UK: Transaction Publishers, 2009.

Power, Elaine M. "De-centering the Text: Exploring the Potential for Visual Methods in the Sociology of Food." *Journal for the Study of Food and Society* 6, no. 2 (Winter 2003): 9–20.

Raviv, Yael. "Food, Art, and the Challenges of Documentation." *Liminalities: A Journal of Performance Studies* 16, no. 4 (2020): 1–19.

Ray, Krishnendu. *The Ethnic Restaurateur.* London: Bloomsbury Academic, 2016.

Reimer, Bill. "The Informal Economy in Non-Metropolitan Canada." *The Canadian Review of Sociology and Anthropology* 43, no. 1 (February 2006): 23–49.

Reiter, Esther. *Making Fast Food: From the Frying Pan into the Fryer.* 2nd ed. Montreal: McGill-Queen's University Press, 1996.

Robidoux, Michael A., and Courtney W. Mason, eds. *A Land Not Forgotten: Indigenous Food Security and Land-Based Practices in Northern Ontario.* Winnipeg: University of Manitoba Press, 2017.

Russell, Peter A. *How Agriculture Made Canada: Farming in the Nineteenth Century.* Montreal and Kingston: McGill-Queen's University Press, 2012.

Russell, Polly. "Archives, Academy, and Access: Food Producer Life Stories." *Gastronomica* 15, no. 3 (Fall 2015): 53–58.

Sapoznik, Karlee. "Where the Historiography Falls Short: La Vérendrye Through the Lens of Gender, Race and Slavery in Early French Canada, 1731–1749." *Manitoba History* 62 (Winter 2009). http://www.mhs.mb.ca/docs/mb_history/62/laverendrye.shtml. Accessed 7 June 2023.

Schlosser, Eric. *Fast Food Nation: The Dark Side of the All-American Meal.* New York: Perennial, 2002.

Seitz, Brian, and Ron Scapp. *Eating Culture.* New York: State University of New York Press, 1998.

Sharpless, Rebecca. "Cookbooks as Resources for Rural Research." *Agricultural History* 90, no. 2 (Spring 2016): 195–208.

———. *Cooking in Other Women's Kitchens: Domestic Workers in the South, 1865–1960.* The John Hope Franklin Series in African American History and Culture. Chapel Hill: University of North Carolina Press, 2010.

Smith, Andrew F. *Hamburger: A Global History.* London: Reaktion, 2008.

———. ed. *The Oxford Companion to American Food and Drink.* Oxford: Oxford University Press, 2007.

———. *Popped Culture: A Social History of Popcorn in America.* Columbia: University of South Carolina Press, 1999.

Smith, Nicole F., Dana Lepofsky, Ginevra Toniello, Keith Holmes, Louie Wilson, Christina M. Neudorf, and Christine Roberts. "3500 Years of Shellfish Mariculture on the Northwest Coast of North America," *PLoS ONE* 14, no. 2 (27 February 2019). https://doi.org/10.1371/journal.pone.0211194. Accessed 7 June 2023.

Spitznagel, Eric. *Junk Food Companion: The Complete Guide to Eating Badly.* New York: Penguin, 1999.

Steeves, Paulette F.C. *The Indigenous Paleolithic of the Western Hemisphere.* Lincoln: University of Nebraska Press, 2021.

Stern, Jane and Michael Stern, *500 Things to Eat Before It's Too Late and the Very Best Places to Eat Them.* Boston. Houghton Mifflin Harcourt, 2009.

Stevenson, Allyson D. *Intimate Integration: A History of the Sixties Scoop and the Colonization of Indigenous Kinship.* Toronto: University of Toronto Press, 2021.

Strong, Liz H. "Shifting Focus: Interviewers Share Advice on Protecting Themselves from Harm." *Oral History Review* 48, no. 2 (2021): 196–215.

Sunahara, Ann Gomer. *The Politics of Racism.* Burnaby: Nikkei National Museum and Cultural Centre, 2020.

Tachibana, Rumiko. "'Processing' Sushi/Cooked Japan: Why Sushi Became Canadian." MA thesis, University of Victoria, 2008.

Teillet, Jean. *The North-West Is Our Mother: The Story of Louis Riel's People, the Métis Nation.* Toronto: HarperCollins, 2019.

Teitelbaum, Sara, and Thomas Beckley. "Harvested, Hunted and Home Grown: The Prevalence of Self-Provisioning in Rural Canada." *Journal of Rural and Community Development* 1 (2006): 114–30.

Thiessen, Janis. "From Faith to Food: Using Oral History to Study Corporate Mythology at Canadian Manufacturing Firms." *Oral History* 42, no. 2 (Spring 2014): 59–72.

———. *Snacks: A Canadian Food History.* Winnipeg: University of Manitoba Press, 2017.

Thiessen, Janis, Kent Davies, and Kimberley Moore. "Rhymes with 'Truck': The Manitoba Food History Project." *Oral History Review* 50, no.1 (2023): 41–61.

Thompson, Edward Palmer. *Whigs and Hunters: The Origin of the Black Act.* New York: Pantheon Books, 1975.

Thompson, Paul, Tony Wailey, and Trevor Lummis. *Living the Fishing.* London: Routledge, 1983.

Tipton-Martin, Toni. *Jubilee: Recipes from Two Centuries of African American Cooking.* New York: Clarkson Potter, 2019.

Truderung, Diane. *Transcona's Story: 100 Years of Progress.* Winnipeg: Bond Printing Ltd., 2012.

Truth and Reconciliation Commission of Canada. *Canada's Residential Schools: The Legacy.* Montreal and Kingston: McGill-Queen's University Press, 2015.

———. *A Knock on the Door: The Essential History of Residential Schools from the Truth and Reconciliation Commission of Canada.* Winnipeg: National Centre for Truth and Reconciliation and University of Manitoba Press, 2016.

Tuck, Eve. "Suspending Damage: A Letter to Communities." *Harvard Educational Review* 79, no. 3 (2009): 409–28.

———, and K. Wayne Yang. "Decolonization Is Not a Metaphor." *Decolonization: Indigeneity, Education and Society* 1, no. 1 (2012): 1–40.

Turner, Katherine Leonard. "Buying, Not Cooking: Ready-to-eat Food in American Urban Working-class Neighborhoods, 1880–1930." *Food, Culture and Society* 9, no. 1 (Spring 2006): 13–39.

Twitty, Michael W. *The Cooking Gene.* New York: HarperCollins, 2017.

Valverde, Mariana. *The Age of Light, Soap, and Water: Moral Reform in English Canada, 1885–1925.* Toronto: McClelland and Stewart, 1991.

Van de Vorst, Charlotte. *Making Ends Meet: Farm Women's Work in Manitoba.* Winnipeg: University of Manitoba Press, 2002.

Vennum, Thomas. *Wild Rice and the Ojibway People.* St. Paul: Minnesota Historical Society Press, 1988.

Vernon, Karina. "Introduction." In *The Black Prairie Archives: An Anthology,* edited by Karina Vernon, 1–35. Waterloo: Wilfrid Laurier University Press, 2020.

Vlassis, George D. *The Greeks in Canada.* 2nd ed. Ottawa: n.p., 1953.

Vowel, Chelsea. *Indigenous Writes: A Guide to First Nations, Métis & Inuit Issues in Canada.* Winnipeg: HighWater Press, 2016.

Waisberg, Leo G., and Tim E. Holzkamm. "'A Tendency to Discourage Them from Cultivating': Ojibwa Agriculture and Indian Affairs Administration in Northwestern Ontario." *Ethnohistory* 40, no. 2 (Spring 1993): 175–211.

Walker, Barrington. "Critical Histories of Blackness in Canada." In *Unsettling the Great White North: Black Canadian History,* edited by Michele A. Johnson and Funké Aladejebi, 31–49. Toronto: University of Toronto Press, 2022.

Ward, W. Peter. "The Japanese in Canada." The Canadian Historical Association Immigration and Ethnicity in Canada Series, no. 3. Ottawa: The Canadian Historical Association, 1982.

Watts, Vanessa. "Smudge This: Assimilation, State-Favoured Communities and the Denial of Indigenous Spiritual Lives." *Journal of Child, Youth and Family Studies* 7, no. 1 (2016): 148–70.

Wheeler, Winona. "Reflections on the Social Relations of Indigenous Oral Histories." In *Walking a Tightrope: Aboriginal People and Their Representations,* edited by Ute Lischke and David T. McNab, 189–213. Waterloo: Wilfrid Laurier University Press, 2005.

Wilmshurst, Sara. "How to Eat Like a Canadian: Centennial Cookbooks and Visions of Culinary Identity." *Cuizine* 4, no. 2 (2013). https://doi.org/10.7202/1019317ar.

Winks, Robin W. *Blacks in Canada: A History.* 50th anniversary ed. Montreal and Kingston: McGill-Queen's University Press, 2021.

Women's Auxiliary of the Chapel of the Good Shepherd and the Ladies of St. Paul's Anglican Mission. *Northern Kitchen.* Rev. ed. Churchill: The author, 1992.

Yee, Paul. *Chinatown: An Illustrated History of the Chinese Communities of Victoria, Vancouver, Calgary, Winnipeg, Toronto, Ottawa, Montreal and Halifax.* Toronto: James Lorimer and Co., 2005.

Zembrzycki, Stacey. "'We Didn't Have a Lot of Money, but We Had Food': Ukrainians and Their Depression-Era Food Memories." In *Edible Histories, Cultural Politics: Towards a Canadian Food History,* edited by Franca Iacovetta, Valerie J. Korinek, and Marlene Epp, 131–39. Toronto: University of Toronto Press, 2012.

Index